God and Dreams

God and Dreams

Is There a Connection?

JOHN PRATT BINGHAM

RESOURCE *Publications* • Eugene, Oregon

GOD AND DREAMS
Is There a Connection?

Copyright © 2010 John Pratt Bingham. All rights reserved. Except for brief quotations in critical publications or reviews, no part of this book may be reproduced in any manner without prior written permission from the publisher. Write: Permissions, Wipf and Stock Publishers, 199 W. 8th Ave., Suite 3, Eugene, OR 97401.

Resource Publications
An Imprint of Wipf and Stock Publishers
199 W. 8th Ave., Suite 3
Eugene, OR 97401
www.wipfandstock.com

ISBN 13: 978-1-60608-667-4

Manufactured in the U.S.A.

The Scriptural quotations contained herein are from the New Revised Standard Version Bible, copyright © 1989 by the Division of Christian Education of the National Council of Churches of Christ in the U.S.A., and are used by permission. All rights reserved.

To my wife, Barbara;

Our children: Ken, Erich, Jennifer, Kimberly, Katy & Sarah;

Our grandchildren: Willow, Samantha, Sarah, Sydney, Joshua, Emma, Madeleine, Katrina and Megan;

And to all my teachers, mentors, students, and clients.

Contents

Acknowledgements ix
Foreword xi
Introduction: Discerning the Will of God xv

1. Historic Perspectives 1
2. Jewish Perspectives 15
3. Christian Perspectives 34
4. Islamic Perspectives 52
5. A Few Other Religious Perspectives 63
6. Some Non-Religious Perspectives 72
7. Another Perspective 99

Appendix A   Six Characteristics of Doing God's Will 111
Appendix B   Some Characteristics of a Revelation 114
Bibliography 119
Index 143

Acknowledgments

I WANT TO THANK all of the people who have taught me about dreams. I especially want to express my appreciation to those who have worked with me on mine: Glenn Foy, Ph.D., the Reverend John A. Sanford, Robert Johnson, Melvin Kettner, M.D., and Paul Turner, Ph.D. I also want to acknowledge those individuals who made history come alive for me. Chuck Clustka and the Rev. Dr. John Gill at Harvard School, Dr. Francis Markus at Willamette University and Dr. John Woolverton at the Virginia Theological Seminary. Dr. John Fletcher, also at the Virginia Theological Seminary, helped to open my eyes with regard to the ethical implications of Christianity and how to not be afraid to think unpopular thoughts. I also want to acknowledge Dr. Harvey Mindess who was the chair of my graduate program at Antioch University in Los Angeles. He too was an influence on my psychological development.

I want to thank Dr. Turner, the Reverend Dr. Scott R. A. Starbuck, Dr. Bart Koet, Imam M. A. Azeez and Richard Smoley for their careful reading of an earlier version of this material and for their recommendations. I appreciate Dr. Kelly Bulkeley's assistance with this project. The Rev. Joan Stock also provided helpful input as did the Rev. Roy Hayes and Emile Carriere.

I want to thank Elisabeth Thompson and Betty Ann Beauchamp for their careful editing of the manuscript. Their knowledge and skill is truly appreciated.

I want to express my gratitude to Peter and Vicki Bergstrom and the staff of Camp Stevens in Julian, California, who encouraged my work on this material for several decades, as did Don Evans of All Souls Episcopal Church in Point Loma, California. Also my appreciation goes to the staff and students of MiraCosta College in Oceanside, California; Trinity Episcopal Church in Sutter Creek, California; Trinity Episcopal Cathedral, Sacramento, California; Bethesda-by-the-Sea Episcopal Church, Palm

Beach, Florida; and Holy Trinity Episcopal Church, Juneau, Alaska for their interest and input.

I want to thank the Author's Guild of America for their legal advice without which I would have been tremendously handicapped.

Finally, I want to thank Jim Tedrick and Christian Amondson at Wipf *and* Stock *Publishers* for their assistance in the publishing process.

Foreword

EVERY HUMAN CULTURE HAS its dream teachers, its highly experienced guides into the mysterious realms of nocturnal experience. Whether we call them shamans, mystics, diviners, or prophets, these dream teachers provide valuable services and leadership to their communities. They mediate between the human and trans-human realms, helping the people in their group understand the ultimate powers that shape their lives. They reflect to the community its highest ideals, and its darkest fears. They call attention to neglected problems, and envision new possibilities for individual and collective growth. They focus on the health of the body and the vitality of the spirit. They understand the ever-lasting influence of the ancestral past, and they boldly cast their vision toward the farthest horizons of the future.

Modern western society seems to have little place for dream teachers like these. The incredibly rapid pace of contemporary life, the overwhelming stimulation of electronic entertainment, the rising pressure of economic anxieties—we live in times that are not favorable to the dreaming imagination. Sleep deprivation has become a chronic condition for increasing numbers of people, making it harder and harder to maintain a healthy relationship with dreaming experience. Added to that, authoritative scientists repeatedly claim that dreams are nonsense, despite extensive empirical evidence to the contrary. The impact of these misstatements is to belittle any attention to dreams, to dismiss them from serious consideration, to banish them from the real concerns of normal people.

And yet, people in the modern world continue to dream, and they continue to seek knowledgeable, trustworthy guidance in better understanding their dreams. I am pleased to report that John Bingham is one of these rare teachers of dreaming. His book, *God and Dreams: Is There a Connection?* is historically grounded, theologically ambitious, and clinically valuable. It gathers in one volume the insights of someone who knows what he knows not only from extensive research but also from deep self-reflection and personal experience. For those who are called in their dreams to seek a deeper understanding of themselves, the world, and the divine, John Bingham has something to teach you.

Kelly Bulkeley
February 13, 2008
Kensington, California

*He whose vision cannot cover
History's three thousand years,
Must in outer darkness hover,
Live within the day's frontiers.*

—*Goethe*

Introduction

Revelation is the soul of religion.
—Maulana Aftab-ud-Din Ahmad Sahib[1]

A PERSONAL NOTE

My first awareness that God communicates through dreams happened in the early 1970s. I was a newly ordained Episcopal priest, full of the excitement that accompanies the start of a long-desired career. The war in Vietnam was winding down; my first-born daughter was about 18 months old and my wife was pregnant with our second daughter. Life was good. In a dream I was walking across the intramural field at Willamette University. This is something I did hundreds of times during my years there in the 1960s. There was nothing unusual about it. In the dream while I am crossing the field on a bright, clear day a bolt of lightning strikes the ground a few yards in front of me. I am stunned and paralyzed with fear. I can walk no farther. I awaken.

This dream made a very lasting impression on me even though I had no idea what it meant. My Jungian analyst, Dr. Glenn Foy, suggested it showed the presence of God in my life and that I needed to pay careful attention to this dream. His words sent a shiver through me as I intuitively knew he was correct. Even though I was already ordained and functioning as a parish priest, this dream brought home to me the power and presence of God in a most personal way. This wasn't the first time I'd felt God break into my life unexpectedly. A vision I had when I was 16 called me to the priesthood. With the passage of time, however, I'd come to question that experience. Did that vision truly happen? Perhaps it was just the over-stimulated imagination of an impressionable teenager. But this dream brought back the intensity of that vision and reminded me not to be so casual in my relationship with God. The dream was a wake-up call to take this dimension of life seriously. In that moment, God was numinous again. Whenever my faith starts to get casual, the memory of that lightning bolt returns.

This and other dreams I have had, along with the dreams clients of mine have shared, have left no doubt in my mind God does indeed speak through dreams. My exploration of God and dreams is more than an intellectual exercise for me. It is an attempt to understand experiences that have been a part of my life.

When I began my investigation, I was interested in the experience of others. How common is it to have God in a dream? What I have discovered both surprised me and confirmed my experience: there is a long history of God communicating through dreams. Indeed, Judaism, Christianity and Islam each got their start with a revelation from God that was communicated through a dream. The story of God's involvement with dreams unfolds in the chapters that follow. My hope in presenting this material is not only to remind the reader that God does indeed continue to speak through dreams but to encourage the reader to look for the spiritual dimension of his or her dreams.

I approach this topic as a Christian, not as a Jew or Muslim. I am a total outsider to Islam, but part of my ancestry is Jewish. I have tried to be open to each tradition and have sought to present their history and teachings with respect and with an appreciation for their contributions. I have by necessity drawn on the scholarship of others. Any misrepresentations, distortions or errors in the book, however, are entirely of my own doing.

WHAT IS A DREAM?

Dreams are a succession of images, sensations, emotions or thoughts present to us while we are asleep. Dreams are an involuntary, autonomous, natural phenomenon. A dream can be a single image or an elaborate, vivid story. Everyone dreams whether the dreams are recalled or not. On the average, each adult dreams three to five times a night. Infants and young people dream more than this average while older individuals dream less.

YEARNING FOR GOD

The exploration of God and dreams satisfies, I believe, the deep-seated yearning for God most people seem to have. Currently this yearning, surveys indicate, is not being met by organized religion. Numerous polls conducted over the last decade have found increasing numbers of people are leaving organized religion to become either "spiritual" or nothing at all. A poll[2] conducted in 2001 found that there are significantly fewer Christians in the United States than there were in 1990 (76.5% to 86.2%). This poll also found that those who do not follow any organized religion increased from 8% to 14.1%. Another poll conducted jointly by USA Today and the Gallup Organization found similar trends. There was a 4% decrease between December, 1999 and January, 2002 among American adults who identified with an organized religion (54% to 50%). The poll also found during the same period there was an increase in those individuals who regard themselves as "spiritual" but not religious (30% to 33%). Another 10% of those polled identified themselves as neither spiritual nor religious.[3] Reflecting on these findings, marketing researcher George Barna suggested that there is an unmet need to have "a deeper and more meaningful relationship with God."[4]

Dreams can provide a deeper and more meaningful relationship with God. This relationship can be accomplished by developing an emotional connection with the images present in the dream; by recognizing that dreams speak a symbolic language, not a literal one; and by paying attention to the patterns that emerge in a series of dreams.[5] Yet few people take advantage of their dreams to grow closer to God. Why is this? Two explanations come to mind.

One explanation is that there are not many people who still believe dreams actually come from God. While not believing dreams come from God is a common attitude today, it has not always been the typical viewpoint. For more than two thousand years there was widespread acceptance that God does communicate through dreams. This perception was essentially unquestioned. The third-century Christian theologian Quintus Tertullian illustrates this conviction when he observed: "Is it not known to all people that the dream is the most usual way that God reveals himself to man?"[6]

About fifteen hundred years ago, a shift in thinking began that led to the belief that God has nothing to do with dreams. King William II of England expressed this attitude in the eleventh century when he said, "They are not good Christians that regard dreams." That God has nothing to do with dreams continues to be what many people believe.

This perception is starting to change again. As a result of discoveries made during the twentieth century in psychology and theoretical physics, the assumptions that led to the belief that God has nothing to do with dreams have been shown to be incorrect. At the start of the twenty-first century, it once again makes sense to be open to God's role in dreams.

A second explanation as to why people do not utilize their dreams to draw closer to God stems from a misunderstanding of dream language. If the images in dreams are interpreted literally, then more often than not dream messages do not make sense. But if the images are understood to be symbols, then their messages can be more readily comprehended.

DREAM IMAGERY

One of the significant shifts in the understanding of dreams that occurred during the twentieth century involved the language of dreams. Whereas for thousands of years dream language was understood literally, with the advent of psychology, dream language came to be understood as symbolic. With the literal interpretation of dreams, only those dreams whose messages were understood and came true were regarded as divine in origin. Other dreams were assumed to have their origins in the body or in the influences of the environment. When psychology discerned that dreams arise from the unconscious, it became apparent that dream imagery is more descriptive of the dreamer's psyche than it is of the dreamer's exterior life. Psychology has shown that when we dream we participate in a world of image and symbol. It has been known since at least the time of Jesus that God's will is revealed through the use of image and symbol. This is one of the reasons Jesus used parables to teach.

While God on occasion does speak literally, more often than not God uses symbols to convey His message. Symbols are images that are pregnant with energy and meaning. As C.G. Jung noted, symbols don't define or explain but point beyond the familiar they depict to a greater reality that cannot be expressed in any other way. Symbols are capable of imaging the ineffable because they have their roots in the depths of the mystery they portray. Literal language can't convey knowledge that is still beyond its grasp. Symbols can. Symbols make it possible for dreams to initiate people into new levels of awareness. Symbols make it possible for *all* dreams to be instruments of God's revelation.[7]

DREAMS ARE MYSTERIOUS AND SACRED

Dreams are both mysterious and sacred. The original meaning of *mystery* was to be initiated into the knowledge of something through an experience of that mystery. That is, something remains mysterious until a person has an experience of it. This kind of awareness can not be achieved by attending a lecture, by talking about it with someone, or by reading about another person's experience. This awareness happens only as a result of one's own experience. Love, grace, drug highs or jumping out of an airplane are examples of mysterious things. Dreams are mysterious because they show or tell us things we do not know. Dreams initiate their recipients into new levels of awareness.

Dreams are sacred because they give image to God's will for our lives. When an individual pays attention to the imagery in his dreams and studies the patterns present in a series of dreams, what is discovered is an autonomous other that is reaching out and offering guidance that is intimate. This experience is energizing, numinous and humbling. It is by relating to the symbolic nature of a dream's imagery and by paying attention to the patterns that emerge in a series of dreams that people are able to experience the Holy in everyday life.

REASON AND REVELATION

A healthy relationship with God contains a tension between reason and revelation. Reason keeps seekers grounded in the reality of what is, while revelation exposes individuals to new possibilities. Too much reason leads to a dry rigidity of thought with limited horizons. Too much revelation leads to airy speculations that lack credibility.

The relationship between reason and revelation has found expression theologically in orthodoxy and mysticism. As orthodoxy applies reason to revelation, clarity, knowledge and meaning follow. On occasion, however, orthodoxy transforms religious symbols into facts. When this occurs, an image's symbolic content is lost. The more literal the images are regarded, the less able the images are to connect beholders with the preconceptual, spiritual dimensions of life.

Mysticism expands spiritual horizons by revealing God's presence at moments when it was not expected. On occasion, however, mysticism fails to make spiritual reality's symbols pertinent to everyday life. Without a practical application, mysticism becomes inconsequential.

Dreams offer the best of both reason and revelation by combining access to the spiritual dimensions of life with everyday practicality. Dreams release individuals from bondage to their ego's perspective and expose them to new ways of seeing and experiencing life. A dream not only discloses the transcendent spiritual reality that underlies the realm of sense-experience, but also enables participation in it. Participation in the spiritual domain becomes possible when an emotional connection is made with the dream's images and the energy of that connection is allowed to vibrate within us. Because dreams offer this opportunity, they make it possible for each of us to discern the will of God for our lives.

DISCERNING THE WILL OF GOD

"What is God's will?" is a question that has been pondered for thousands of years. The search for an answer has evolved differently between the East and the West.

In the East, Buddhists, Confucians and Taoists believe divine wisdom such as their founders possessed originates solely from within the psyche. Truth exists within each of us because truth is a basic component of being. Inspiration is the process by which an individual connects with divine or eternal truth. For Hindus everything happens according to the will of God. God's will is discerned by disciplined minds using meditative skills. Some Sikh devotions open with the following words:

> God is not to be comprehended by human thought,
>   Though we may try it a hundred thousand times.
> Outward silence cannot still the mind's search for truth,
>   Though we absorb ourselves in meditation long and deep.
> Our hunger for God can never be satisfied,
>   Even if we acquire everything the universe has to offer.
> If we increase our wisdom beyond measure,
>   It is still not enough.
> How, then, can we come to know the truth?
> How can the veil of falsehood be torn asunder?
> By following God's will, O Nanak,
> Which is written within our hearts.

In the West the answer to how a person finds the will of God is different. Judaism, Christianity, and Islam grow out of a shared belief that there is a supreme creator who takes a continuing interest in his creation.

It is the creator who provides information about his will whenever, however, and to whomever he chooses.

Access to God's will in the West has taken two paths: divination and revelation. Divination means a seeker *takes the initiative* to discern what the will of God is. Reading tarot cards or casting the Urim and Thummim are examples of what a seeker might do. Revelation occurs when a seeker *observes* a phenomenon to determine God's will. Studying the movement of the stars, reading sacred texts, and receiving imagery in a vision or dream are examples of how revelation occurs.[8]

The reality common to both divination and revelation is that something normally hidden is revealed. "Revealed knowledge," according to Dr. Keith Ward, a theologian at Oxford University, is "when God directly intends someone to know something beyond normal cognitive capacity, and brings it about that they do know it, and they know that God has so intentionally caused it."[9] It involves a direct, personal experience that conveys information that is not restricted by space-time considerations.

In contrast, science provides the seeker with discovered knowledge. Discovered knowledge comes from the exploration of what is already present.[10] Religion and science need each other. As Dr. Albert Einstein noted, "Science without religion is lame, religion without science is blind."[11]

Discerning the will of God involves both revelation and reason. Dr. Ward suggests the following role for each in the process.

> If . . . revelation is of that which essentially remains mystery, beyond full conceptual clarification; it will be difficult to insist upon very precise conceptual truths as central to revelation. Even those concepts which are taken to be revealed will often be cryptic, carrying hidden meanings which can only be touched upon but never finally unraveled by contemplation and prayer. This means that reason will never have the last word in religion; but it does not mean that reason will have no part to play. The proper function of reason is precisely to clarify its own limits, to warn where those limits are overstepped and to point to the rationality of an ultimate mystery where it cannot reach. Rational reflection on religion not only warns empirical disciplines when they seek to eliminate or articulate too precisely the realm of mystery. It also warns the religious when they seem to turn the mystery into pseudo-science, to confuse unfathomable goodness with primitive science or primitive morality.[12]

Some traditional methods in Judaism, Christianity, and Islam for discerning the will of God are prayer, the study of sacred texts, meditation, fasting, visions, and dream work. What makes each of these methods effective is its ability to alter the normal way reality is perceived so that a new awareness may come.[13.] Some of us are better at discerning God's will than are others.[14.] The teachings of the most gifted individuals are preserved as sacred texts.

REVELATION OR HALLUCINATION?

Because the words, images, sounds, and feelings of a revelation are processed by the psyche, divine messages are sometimes confused with other psychic material. It is vital to distinguish between revelations and hallucinations or delusions, between what is genuine and authentic and what is aimless and groundless. There are a variety of ways to distinguish the true from the false.

John C. Robinson, Ph.D., a clinical psychologist in Sacramento, California, states that what differentiates an authentic religious experience from the hallucinatory or delusional one is the health of the individual's ego. Dr. Robinson advises other psychotherapists:

> Religious beliefs are not infrequently part of more severe psychopathology, especially psychoses characterized by delusions of grandeur (e.g., Jesus identification) religiosity (e.g., obsessive religious ideation), magical thinking (e.g., special powers), and auditory hallucinations (e.g., the voice of God or Satan). It is easy to be entranced by the power and apparent reality of the psychotic process, particularly for someone with a weakened ego or profound feelings of inferiority. A friend or therapist can also be seduced into believing that such religious talk represents a spiritually transforming experience or divine intercession. When this happens religious conversation simply confuses and distracts the patient whose core psychopathology must be managed to recover. Even when mystical consciousness or content is emerging, the major diagnostic question is whether the client's ego functions i.e., reality testing, ego boundaries, are intact enough to integrate it.[15]

Pathology is evident in behaviors such as hallucinations and delusions. An hallucination is a perception without external stimuli and that has no existence in reality. The brain is making up what it hears, sees, feels, smells, or tastes although such experiences are very real to the person having the hallucination. The individual having a religious hallucination will display psychosis in other parts of his or her life as well, whereas individuals having authentic experiences of God will be in touch with reality in the other parts of their lives too.

Delusions are false ideas believed by a person but not by other people in his or her culture and which cannot be corrected by reason. Delusions are usually based on some kind of sensory experience that the individual misinterprets. For example, a delusional person interprets a stranger using a leaf-blower to clean his yard to mean that the stranger wants to "blow me away." In contrast to delusional thinking, a genuine experience of God is grounded in that which is actual.

There is also a sterility of thought which characterizes psychopathology. Such a person is not in touch with "truth" but with images and ideas that give expression to the pathology. One way of telling the difference is that there will be no general consensus that lasts over the centuries that this person's experience is authentic. In contrast to the sterility of pathology, vitality characterizes authentic experiences of God. These experiences produce an extensive following that sustain over time.

Psychoanalyst Silvano Arieti, M.D. (1914–1981) uses the following three criteria to distinguish between a religious experience and one rooted in schizophrenia. Whereas religious experiences are usually visual, schizophrenia predominately involves auditory experiences. Second, whereas religious experience usually involves a benevolent guide or advisor who issues orders to the person, a person with schizophrenia hears sounds, often a voice or voices that are frequently loud and incoherent, sometimes continuous and accusatory. Third, whereas religious experience is usually pleasant, having schizophrenia is unpleasant: You cannot trust what your brain is telling you.[16]

SUMMARY

For more than two thousand years it was widely accepted that God communicates through dreams. This belief changed about fifteen hundred years ago until it was no longer accepted that God had anything to do with dreams. Discoveries in psychology and theoretical physics during the twentieth century show that the assumptions, which underpin the belief God has nothing to do with dreams, are incorrect. A reconsideration of God's involvement with dreams is now warranted, especially since it is now possible to distinguish genuine religious experience from psychopathology.

Dreams are one form of God's revelation. Dreams are able to function as such for a couple of reasons. First, sleepers are in an altered state of consciousness. This frees the individual from the limitations of their ego's perspective. This altered state of consciousness allows an experience of the ineffable to be received.

A second contributor to the revelatory capacity of dreams is the symbolic nature of dream images. It is the symbols that initiate the individual into new levels of awareness, which enables the hidden to be revealed. The symbolic dimension is the link between the image itself and the mystery the images portray.

When both individual dreams and series of dreams are reflected upon and interacted with seriously for a period of time, there arises the awareness that an autonomous other is reaching out to the dreamer. Paying attention to dreams is a way of satisfying the yearning for a personal connection with God.

ENDNOTES

1. Maulana Aftab-ud-Din Ahmad Sahib is a twentieth century Muslim who lives in India.

2. "American Religious Identification Survey," by *The Graduate Center of the City University of New York*. The poll also found about 16% of American adults changed their religious identification sometime during their lives, with the largest percentage of this group abandoning religion altogether. The percentage of Americans who change their religious affiliation increased dramatically according to a 2007 poll conducted by the Pew Forum on Religion & Public Life which was released in February, 2008. 44% of those polled either switched their religious affiliation, moved from being without a religious affiliation ("unaffiliated") to identifying with a particular faith, or dropped their religious affiliation entirely to become "unaffiliated." This religious movement in every direction suggests that the current religious practices are not satisfying individuals yearning for God. Jane Haldane interviewed 18 lay people, including 12 newcomers, who attended St. Columba's Episcopal Church in Washington, D.C. over a 15-month period in the early 1970s. She found that these people's religious pilgrimage was considered by them to be a private affair that was fed from a variety of sources that were mostly unknown to others and shaped by the individual's personal history and crises. Their religious journey happened "on the side in terms of the Church" which did not ask its members how they were doing. Mrs. Haldane found that the primary place where those she interviewed lived their faith was in the world, not in the Church. While her study focused on only one congregation, it is likely that her findings are true for many congregations, especially mainstream Christian ones.

3. Cathy Grossman, "Charting the Unchurched in America."

4. The Barna Group, "Survey."
5. A variety of ways of how to do this are found in books that address dream interpretation.
6. Morton T. Kelsey, *Dreams, A Way to Listen to God*, 74. Copyright © 1978 by The Missionary Society of St. Paul the Apostle in the State of New York, Paulist Press, Inc., New York/Mahwah, N.J. Used with permission of Paulist Press.
7. An example of the three different ways of understanding the origin of dreams can be seen in the story of Rabbi Eisik of Cracow.

The pious rabbi, Eisik of Cracow, had a dream telling him to go to Prague, where, beneath the great bridge leading to the royal castle, he would find a buried treasure. The dream recurred three times, and the rabbi resolved to make the journey. He arrived in Prague and found the bridge, but it was guarded night and day by sentries. So Eisik didn't dare to dig beneath it. His constant prowling finally drew the attention of the captain of the guard.

The captain asked him in a friendly way, if he had lost something. The rabbi, a simple man, recounted his dream. The officer burst out laughing: "Really, my poor chap," he said to the rabbi, "you haven't actually worn out all that shoe leather coming here simply on account of a dream, have you? What rational person would believe in a dream?"

Now it seems that the officer himself had heard a voice in a dream too. "It went on about Cracow, telling me to go there and look for a great treasure in the house of a rabbi called Eisik, Eisik, son of Jekel. I was supposed to find this treasure hidden in a dusty recess behind the stove." But the officer put no faith in dream voices; the officer was a rational man.

The rabbi bowed very low, thanked him, and hurried back to Cracow. He searched in the walled-up recess behind his stove and uncovered the treasure that put an end to his poverty."

The rabbi's perspective represents the historic understanding of dreams: the dream comes from God because it predicts an event that actually happens. The rabbi is told in his dream of a treasure and he is able to find it. The captain of the guard's attitude represents the perception of dreams that has been popular for the last fifteen hundred years: dreams are nonsense. The guard tells the rabbi not to bother with his dreams because they have nothing of value to offer. The third perspective, one that is reflective of a good deal of twentieth century clinical psychology, places its emphasis on the internal, symbolic nature of the dream. The treasure is to be found in the unconscious, walled-up in the recesses of the rabbi's psyche. It is an inner treasure the holy man seeks, not an outer one.

Heinrich Zimmer told this story. He took it from Martin Buber's book, *Tales of the Hasidim*. I found the story in Mircea Eliade's, *Ordeal by Labyrinth, Conversations with Claude-Henri Rocquet*, 194–95.

8. Marie-Louise von Franz, *On Divination and Synchronicity*, wrote that the Chinese had two ideas about time: timeless time or eternity and cyclic time. While the ego lives in cyclic time, there is an eternal time underneath the ego's perception that sometimes interferes with cyclic time.11 The ancient Chinese developed a way to access the intersection of the two through divination. On a round plank was drawn a line that represented the heavenly order of eternal time. On a square plank, another line was drawn that represented the heavenly order of cyclic time. Through a whole in the middle of each a stick was placed. The individual seeking divination would rotate the two against each other. When they stopped, the situation inquired about would be addressed with the information revealed by the way the two combined. 97

Joseph Campbell, the American twentieth century teacher of mythology, suggested the first revelation of God might have occurred when thunder cracked.

9. Keith Ward, *Religion and Revelation*, 16. Dr. Ward is Regius Professor of Divinity at the University of Oxford. I disagree with Dr. Ward's contention that part of the defining aspect of a revelation is that the individual *always* knows "that God has so intentionally caused it." Certainly this component of a revelation is present in a variety of ways but not all of them are recognized for what they are. Many prayers are answered but the response is not recognized because the answer is not what was anticipated. When God's revealed will is not recognized, does this mean a revelation did not occur? I don't think so. Revelations happen whether the recipient recognizes them or not. Experiences of synchronicity and dreams are two other examples of revelation that frequently go unrecognized for what they are.

10. "Science is the century-old endeavor to bring together by means of systematic thought the perceptible phenomena of this world into as thorough-going an association as possible. To put it boldly, it is the attempt at a posterior reconstruction of existence by the process of conceptualization. Science can only ascertain what is, but not what should be, and outside of its domain value judgments of all kinds remain necessary." Albert Einstein, *Science, Philosophy and Religion: A Symposium*, ch. 13.

11. Albert Einstein, *Science, Philosophy and Religion: A Symposium*, ch. 13.

12. Keith Ward, *Religion and Revelation*, 98.

13. William James, in 1929, wrote: "Our normal waking consciousness . . . is but one special type of consciousness, whilst all about it, parted from it by the filmiest of screens, there lie potential forms of consciousness entirely different. We may go through life without suspecting their existence; but apply the requisite stimulus, and at a touch they are all there in all their completeness, definite types of mentality which probably somewhere have their field of application and adaptation. No account of the universe in its totality can be final which leaves these other forms of consciousness quite disregarded. How to regard them is the question – for they are so discontinuous with ordinary consciousness. Yet they may determine attitudes though they cannot furnish formulas, and open a region though they fail to give a map. At any rate, they forbid a premature closing of our accounts with reality." This quotation is from Charles T. Tart, ed., *Altered States of Consciousness*, 32.

14. Rumi, a thirteenth century Sufi, taught that the ears of men are ranked. Not all men have equal ability to hear.

15. John C. Robinson, *But Where Is God?*, 24.

16. E. Fuller Torrey, M.D., *Surviving Schizophrenia*, 62.

1

Historic Perspectives

> Most of the late-antique theorists of dreams agree that dream-speech was divine speech. Apart from nightmares and nocturnal visions inspired by demons or anxiety, dreams were thought to be somehow significant and divinely appointed, although the mechanics of their relation to the gods was subject to debate.[17]

INTRODUCTION

THE STORY OF GOD's involvement with dreams begins with some of the earliest preserved writings. It is fortunate that records preserved in the Near East during the 2,200 years before the birth of Jesus include passages that describe dreams in detail. Typically these records contain a description of the setting of the dreams, including who experienced them, when, where, and under what noteworthy circumstances the dream occurred, as well as the content of the dreams. It was not uncommon for these texts to include the reactions of the dreamer. The preserved texts also note how the dream was actually fulfilled if it contained a prediction or promise. It is typical of these reports to begin with the words that the dreamer "has gone to bed and is deeply asleep." These records make it possible to understand the attitudes these people had about God and dreams. This chapter surveys the more common attitudes from this ancient period.

ANCIENT NEAR EAST ATTITUDES ABOUT GOD AND DREAMS

Indicative of the attitudes about God's involvement with dreams are those found in Mari,[18] one of the great city-states of Mesopotamia during the Early Bronze age. Archeological research has found many documents, written in Akkadian, that were created there between 1800 and 1750 B.C. E.[19] Scholar Dr. Abraham Malamat studied these documents. He observed:

> The divine-prophets at Mari were of two types: professionals, recognizable by their distinctive titles. . . and lay people with no title whatsoever. . . . More than half of the "prophetic" documents from Mari deal with lay persons not functioning as professionals attached to a sanctuary. . . . Among the lay prophets the dream is prevalent as a prophetic means, while this medium is totally absent among the professionals. . . . The professional prophets enjoyed direct revelations while awake; the lay persons . . . were usually dreamers of dreams. . . . From a third to half of all published prophecies from Mari originated in dreams. . . . The credibility of prophetic revelation was obviously a sensitive matter, not to be taken for granted. Thus it was often verified by means of accepted mantic devices, which were considered more reliable and preferable to intuitive prophesying. . . . In contrast, in Israel the prophetic word . . . is never subjected to corroboration by cultic means; it is simply vindicated by the test of fulfillment (cf. Deut.18:22; Jer. 28:9; Ezekiel 33:33)[20]

TYPES OF DREAMS

Another scholar of the dreams from this period was Dr. Leo Oppenheim. Dr. Oppenheim identified three types of dreams preserved in the ancient Near East: message dreams, symbolic dreams and mantic dreams.

Message Dreams

Message dreams provide a command or warning to the dreamer from the dreamer's god.[21] It did not matter which god the dreamer worshipped, since it was a commonly accepted fact among all the people of the region that all gods communicate through dreams.

A distinguishing characteristic of message dreams is their clarity. The meaning of these dreams was so obvious that they did not need an interpretation. For example the Hittite King Hattushili wrote that he married his queen "not blindly but I took her [as wife] upon the command of the deity. The deity assigned her to me in a dream." Truly this was a marriage made in heaven![22]

Message dreams typically contained either a reference to the presence of god being in the dream or that god sent a spirit to function as a messenger. Frequently a description of the towering size and beauty of the deity or messenger was included in the report. Sumerian, Akkadian, and Greek message dreams shared a common phrase that means the appearing deity "stood at the head of the sleeper." Greek accounts, in particular, give the impression that the god *actually* entered the sleeper's room. They also indicate the voice of the visiting god was heard at the very moment of awakening. Some later Nordic dream accounts say the sleeper, after awakening suddenly, caught a glimpse of a "person just leaving his room."

Another feature shared among the various reports of message dreams was that of the sleeper hearing his or her name called by their god before the god presented the message. The story of Samuel found in Hebrew Scripture is an excellent illustration.[23] Message dreams often began with the deity or messenger saying, "Be not afraid!"[24]

It was common also for dream reports to conclude with wording that indicated the dreamer was startled awake by the experience of encountering a divine presence in their dream. One of the oldest dreams in literature, the second preserved dream of the great Mesopotamian King Gudea (2141–2122 B.C.E.), is an illustration of this numinous experience. The King's dream concludes, "He woke up with a start, it was (but) a dream!"[25] King Gudea believed his god spoke to him through his dreams. In another of the King's dreams he was instructed by his god to build the Temple Erinnu in his city-state capital of Lagash (southeast Iraq). In response to his god's directive, King Gudea built the temple using precious stones, copper, and tin.

Symbolic Dreams

Dr. Oppenheim identified a second type of dream from the ancient Near East, the "symbolic" dream. He wrote:

> In such dreams man meets a world whirling with strange objects and unprecedented activities and happenings, teeming with gods, demons, humans and beasts; a world which extends in sweep, variety and intricacy far beyond that to which the duller senses of man's waking consciousness grant him access.[26]

Dr. Oppenheim noted that whereas message dreams were addressed to men almost exclusively, symbolic dreams tended to be more frequently experienced by women.

Unfortunately, Near Eastern censorship was rigorous. Not many symbolic dreams were preserved. The dream's images, in spite of Dr. Oppenheim's name for this type of dream, were understood literally. Consequently the dream's content and message was baffling. Nevertheless, symbolic dreams were so impressive that the dreamer had no doubt they were full of meaning. Dr. Oppenheim found that the meaning of the dreams always dealt with future events, never the past or present.[27] It was probably because these dreams so emotionally touched their recipients that the dreams were recorded and preserved. To gain access to the dream's meaning, symbolic dreams needed to be interpreted. The dream and its interpretation were usually preserved together as a unit.

In the Hebrew Scriptures, Dr. Oppenheim noted, symbolic dreams are reserved for Gentiles. God sent the Egyptian Pharaoh of the Exodus and Nebuchadnezzar such dreams but also provided them with an interpreter—Joseph and Daniel, respectively—to make his message understandable. Most of the symbolic dreams found in the Hebrew Scriptures emphasize not the importance of the dream message, but the piety and interpretative capacity of the god-inspired interpreter.[28]

Because symbolic dreams were difficult to understand and inspired interpreters hard to find, elaborate rules were created and collected into handbooks to guide clergy in dream interpretation. Some of these handbooks have been discovered in Assyria and Babylonia.

Mantic Dreams

Mantic or predictive dreams are the third type of dream Dr. Oppenheim identified from the Ancient Near East. Dreams containing predictions were believed to occur slightly before dawn. In Akkadian literature some predictions are public and some are private. Public predictions concern the king and the country. Private predictions concern individual citizens. The Mesopotamian attitude, according to Dr. Oppenheim, was that mantic dreams were warnings sent by a concerned god to those who paid attention to their dreams and could understand them. When a mantic dream predicted a misfortune, the recipient could protect himself by means of apotropaic rituals. The correct ritual was considered potent enough to obviate all of the bad consequences suggested in the dream.

Dr. Oppenheim wrote about the following incident which illustrates the perceived power of rituals to cleanse the bad consequences a dream may bring.

> The Hittite king Murshili was traveling to a distant city dressed in festive garments for some sort of a cultic ceremony when there was an especially loud thunderclap. The experience shocked Murshili so severely that he lost his ability to speak (aphonia). With time Murshili recovered and forgot the entire incident. After several years, however, Murshili began to dream of this thunderstorm. Each time he did he re-experienced the original shock. Finally Murshili had such an intense dream that it felt like the 'Hand of God', to use Murshili's own words, struck him. When he awoke he could not speak at all.
>
> What follows are a series of ritualistic attempts to cure the troubled king. One of these rituals involved taking the contaminated garments of the king's, along with his chariot and the horses involved in the thunderstorm and sacrificing them to the Weather-god. The royal paraphernalia involved included also the king's shoes, weapons, the very table, bed, bowl and wash basin and every utensil he used. All of these were taken to the temple of the Weather-god and were burnt as an offering. A substitute for the king himself was used: a bull upon whom Murshili laid his hands. This ritual cleansing worked and the king was healed—the dreams stopped.[29]

EGYPT

During the two millennia before the birth of Jesus, Egypt was a place where dreams were highly regarded. Egyptians believed many dreams came directly from God. A seventh century B.C.E. Egyptian writing expressed it well: "(God) has created remedies to cure disease, wine to cure sorrow, and he has created dreams to guide him who experiences them. . . ."[30] It was in Egypt around 2000 B.C.E. that the oldest known dream book, the papyrus of Deral-Madineh, was written. It contains dreams that are regarded as divine revelations.[31]

Some of the divine dreams provided healing. If an individual wanted to increase the likelihood of receiving such a dream, that person might go to sleep in a specially designated area of a Sleep or Dream Temple. In these holy places the temple clergy put supplicants in a trance-like sleep.

6   GOD AND DREAMS

When the individual awoke, their dream would be interpreted with the expectation of finding out more about the person's illness or of perhaps identifying a possible cure.[32] Egyptian priests of the second century B.C.E. who specialized in dreaming were known as "Learned Ones of the Magic Library."[33] Egypt was also the place that most respected dream interpreters were found. For several centuries in Assyria and Palestine, an interpreter of dreams had to be from Egypt in order to be acceptable.

During the earliest periods of Egyptian history, anyone could receive a message from the gods through their dreams.[34] Not surprisingly though, it was the dreams of the Egyptian royalty that were the ones most often preserved. Dr. Leo Oppenheim wrote about one of the earliest preserved royal dreams. It dates from the end of the fifteenth century B.C.E. and was a dream of a young man named Thutmose. Thutmose had gone hunting and decided to take a nap around noon. He fell asleep in a quarry in the shadow of the Great Sphinx, which was mostly buried in sand at the time. In the dream, the Sphinx spoke to Thutmose saying the sand was choking the Sphinx and that if Thutmose would clear the sand away, his reward would be to become Pharaoh someday. The young Thutmose obeyed his dream. He did what the Sphinx requested. Later he became Pharaoh Thutmose IV.[35] Thutmose's dream is the only one preserved from this period that did not happen at night. The report of the dream stresses how his sleeping at this time of day was unusual.[36]

Many of the royal dreams preserved in Egypt come from the seventh century B.C.E. So remarkable were the dreams of the Egyptian royalty that the Greek historians Herodotus and Plutarch made note of them many centuries later.[37]

BABYLONIAN REFERENCES

Babylon, which means *gate of god*, was a close second to Egypt with regard to people's interest and skill with dreams. Its interpreters were considered to be highly specialized also (see Daniel 1:17). Mamu was an ancient Sumerian god of dreams that the Babylonians continued to worship. Babylonians believed Mamu provided divine oracles through dreams and visions.

Nebuchadnezzar II (605–562 B.C.E.) was the greatest king of Babylon. He was famous for expanding its empire, building up its capital, and for constructing the Hanging Gardens to please his homesick wife. Nebuchadnezzar II valued his dreams, especially the vivid, spectacular ones documented in the Book of Daniel. One of his sons, Nabonidus (555–539 B.C.E.) also paid attention to his dreams. When Nabonidus was King of Babylon, he had a divine dream that instructed him to rebuild the temple Ehulhul.[38]

Babylon is where the Gilgamesh Epic took place. It is the world's oldest written story, dating from at least 2000 B.C.E. In the story, King Uruk is helped repeatedly by dreams given him by heavenly powers.

HITTITE REFERENCES

Another early text containing dream communications from god was found in Hittite Asia Minor. The text was King Hattushili's autobiography (twelfth century B.C.E.). Dreams were so important to the King that when he told the story of his life he included many of them. Dreams, King Hattushili believed, were used by his god to both direct his rise to power and to give credibility to his reign.

King Hattushili's wife was also the recipient of message dreams. The queen was in Boghazkeui, the capital of the Hittite Empire, sometime between 1290 and 1250 B.C.E. when she received the message from her god.

CANAANITE REFERENCES

A fourteenth century B.C.E. Canannite text tells the story of King Kret. Discovered in 1931 in Syria, *The Epic of Kret* was recorded on three clay tablets. The story tells how Kret was a king who had lost both his estate and eight successive wives before any of them could give birth to an heir. Distraught, the king is said to have fallen asleep in tears. His god, El, appeared to him in a dream. To lessen his sorrow, El offered Kret in the dream an expanded kingship and new riches. El also gave Kret a set of instructions. These instructions included the directive that Kret should lay siege to the city of Udm. Not only that, but Kret was told to take Huray, the daughter of the Udm's king, to be his wife. Kret did as he was instructed and all went well. Riches, a new wife, and eight sons followed. Later in his life when Kret became very ill and near death, El gathered the Divine Assembly on Kret's behalf and arranged to have Kret cured.[39]

8 GOD AND DREAMS

ANCIENT GREEK AND ROMAN REFERENCES

Homer is considered to be the earliest known Greek poet. The *Iliad* and the *Odyssey* are generally acknowledged to be his writings. Herodotus believed Homer lived around 850 B.C.E. though others dispute this date. Toward the end of Book XIX of the *Odyssey* is found Homer's reference to the two gates of sleep through which dreams pass. Homer had Penelope, Odysseus' wife, say:

> Truly dreams are by nature perplexing and full of messages which are hard to interpret; nor by any means will everything [in them] come true for mortals. For there are two gates of insubstantial dreams; one [pair] is wrought of horn and one of ivory. Of these, [the dreams] which come through [the gate of] sawn ivory are dangerous to believe, for they bring messages which will not issue in deeds; but [the dreams] which come forth through [the gate of] polished horn, these have power in reality, whenever any mortal sees them.[40]

Homer spoke of *seeing* a dream, not of *having* a dream because a dream image for him was independent of the dreamer, existed objectively in space, and presented itself to the dreamer.[41] Dream images for Homer were connected with divine beings who sent or were in the dreams themselves, though in disguised form.[42] The Greek playwright Sophocles (496?–406B.C.E.), while not speaking of the divine origins of dreams, did have a personal experience with at least one dream message that came true and also included dreams that came true in his writings. In his personal life Sophocles had a dream that was both recurring and predictive. The dream concerned the theft of a heavy gold dish from the temple of Hercules. Sophocles ignored the dream the first two times he had it. When the dream occurred a third time, Sophocles went to the authorities and told them the name of the individual the dream identified as the thief. The authorities arrested the man, who then confessed and returned the dish.[43] In *Oedipus the King*, Sophocles included a dream that accurately foretold the future. Jocasta tells her son and husband, Oedipus: "How often it chances that in dreams a man has wed his mother! He who least regards such brainsick fantasies lives most at ease."[44]

Another Greek who had predictive messages come to him in his dreams was Socrates (470?–399 B.C.E.). Tradition indicates that Socrates dreamed on the night before he met Plato of "a young swan settled in

[my] lap and, developing at once into a full-fledged bird, it flew into the open sky uttering a song that charmed all hearers."[45]

Plato (427?–347 B.C.E.), whose attitudes about dreams were often contradictory, wrote in *Timaeus*:

> No one achieves true and inspired divination when in his rational mind, but only when the power of his intelligence is fettered in sleep or when it is distraught by disease or by reason of some divine inspiration. But it belongs to a man when in his right mind to recollect and ponder both the things spoken in dream or waking vision by the divining and inspired nature, and all the visionary forms that were seen, and by means of reasoning to discern about them all wherein they are significant.[46]

Aristotle (384–322 B.C.E.), on the other hand, did not believe that dreams are messages from God but are products of the interaction between the body and the mind. Dreams for Aristotle were a re-experiencing of impressions left by the previous day's activities.[47] Yet even Aristotle could not refrain from reporting a dream incident that showed dream predictions could be substantiated by the events that followed. In Aristotle's view of the world a dream coming true was the result of good guessing, luck or coincidence. Nevertheless, recounting the report, Cicero wrote:

> And Aristotle, who was endowed with a matchless and almost godlike intellect,—is he in error, or is he trying to lead others into error in the following account of his friend, Eudemus the Cyprian? Eudemus, while on his way to Macedonia, reached Pherae, then a very famous city of Thessaly, but groaning under the cruel sway of the tyrant, Alexander. There he became so violently ill that the physicians despaired of his recovery. While sick he had a dream in which a youth of striking beauty told him that he would speedily get well; that the despot Alexander would die in a few days, and that he himself would return home five years later. And so, indeed, the first two prophecies, as Aristotle writes, were immediately fulfilled by the recovery of Eudemus and by the death of the tyrant at the hands of his wife's brothers.[48]

In the second century of the Christian era, Artemidorus devoted his life to the study of dreams. According to tradition, he traveled extensively to gather information about dreams. The result was a five volume *Interpretation of Dreams* known in Greek as *Oneirocritica*. This is the longest of the ancient dream books. Artemidorus paid careful attention to the images and details of a dream in order to show how the dream predicted the future.

Marcus Tullius Cicero (106–43 B.C.E.), a Roman lawyer, orator, politician and philosopher agreed with Aristotle that dreams result from the interaction of the body and the mind. Like Aristotle, Cicero was a man who valued logic. He thought of religion as being nothing more than an attitude that developed when a person felt awe in the presence of the frightening unknown. Accordingly, Cicero did not believe in divination. The year before he died, Cicero wrote *On Divination* in which he maintained that divination is a superstition that "should be torn up by the roots." Dreams, he said, were merely a form of superstition that took advantage of human weakness to cast a spell over people.[49] "It must be understood," he argued, "that there is no divine power which creates dreams."[50] Those individuals who sanction divination, he went on to say, "Were influenced more by actual results than convinced by reason."[51] It is possible that Cicero's attitudes later influenced Jerome's translation of the Bible.

DREAMS THAT HEAL

As they are today, dreams in this ancient period were interpreted for therapeutic reasons. The word *chalom* or the verb *chalam* (dream) etymologically is related to the Aramaic and Hebrew verb "to be made healthy or strong."[52] One example of a dream being used for healing is the Egyptian story of Mehwesekht, the wife of Ramses II's son, Setme Khamuas.[53] Mehwesekht was unable to become pregnant, so she went to the temple of Imhotep in Memphis to seek a cure. In the temple, Mehwesekht offered a prayer and fell asleep. In response to her prayer Mehwesekht received a dream which contained the cure for her sterility. In another example Dr. Oppenheim wrote about a Hittite man healed of his impotence when he dreamed he slept with a goddess.[54]

Frequently it was necessary for someone to translate the dream images into a message the dreamer could understand before the healing occurred. The confusion created by the literal understanding of the images disappeared as the dream was interpreted. In Mesopotamia and Asia Minor women functioned most often as the dream interpreters. Their role was not to analyze a dream, but to clarify it.

Like the Egyptians before them, the ancient Greeks also had a therapeutic attitude about dreams. The Asklepian site at Epidaurus[55] was based on the ritualistic use of dreams. This approach to healing was so successful that it was practiced for more than 1,000 years. Later, the Romans also had temples that used dreams for healing. Their temples were dedicated to Apollo and were spread throughout the entire Roman Empire. One of these temples was discovered in Britain in 1928 in Lydney Park, Lydney, Gloucestershire.[56]

SUMMARY

It was common for dreams in antiquity to have a religious significance. Some were regarded as revelatory. The prevailing attitude was that if God could and did speak to a person this way, it was better to pay attention to what was being said than not to do so. It was such a widely accepted perspective that it did not matter whose god was the source of the dream.

Dreams were recalled, discussed, analyzed and acted upon. Different types of dreams were identified, and dream interpretation was common. Dreams offered comfort and guidance, alerted people to impending danger, gave glimpses into the future, inspired creativity and healed. Manuals for how to interpret dreams were created and widely distributed. Not everyone believed dreams came from God, but the general attitude was that at the very least, some dreams do

ENDNOTES

17. Patricia Cox Miller, Dreams in Late Antiquity, Studies in the Imagination of a Culture, 65–66.

18. Mari is also known as Tell Hariri. It dates back as far as the third millennium before Christ and was a commercial, political and artistic center around 1800 B.C.E. Its power extended over 300 miles. In the Hebrew Bible they are referred to as the Amorites. Hammurabi conquered Mari around 1700 B.C.E. and it never regained its former status. This information was found at http://ancientneareast.tripod.com/Mari_Hariri.html.

19. B.C.E. stands for "Before Christian Era." When C.E. is used, it means "Christian Era."

20. A. Malamat, 'A Forerunner of Biblical Prophecy," 33–52. Dr. Bart Koet has found that the Jews in addition to the test of fulfillment to show that a dream truly came from God used scriptural references. "References to Scripture can take several forms: a quotation, a reference to the whole of Scripture, a part of it, or only the whole of one book. It can even be an allusion." Koet, "Trustworthy Dreams?," 87–107.

21. In Mari and in the Hebrew Bible (Num. 12:6; Jer. 23:25–32; 29:8; Zech.10:2) some message dreams were not intended for the dream recipient but for someone else. Malamat, "Forerunner of Biblical Prophecy."

22. Information on dreams in the Near East from the period prior to the birth of Jesus comes from L. Oppenheim, *The Interpretation of Dreams in the Ancient Near East*. The

story of King Hattushili's dream report was found on page 197. Used with permission. Of Dr. Oppenheim's three types, message dreams were the ones most often preserved. Dr. Oppenheim wrote that some message dreams helped artists with their creativity. 192 Later scholars like Dr. Scott Noegel of the University of Washington are critical of Oppenheim's division of dreams because he made no distinction between textual genres, did not place his data into an historical context, and because the dreams do not really fit neatly into his categories. Nevertheless, Dr. Oppenheim's categories are used here because they are helpful teaching aides. See Dr. Noegel's review of Ruth Fidler's book, *Dreams Speak Falsely*.

23. First Samuel 3. Dr. Malamat interprets this event with a different emphasis. "In general, novice and inexperienced prophets were unable to identify revelations when they first encountered them ... hence the repetition of the manifestation. . . ." Malamat, "Forerunner of Biblical Prophecy."

24. Oppenheim, *Dreams*, 188. See Luke 1:13, 30 for the New Testament continuation of this reassurance offered by God when making an appearance in a person's life.

25. Oppenheim, *Dreams*, 188–91.

26. Oppenheim, *Dreams*, 184.

27. Even dreams that were professionally interpreted on occasion required divine confirmation through some sort of a sign. Dr. Oppenheim observed that there are only a few references in Mesopotamia to dream interpreters who were priests or members of a socially prominent class. Oppenheim, *Dreams*, 200–7.

28. Oppenheim, *Dreams*, 203.

29. Oppenheim, *Dreams*, 230–31.

30. This quotation comes from the Papyrus Insigne and found in Oppenheim, *Dreams*, 239.

31. Jon Tolaas and Montague Ullman, "Extrasensory Communication and Dreams," *Handbook of Dreams—Research, Theories and Applications*.

32. David Reeves, "The Roots of Hypnosis."

33. Robert Moss, "Dreaming Like an Egyptian." The priest's title suggests that early Egyptians already appreciated the vast depths from which dreams arise. Today the "magic library" is called the unconscious. Mr. Moss wrote in this article that in Egypt "trained dreamers operated as seers, remote viewers and telepaths, advising on affairs of state and military strategy and providing a mental communications network between far-flung temples and administrative centers. They practiced shapeshifting, crossing time and space in the dreambodies of birds and animals. Through conscious dream travel, ancient Egypt's 'frequent flyers' explored the roads of the afterlife and the multidimensional universe. It was understood that true initiation and transformation takes place in a deeper reality accessible through dream journey beyond the body."

34. Jimmy Dunn, "Piety of the Common Ancient Egyptians."

35. Oppenheim, *Dreams*, 187.

36. Oppenheim, *Dreams*, 187.

37. Herodotus said that the Egyptians were "religious to excess, far beyond any other race of men. . . ." "Herodotus' Second Book of Histories, Euterpe." 10.

38. Oppenheim, *Dreams*, 250.

39. Christopher B. Siren, "Canaanite/Ugaritic Mythology FAQ." Also, *The Epic of Kret*. Dr. Barry L. Bandstra, *Reading the Old Testament*, 464, observed that other fourteenth century B.C.E. Ugaritic texts make reference to a Danel who was a notable Canaanite king. This leader was highly regarded because of his efforts to bring justice to his kingdom. Dr. Bandstra argued that it was this ancient hero that the Hebrew Bible later used as a model or at least as a namesake for the Book of Daniel, which was composed around 164 B.C.E.

Historic Perspectives 13

40. Odyssey 19:560–67. This quotation was found in Miller, *Dreams in Late Antiquity*, 15. The Latin poet Virgil (70–19 B.C.E.) made a significant (and unfortunate) contribution to dream interpretation. Virgil did not agree with Homer that dreams were "by nature perplexing and full of messages which are hard to interpret." Virgil believed dreams were either true or false. He altered Homer's image of the two gates from representing the fact that some dreams come true while others do not to representing some dreams are true while others are false. Virgil's contribution to dream interpretation was the introduction of value judgments about a dream's truth. Miller, *Dreams in Late Antiquity*, 26.

41. Miller, *Dreams in Late Antiquity*, 17, references the work of E.R. Dodds, *The Greeks and the Irrational*, 104 and A. H. M. Kessels, *Studies on the Dream in Greek Literature*, 178–79.

42. Miller, *Dreams in Late Antiquity*, 18. Again she references Kessels, *Studies*, 86–87, 115n.10.

43. The account of this dream was found in Cicero, *On Divination*, 283.

44. Lines 983–85.

45. Miller, *Dreams in Late Antiquity*, 3. She references Riginos, pp. 21–24.

46. Miller, *Dreams in Late Antiquity*, 39, *Timaeus* 71E.

47. Miller, *Dreams in Late Antiquity*, 43–44. Miller references Aristotle's *De insomniis*, *De somno*, and *De divinatione per somnum*.

48. Cicero, *On Divination*, I.xxvi.55, 283. Aristotle also writes about lucid dreaming: "For often when one is asleep there is something in consciousness which declares that what then presents itself is but a dream." From Aristotle, *On Dreams*, as found in Stephen LaBerge: *Lucid Dreaming*, chapter 2. For more information about lucid dreaming see chapter 6.

49. Cicero, *On Divination*, II.lxxii.149, 537.

50. Cicero, *On Divination*, II.lx.125, 511.

51. Cicero, On Divination, I.iii.5, 227. In making his arguments Cicero identified many people who did believe in divination. Among the believers he cited were Pythagoras; Democritus; Dicaearchus the Peripatetic (who accepted divination by dreams); and Cratippus, also a Peripatetic. Cicero noted that the Stoics defended divination and that Chrysippus wrote two books on the divination, one of which was on dreams. Diogenes of Babylon wrote a book on divination, Antipater wrote two books, and Posidonius wrote five.

52. In contrast, the Egyptian word for dreams, *RSWT*, etymologically means, "to be awake." An open eye represents the dream state. According to Dr. Oppenheim, dreams for Egyptians are a state of consciousness that exists between the eclipse of sleep and the dull reality of day. *Dreams*, 190.

53. The account comes from "The Second Story of Khamuas: Prince Khamuas and Si-Osiri.

54. Oppenheim, Dreams, 192.

55. Other sites where dream incubation took place included the Cave of Trophonius, which was located in the Grove of Leivadia in Viotia. Trophonius was the Greek god of architecture who was swallowed by earth. Trophonius gave oracles about the future. The mental shock of receiving an oracle at his cave sometimes resulted in people developing melancholia. The Egyptian Temple of Serapis in Alexandria was a second location. Serapis was god of the underworld and was worshipped by both Greeks and Egyptians. His statue was moved to Alexandria when Ptolemy Soter had a dream telling him to move it there. A third location was the Egyptian Temple of Hathor in the Sinai Peninsula.

Hathor was the goddess of music, dance and the arts who was consulted through dreams for aid in creativity.

56. Reeves, "The Roots of Hypnosis." Reeves adds that one of the people assisting with the excavation was a young professor named J. R. R. Tolkien.

2

Jewish Perspectives

As the sun was going down, a deep sleep fell on Abram. . . . On that day, the Lord made a covenant with Abram, saying, "To your descendents I give this land, from the river of Egypt to the great river, the river Euphrates, the land of the Kenites, the Kenizzites, the Kadmonites, the Hittites, the Perizzites, the Rephaim, the Amorites, the Canaanites, the Girgashites, Hivites and the Jebusites."

—Genesis 15:12, 18–21

INTRODUCTION

THE EXPLORATION OF GOD'S involvement with dreams next turns to Judaism. God's relationship with the Hebrew people and their descendents can be characterized as a continuing conversation. Significantly, one of the ways God conveyed His messages to the Hebrew people was through dreams. The people of the Hebrew Bible shared the same attitude about dreams that their neighbors did: God does speak through dreams. Because of the special relationship the Hebrew people had with God, they considered their dreams trustworthier than the dreams other people had.

The Hebrew Bible[57] contains many references to God communicating through dreams. Some of these messages were prophecies, some warnings. While most dream messages from God were positive, some were negative. There are also passages that are critical of dreams for leading people away from God.

The rabbinic traditions kept the conversation uninterrupted after the close of the Hebrew Bible. Later, Jewish orthodoxy, mysticism, and Zionism developed out of these earlier conversations and keep the discourse alive and vital today.

ATTITUDES IN THE HEBREW BIBLE ABOUT GOD AND DREAMS

The dreams found in the Hebrew Bible are regarded in the same way they were by other people of the ancient Near East: some come with God, some do not. It was generally accepted though that dreams were one way of having a direct, personal experience of God. The Elohist source, written about 850 B.C.E., provides the majority of the dream accounts, including Abram's covenant dream.

> Patrick Miller, a scholar of the Hebrew Bible, writes: The will of [Yahweh] was conveyed by means of oracle inquiry and prophetic audition or vision. Dreams, casting of lots within the sacred assembly, and prophetic revelation were legitimate means of discerning the divine will or direction. Divination, soothsaying, and necromancy, however, were prohibited. That is, there were both prescribed and proscribed techniques for consultation of the deity.
>
> Even dreams, which were regularly a vehicle for Yahweh's authentic communication, at times became suspect, usually because they were perceived as vehicles of lies. Indeed, much of the prophetic condemnation of dreams, prophetic visions, and divination is less because of an inappropriate medium being used than because of its false product.[58]

In the Hebrew Bible divine dreams were distinguished from other kinds of dreams by their ability to accurately predict the future. A dream's reliability was proven when the events foretold came to pass. A dream that did not come to pass was not considered to be from God.

DREAMS AND VISIONS

Although a differentiation is made between a divine dream and a vision in Hebrew Scripture, the source is considered to be the same: both originate in God.[59] Often it is difficult to identify which medium the writer had in mind because there is such fluidity between the two. In the reports of the prophets, the words "heard" and "saw" are used in such a way that it is not easy to distinguish how they received God's message. It was the message, not the medium, which mattered.[60]

DIVINE COUNCIL

It has been argued that before Israel was exclusively monotheistic it shared the belief with several other Near Eastern countries that God was the head of a Divine Council. The undefined nature of the Council's membership allowed other gods to be included in this heavenly host, including those of the surrounding nations. Yahweh was enthroned as King and Judge and presided over the Council's deliberations. The other members were called "angels" (messengers); "ministers"; "servants"; "holy ones"; and "sons of God" meaning "divine beings."[61]

The Divine Council met at least once a year, perhaps on New Year's Day, to pronounce judgment on sin and rebellion. It was the prophet's responsibility to be the spokesman for the Council. The true prophet discerned the divine sentence and commission (Isaiah 6:8), whereas the false prophet did not (Jeremiah 23:16–18). One way a prophet received the Council's message was through a dream.

THE PATRIARCHS AND DREAMS

Abraham, who appears to have lived sometime between 2000–1550 B.C.E., was the first person in Hebrew Bible whose dreams were recorded. God makes His historic covenant with Abram in the dream quoted in Genesis 15 that pledges the Promised Land to him and to his descendents.

According to the Genesis narrative, another Patriarch who was a dreamer was Jacob. Two of his dreams in particular deeply influenced his life. According to the account in Genesis, the first of these dreams occurred when he was in despair. In the dream (Gen. 28:10–19) God appeared and reaffirmed the three-fold promises He made to Abram. God spoke directly and personally to Jacob, twice (28:15, 29) telling him, "I will be with you."[62] Years later when Jacob had the dream of wrestling with an angel (Genesis 32:26–29), he named the isolated place where the dream occurred, *Peniel*, "because I have seen God face to face and I have survived."

One of Jacob's sons, Joseph, also believed God spoke through dreams. Indeed, the entire scriptural account of Joseph revolves around his ability to interpret the dreams of others as well as his own. His success as a leader was due in large measure to his ability to work with dreams; a trait appreciated more in Egypt than at home.

OTHER DREAM REFERENCES IN THE TORAH

According to the book of Genesis Jacob's clan lived in Egypt for approximately 450 years. Around 1280 B.C.E., according to the book of Exodus, Moses led the Hebrew people out of Egypt toward the Promised Land. In chapter three of the book of Numbers, when Moses was criticized for not getting to the Promised Land quickly enough, one of his supporters offered this defense for him. "How dare you criticize Moses. God speaks face-to-face with him. To us He only speaks in dreams. . . ." It is clear that the people of the exodus believed God communicated through dreams.

Numbers 22–24 tells the story of Balaam and his talking ass. Balaam's animal saw visions of an angel before Balaam did. But God spoke with Balaam at night, probably through his dreams. As a result, Balaam did God's will—in spite of being offered a house full of gold and silver to do otherwise. Balaam regarded his dreams from God with the utmost seriousness.

Dreams and their interpretations are important also in the book of Judges. After Moses died, the Israelites entered Canaan under the leadership of Joshua and began settling there. When Joshua died, there was no one to take his place. A loosely organized federation of tribes emerged. When problems arose with the tribe's neighbors, an individual inspired by God, called a judge, assumed leadership of the tribes. The judge's role was to lead the tribes into battle and defeat the enemy. In one account, Judges 7:13–23, Gideon won a battle because of a dream.[63]

The prophet Nathan spoke to King David in the name of the Lord in 2 Samuel 7 and I Chronicles 17. Nathan's message was that God did not want David to build a "home" for the Ark of the Covenant. Instead, God would build David's family into an everlasting dynasty.[64] This prophecy of Nathan's came to him in a nighttime vision.

First Kings 3:5–15 records a dream that King Solomon had in which he dialogues with God. Solomon, being a new king, traveled six miles northwest of Jerusalem to the shrine at Gibeon to participate in what appears to have been the ancient tradition of dream incubation: sleeping in a holy place in anticipation of receiving a dream from God. Solomon began his dream preparation by offering a substantial sacrifice to God. In his dream, Solomon asked God for "an understanding mind to govern your people, able to discern between good and evil; for who can govern this your great people?" God's response in the dream was to grant Solomon's request: "I give you a wise and discerning mind; no one like you shall arise after you." Upon waking, Solomon returned to Jerusalem, made another sacrifice to God, and then held a "drinking-feast" where he told others of the blessings God promised him in his dream.

Psalm 3 is another example of dream incubation.⁶⁵ The author is a ruler, probably a king, who is in a frightening situation. He faced a large number of enemies and was told "there is no help for you in God." The king went to a holy place, offered a prayer, and then slept. While asleep the king dreamed of God's presence offering him the assurance of support. He awakened full of confidence that the "Lord sustains me."

> I cry aloud to the Lord,
> and he answers me from his holy hill.
> I lie down and sleep;
> I wake again, for the Lord sustains me.
> I am not afraid of ten thousands of people
> who have set themselves against me all around.

Psalm 126:1–3 also addresses the importance of dreams:

> When the Lord restored the fortunes of Zion,
> we were like those who dream.
> Then our mouth was filled with laughter,
> and our tongue with shouts of joy;
> then it was said among the nations,
> "The Lord has done great things for them."

This hymn of joy and expectation was written during a very dark moment for the Israelites.⁶⁶ The Psalm writer recognized the hope of Israel rested on God's initiative, not their own. The people of Israel were open to God doing great things for them. In this way they are like those who dream.

NEGATIVE MESSAGES FROM GOD

Negative messages from God are of two kinds: those that tell the dreamer something the dreamer does not want to hear and those that deny the dreamer what the dreamer wants.⁶⁷

Job 7:13–14 is an example of a dream that communicates something the dreamer does not want to hear. Job, miserable due to his suffering, protests to God:

> When I say, 'my bed will comfort me,
> my couch will ease my complaint,'
> then you scare me with dreams
> and terrify me with visions.

The account of Samuel's dream in I Samuel 3 is an example of a dream that is both positive and negative. It is positive because in the dream Samuel received his call to God's service. The early chapters of the book of Samuel depict him as a young man watching, learning and practicing priestly activities in Shiloh. Then he had the dream that called him to a larger destiny: Samuel was to become the most important Hebrew priest and leader of his time. Samuel was so distinguished that two books in the Hebrew Bible are named after him. What made Samuel's dream especially significant was that it occurred at a time when revelations were rare. A consequence of Samuel's experience was that Shiloh became well known as a place where revelations occur.

On the other hand, Samuel's dream also contained a negative message. It told him something he did not want to hear. The dream told Samuel about Eli and his clan's future. Eli's sons had blasphemed God and Eli had done nothing about it. God told Samuel in the dream that Eli and his family were about to be severely punished for the offense. The house of Eli was to fall, the Ark of the Covenant captured, and Shiloh destroyed by Eli's enemy, the Philistines. When Eli heard this from Samuel, he said: "It is the Lord; let him do what seems good to him." Eli, a distinguished priest and mentor for Samuel, accepted messages from God that were received through dreams.

The story of Abim'elech is an illustration of a dream whose message denies the dreamer his desires. Genesis 20 tells how Abim'elech, King of Gerar, wanted to have sex with Sarah, who was his houseguest. Before the sexual activity began, Abim'elech had a dream. In the dream God told Abim'elech that "you are about to die because of the woman whom you have taken; for she is a married woman." Abim'elech objected and pleaded his innocence. (Abim'elech did not know that Sarah was Abraham's wife because Abraham had introduced Sarah as his sister.) In the dream God was responsive to Abim'elech's pleas and revised his judgment. God told Abim'elech: "Yes, I know that you did this in the integrity of your heart; furthermore it was I who kept you from sinning against me ... Return the man's wife... and you shall live. But if you do not restore her, know that you shall surely die, you and all that are yours." King Abim'elech obeyed the dream even though it denied him the sex he wanted. When he awoke, he immediately restored Sarah to Abraham.

Another instance of a dreamer being denied what he wanted involved Saul, Israel's first king. We learn in I Samuel 28:6–19 that shortly before his death, Saul was very distressed because God no longer offered him guidance through his dreams. Without these messages, Saul was lost. Doom would not be far away. The next day Saul's army was defeated by the Philistines and Saul and his sons were killed.

BIBLICAL PASSAGES CRITICAL OF DREAMS

Not all dreams in the Hebrew Bible come from God. Those that do not, we are told, should not be given any positive regard. For example, on a few occasions the Hebrew Bible uses dreams as a simile for an elusive, ephemeral experience.[68] This can be seen in Isaiah 29:7–9. Isaiah likens those who fight against Mount Zion to a dream, which seems powerful and real while asleep, but upon waking turns out to be nothing.

> Just as when a hungry person dreams of eating
> and wakes up still hungry,
> or a thirsty person dreams of drinking
> and wakes up faint, still thirsty,
> so shall the multitude of all the nations be
> that fight against Mount Zion.

Job 20:4–9 uses the transient nature of dreams as an image for how the triumph of the wicked is short-lived.

> Do you not know this from of old,
> ever since mortals were placed on earth,
> that the exulting of the wicked is short,
> and the joy of the godless is but for a moment?
> Even though they mount up high as the heavens,
> and their head reaches to the clouds,
> they will perish forever like their own dung;
> those who have seen them will say,
> 'Where are they?'
> They will fly away like a dream,
> and not be found;
> they will be chased away
> like a vision of the night.
> The eye that saw them

will see them no more,
nor will their place behold them
any longer.

Psalm 73:18–20 also addresses the difficulty of seeing the wicked prosper. Here again dreams are used as a simile for the transitory nature of events.

Truly you set them in slippery places;
you make them fall to ruin.
How they are destroyed in a moment,
swept away utterly by terrors!
They are like a dream when one awakes;
on awaking you despise their phantoms.

Other passages of the Hebrew Bible are critical of how dreams are utilized. One example is Deuteronomy 13:1–5.

If prophets or those who divine by dreams appear among you and promise you omens or portents, and the omens or the portents declared by them take place, and they say, "Let us follow other gods" (whom you have not known) "and let us serve them," you must not heed the words of those prophets or those who divine by dreams; for the Lord your God is testing you, to know whether you indeed love the Lord your God with all your heart and soul. The Lord your God you shall follow, him alone you shall fear, his commandments you shall keep, his voice you shall obey, him you shall serve, and to him you shall hold fast. But those prophets or those who divine by dreams shall be put to death for having spoken treason against the Lord your God—who brought you out of the land of Egypt and redeemed you from the house of slavery—to turn you from the way in which the Lord your God commanded you to walk. So you shall purge the evil from your midst.

The book of Deuteronomy does not identify dreams as the problem. It is the use of dreams by false prophets to lead the faithful astray that is Deuteronomy's concern. Apparently dream messages were so convincing that a distinction between true and false prophets and their use of dreams is deemed necessary.[69]

Jeremiah was prophesying at the same time the book of Deuteronomy was being written. Similar themes, styles and language exist between the two books. One of the shared themes was a concern how false prophets were leading the gullible astray. Many of the false prophets used dreams to persuade their listeners as to the authenticity of their message. Jeremiah 29:8-9 captures this concern.

> For thus says the Lord of hosts, the God of Israel: Do not let the prophets and the diviners who are among you deceive you, and do not listen to the dreams that they dream, for it is a lie that they are prophesying to you in my name; I did not send them, says the Lord.[70]

The book of Zechariah 10:2[71] also speaks of dreams in the context of being critical of prophets who speak falsely in the name of God.

> For the teraphim utter nonsense,
> and the diviners see lies;
> the dreamers tell false dreams,
> and give empty consolation.
> Therefore the people wander like sheep;
> they suffer for lack of a shepherd.

While the passages from Deuteronomy, Jeremiah and Zechariah warn the faithful not to be gullible and believe the alleged divine messages contained in the dreams of false prophets, there was no general prohibition against paying attention to dream messages. In fact, other biblical writers from this same period spoke of how they received messages from God in their dreams.

DREAM REFERENCES DURING THE EXILE AND POST-EXILIC PERIOD

The book of Job appears to have been written between 600–400 B.C.E. Since the author is unknown, the date of composition is difficult to pinpoint. In chapter 33:14-16 the author has Elihu give Job the following advice.

> For God speaks in one way,
> and in two, though people do not perceive it.
> In a dream, in a vision of the night,
> when sleep falls on mortals,
> while they slumber on their beds,
> then he opens their ears,
> and terrifies them with warnings. . . .

The prophet Joel spoke to the Jewish population in the period 400–350 B.C.E. At this time Judea was a Persian province. Joel spoke of the coming of a new age, a time when God's spirit would be available to everyone.

> Then afterward
> I will pour my spirit on all flesh;
> your sons and daughters shall prophesy,
> your old men shall dream dreams,
> and your young men shall see visions.
> Even on the male and female slaves,
> in those days, I will pour out my spirit. (2:28–29)

Joel associated the outpouring of God's spirit with the receiving of dreams and visions. This gift, Joel foresaw, would be available to everyone.

The last text of the Hebrew Bible written before the scriptures became fixed was the book of Daniel.[72] The book of Daniel is apocalyptic literature[73] that was intended to encourage faithfulness to the Torah at a time when Hellenism sought to assimilate Jews into its culture. A strong theme in the book of Daniel is that it is God's initiative that will bring about the kingdom of God, not human effort.[74]

With the development of apocalyptic writings, there was a shift in how dreams in the Hebrew Bible were understood. Previously dreams were considered divine if they foretold an event that indeed came to pass. In the book of Daniel the dream images were not interpreted literally, but symbolically. Images of strange animals, numbers, and secret codes were present in the dreams. The uninitiated dreamer could not comprehend what was being communicated. Consequently, dream interpreters, usually angels, appeared to make sense of the dream messages. A member of the Divine Council interpreted Daniel's dream in chapter 7 for him.

INTERTESTAMENTAL PERIOD

There were many religious writings composed between roughly 2 B.C.E. to 1 C.E. that were not included in the Jewish canon. In some of these writings dreams were identified as a medium that God used to deliver His messages. 2 Esdras, The Additions to Esther, The Wisdom of Solomon, and II Maccabees spoke of dreams as communications from God while Tobit spoke of a vision being the medium God uses.

An early expression of Jewish mysticism that emerged during the first century B.C.E. was the *Merkavah* (Chariot). The Merkavah were individuals who sought a vision of God's throne like the prophet Ezekiel described in the first chapter of his book. Their method for achieving this holy vision was through studying the Torah and by meditating on Ezekiel's fiery chariot. A committed scholar, they believed, was capable of having such a vision.[75] The Merkavah believed it is possible to commune with God on a physical, emotional and intellectual level.

A prominent Jewish scholar was Flavius Josephus (37–101 C.E.). Josephus was both a priest and an historian. Not only did he believe some dreams come from God, but Josephus had several divine dreams himself.[76] As a priest, Josephus interpreted dreams, believing himself to be a mediator of divine knowledge. As an historian, Josephus reported other people's dreams from God.[77]

Following the destruction of the Temple in Jerusalem in 70 C.E. it was believed that God no longer spoke directly to people as He had done in earlier times. Dreams, therefore, lost their religious significance.

THE ROLE OF LAW IN JUDAISM

In Exodus 19–25 God promised Moses that if the Hebrew people obeyed his voice and kept his covenant they would be God's "own possession among all peoples" and a "kingdom of priests and a holy nation" (19:5–6). To protect and preserve the promises delineated in these verses, laws were given to Moses for the Hebrew people and their descendents to obey.[78] The Law did not create the relationship; it safeguarded the relationship that already existed.

Accordingly, from Moses onward the understanding and application of Jewish Law passed intact from generation to generation. Each new generation enters into the conversation with God by studying[79] and fulfilling the Law themselves. This study acquaints the person with God and enables the individual to experience the sacred in life. The means for having a direct experience of God now became the scrupulous study of scripture. Dr. Jacob Neusner suggested that for the Jews a holy person is one who is "able to think clearly and penetrate profoundly into the mysteries of the Torah and, especially, of its so very trivial laws. In context, those trivialities contain revelation."[80]

MISHNAH, TALMUD AND HALAKHAH

The Mishnah is one of the first collections of writings about Jewish oral law.[81] According to tradition it was compiled in the second century C.E.

by Rabbi Judah the Patriarch (135?–220?). Because it consists of different opinions about Jewish law, it is more of casebook than a codebook. The opinions of importance not included in the *Mishnah* were gathered in a companion text called the *Tosefta* (appendix or supplement).

The Talmud consists of two collections of writings, each of which has several volumes. One collection is known as the Palestinian or Jerusalem Talmud (in Hebrew, *Yerushalmi*). It contains the teachings and debates regarding the Mishnah that took place among the rabbis who lived in Palestine and were collected around the year 400. The other collection is the Babylonian Talmud (in Hebrew, *Bavli*). These are the teachings and debates regarding the Mishnah that took place among Jewish scholars who lived primarily in Babylon. These discussions were collected into one work around 500. Both collections contain the Mishnah, commentaries, and debates about how to interpret the Mishnah. The Talmud is considered an authoritative guide for living a holy life.[82]

After the Talmud was closed, Jews living in communities around the world wanted to know the specific conclusions of the Talmudic arguments. To delineate the practical laws with precision, additional books of Jewish Law were created and organized thematically into codes[83] known as halakhah (Jewish Law). The Mishnah, Talmud and halakhah continued the conversation with God.

RABBINIC ATTITUDES ABOUT DREAMS

According to Rabbi Aaron Parry[84] scholars of the Talmud were mixed in their attitudes about dreams coming from God. This divergence of opinion is evident in the *Sedar Zera'im* (Seeds), one of the Babylonian Talmud's divisions that addressed agricultural laws. The first tractate, *Berakhot* (Blessings) focuses on the rules for benedictions and daily prayer. The last chapter of Berakhot includes several pages of discussion on dreams and their interpretation. Rabbi Parry argued that so much space devoted to the topic of dreams shows how valuable dreams were regarded to be.

Among the positive examples from the Talmud of God's involvement with dreams are the following. These examples come from Berakhot 55.

1. "There are three things for which one should supplicate," the Berakhot advises: "a good king, a good year, and a good dream." The commentary notes that these three depend directly on the will of God. Pray for a good dream, the text goes on to add, "And make me

to live." Isaiah 38:16 is referenced, indicating the writer connected good dreams with the renewal of one's soul.

2. "A good man is not shown a good dream, and a bad man is not shown a bad dream." Further, "The purpose is to turn the good man to repentance and to give the bad man his reward in this world." Elsewhere in the same chapter we are told "a bad dream is worse than scourging," since it says, "God hath so made it that men should fear before Him. . . . "

3. In another passage we are told to not have a dream for seven days is evil.

4. Another declares, "A dream which is not interpreted is like a letter which is not read." This is because "a dream follows its interpretation." That is, a dream from God predicts events that come true. Not to interpret the dream is to miss the prediction.

5. If a person has a dream but can't recall the details, the following prayer is recommended.

> Sovereign of the Universe, I am Thine *and my dreams are Thine*.[85] I have dreamt a dream and I do not know what it is. Whether I have dreamt about myself or my companions have dreamt about me, or I have dreamt about others, if they are good dreams, confirm them and reinforce them [may they be fulfilled] like the dreams of Joseph, and if they require a remedy, heal them, as the waters of Marah were healed by Moses, our teacher, and as Miriam was healed of her leprosy and Hezekiah of his sickness, and the waters of Jericho by Elisha. As thou didst turn the curse of the wicked Balaan into a blessing, so turn all my dreams into something good for me.[86]

The Berakhot 55 teaches the following kinds of dreams are the ones most likely to have their predictions fulfilled: an early morning dream; a dream which a friend has about you; a dream which is interpreted in the midst of the dream itself; and a recurring dream. It also says, "A man should await the fulfillment of a good dream for as much as twenty-two years." Later Talmud commentaries, Rabbi Parry wrote, "State that the degree of excitement generated by a dream is a measure of its veracity." Rabbi Yedudah Patiah, a nineteenth century scholar of the Kabbalah, suggested a dream in which a person hears the name of God, in any language, is one that is likely to be fulfilled.[87]

Another tractate of the Babylonian Talmud, *Chagigah* 5b, quotes God as saying, "Although I hide My face from them, I shall speak to them in a dream." It is Rabbi Parry's opinion that most of the early scholars of the *Mishnah* believed *all* dreams contain at least some discernible truth. Berakhot 55 qualifies Rabbi Parry's observation when it says in a footnote: "There is reality in every dream save one that comes in a fast."

The following examples from the Talmud suggest dreams do not originate in God. Berakhot 55, besides having positive examples, also contains words of caution concerning dreams. Toward the conclusion of the chapter it says, "A man is shown in a dream only what is suggested by his own thoughts. . . ." We are told in another passage that "there cannot be a dream without some nonsense" and "while a part of a dream may be fulfilled, the whole of it is never fulfilled."[88]

ORTHODOXY, MYSTICISM AND ZIONISM

Since the time of the Talmud three influential movements have developed that in their own way have kept the conversation with God continuing: orthodoxy, mysticism and Zionism.[89] While dreams continued to be a part of everyday Jewish life, for the most part, dreams no longer were seen as God's voice speaking directly to his people.

SUMMARY

From the eighteenth century B.C.E. or earlier until the second century B.C.E. the commonly held perception was that one way God communicated was through dreams. While the vast majority of the preserved dream communications predicted positive events that came true, on occasion divine communications told the recipient information that person did not want to hear or denied the dreamer what he wanted. When the Hebrew Bible is critical of dreams, it is not because it viewed dreams as a medium God did not use but because dreams sometimes were used by false prophets to mislead or deceive others, giving messages that were not true.

Following the close of the Hebrew canon, the rabbinic traditions were open to God speaking through dreams. The openness to God speaking directly to a person through dreams did not continue when Jewish Orthodoxy, mysticism and Zionism deveoped.

ENDNOTES

57. The Hebrew Scriptures and the Old Testament differ in their arrangement. The Old Testament moves the prophets from the middle of the collection to the end. The material presented in this chapter is not intended to be a scholarly review of the Hebrew Bible's use of dreams. It is provided to demonstrate that in this holy text some dreams come from God and that these divine dreams contain important messages.

58. P. D. Miller, *The Religion of Ancient Israel*, 48, 54.

59. Today we would say a dream is an experience of the unconscious while asleep and a vision is an experience of the unconscious while awake.

60. Patrick Miller writes: "The textual evidence from Israel and elsewhere leaves the relationship between vision and dream as prophetic revelatory vehicles very ambiguous. There is no doubt that dreams were a mode of divine revelation in the ancient Near East, and there are texts that associate prophesy and "dreaming." But those that do, specifically Deut. 13:1-6 and I Samuel 28:6, set dreams alongside prophecy and, in one case, Urim and Thummim as *different* modes of divine revelation. The texts suggest differentiation between prophecy and dreaming even more than similarity. In any event, the textual data from Israel and other locales where prophetic activity was apparent do not show any fundamental difference in the character of prophetic vision and reported dreams where both things are actually described." From *The Religion of Ancient Israel*, 184-185. ©2000 Patrick D. Miller. Used with permission from Westminster John Knox Press.

61. See Genesis 3:22; Exodus 15:11; Deuteronomy 32:8-9; Psalms 29, 82 and 89:5-8. Dr. Barry L. Bandstra, *Reading the Old Testament*, 73-74, has an interesting perspective on Genesis 6:1-4. Dr. Bandstra believed in order to illustrate the enormous extent to which sin had grown; the author of Genesis told how angels (called "sons of Elohim [God]") were attracted to human women and having sexually activity with them. God took action to keep this new breed of creatures, the offspring of angels and humans (called "warriors" and "men of a name") from acquiring immortality. God responded by limiting human life to 120 years. At lease some of these lusty angels were members of the Divine Council.

62. This message reaches its climax for Christians in Matthew 28:20 with the promise of the risen Jesus: "And remember, I am with you always, to the end of the age." This divine pledge of assurance is also found in Islam. In the Qur'ān, Sura 8, God tells Mohammad, "I shall be with you." Jacob names the place where he had this dream Beth-El (House of El). Bethel was a location where the activity of God and various members of the Divine Council took place (see Gen. 35).

The Divine Assembly met on a "cosmic mountain" where heaven and earth intersected. It was here that the divine decrees were given. For the Hebrew people, the location of this "cosmic mountain" changed over time from the Garden of Eden to Mount Sinai to Mount Zion. The cosmic center of the earth, the place where heaven and earth intersected, appears to be located wherever God was active. Ugaritic beliefs placed the "cosmic center" on Mount Tsaphan. This information came from "The Meeting Place of the Divine Council." According to Dr. Bandstra, because there are no mountains on the Mesopotamian plains, the Babylonians created one in the form of a *ziggurat* (mountain peak). One of the most famous (Etemenanki) was built by Nebuchadnezzar II around 600 B.C.E. Babylonians believed that they could access the heavens through their ziggurat. This may be the idea behind the story of the Tower of Babel (Genesis 11:1-9). *Reading the Old Testament*, 84. Ziggurats may also be the context for Jacob's ladder dream.

30 GOD AND DREAMS

The idea of a place where heaven and earth intersect can be seen also in the writings of Black Elk (1863–1950), a holy man of the Oglala Sioux. Black Elk at age 12 participated in the battle of the Little Big Horn and was wounded at the massacre at Wounded Knee (1890). He is perhaps most famous for the vision he had in which Harney Peak in the Black Hills of South Dakota was identified as being the earth's "cosmic center." Black Elk went on to say that "anywhere is the center of the world." Neihardt, *Black Elk Speaks*, 20–47. The suggestion that it is in the unconscious that heaven and earth intersect and that dreams are a means of accessing God is a contemporary expression of his ancient perception.

63. This was not an uncommon experience. Non-Israelites also won battles because of dreams. The Assyrian King Assurbanipal (? –626 B.C.E.) indicated the goddess Ištar appeared "in a dream" to his entire dejected army with words of encouragement as they prepared to attack Elam. The dream helped turn the tide of battle. Oppenheim, *Dreams*, 209. Dr. Starbuck, *Court Oracles in the Psalms*, 147–148, wrote that Ištar assured Assurbanipal that she would do the fighting for him: "You shall stay (enthroned) here, where the tent of Nabu is. Eat food, drink beer, stage a festival, revere my divine nature, while I go and do the work so that you will attain the conquests of your heart." How Ištar was going to fight the battle is not made clear. Dr. Starbuck references M. Streck, *Assurbanipal*, 64–68.

64. Historically, David's dynasty was not everlasting. It ended about 587 B.C.E. References to this oracle are also found in Psalm 89:28–29, 35–37 and in Psalm 132:11–12.

65. Fidler, Ruth. "A Touch of Support," 192–212.

66. Dr. Starbuck in his article on Psalm 126 stated that a precise date for the psalm cannot be established. His interpretation of the psalm is based on the observation that for people of the time,

> ... dreams represented potential reality ... a dream could often be an initial sign of what was gradually becoming more and more lasting, solid. ... The possibility that all dreams fell in a continuum between fleeting and actualized gives us some indication of what it was like to receive dreams within the world-view of the ancient Near East. When a person dreamt a good dream he or she would wait with hopeful anticipation for its actualization—hoping that the vision would not turn out to be fleeting. And the converse was also true. A nightmare was certain to provoke fear until it was determined that the dream was fleeting and not moving toward permanence. Thus it is reasonable to assume that waiting upon dreams created a certain amount of anxiety in the dreamer—anxiety caused by the trepidation that a bad dream would be actualized and that a good dream would not ... the anxiety which a dreamer experiences while awaiting the eventual outcome of a dream experience is the same type of heartache that the psalmist's community experiences. ...

67. The idea that God gives negative messages through dreams is found in other religious traditions also. Dr. Oppenheim found that in Mesopotamia and perhaps everywhere in the Near East evil dreams were regarded as coming either from the dreamer's god or from that person's enemy. The recipient could protect himself by performing the appropriate ritual. When the evil dreams stopped or changed into pleasant ones, the dreamer was viewed as having been restored to health and into his god's grace. Hittite rituals used for a woman preparing for childbirth varied depending upon whether or not she'd been contaminated by her dreams. A king who failed to act on his dream message in subsequent dreams would have a variety of people remind him of his negligence. An old Babylonian omen [VAT 7525 of the Berlin Museum] says, "If a man cannot remember

the dream he saw (it means) his god is angry with him." Oppenheim, *Dreams*, 230–231, 193, 232. In the Qur'ān, Sura 8 is the acknowledgement that God may use dreams to deceive the faithful for their own good. In the lowlands of Ecuador and Peru, the Achuar tribe identifies a special kind of dream as being an indication of misfortune. This is true also of the Guajiro tribe of northern Colombia and Venezuela.

68. I owe this insight to Dr. Scott Starbuck's article, *Like Dreamers Lying in Wait*.

69. The book of Deuteronomy was completed during the Exile, around 550 B.C.E. According to Dr. Bandstra, *Reading the Old Testament*, 189, one of Deuteronomy's central themes is God's punishment of the Israelites for their apostasy and for their failure to obey the warnings of the prophets. This theme is evident in the passage quoted. Dr. Bandstra also noted that in the book of Deuteronomy Moses was the model for a true prophet. Like Moses, a true prophet is a person who receives his words directly from God. Accordingly, a true prophet's predictions come true while a false prophet's predictions do not.

70. Another passage in Jeremiah that reflects this same concern is 23:25–32. Dr. Bart J. Koet, "Trustworthy Dreams?," 89, notes that "false prophets speak lies with their motto, "I have a dream, I have a dream."(23:25) The critical point is that these prophets present their dreams as a message from God. (23:32) God's word is opposite to false dreams (23:27) and false prophets falsify God's word."

Hebrew scripture also mentions that there are people who seek to discern God's word through the hum of insects, the whisper of leaves, the flight of birds, the use of lightning or examination of the entrails of sacred birds and animals. (See Deut. 18:14; II Kings 21:6; Isaiah 2:6 and 57:3; Jeremiah 27:9.) These practitioners, like their predecessors at Mari, were empiricists, looking for "scientific" methods to discern the will of God. The word in the Hebrew Bible that describes these practices is 'anan. The Hebrew Bible strongly condemns their use.

71. The book of Zechariah, many scholars believe, was based on the words of two prophets, not just one. First Zechariah was active in Jerusalem between 520–518 B.C.E. Second Zechariah, whose real name remains unknown, was active in the fourth and third centuries B.C.E. His prophecy was based on dreams and visions.

72. The book of Daniel is dated around 164 B.C.E. This is the time when the Maccabees successfully retook Jerusalem, cleansed the temple and resumed the ritual activities prescribed by the Torah. According to Dr. Bandstra, *Reading the Old Testament*, 467–68, the author of the book is unknown. (See footnote 39.) The book of Daniel reflects the cultural influences of the post-exilic time in that the text was written mainly in Aramaic instead of Hebrew. Dr. Bandstra observed: "The Book of Daniel reflects a new approach to dealing with historical experience. It extrapolates from the present and tries to imagine how the future might look, heavy on imagination." 472.

73. Apocalyptic literature addresses issues around the end of time. Dr. Bandstra noted that Daniel, like other apocalyptic literature, kept his dream/visions secret until the events predicted occurred. This is the opposite attitude of the prophets who felt called to tell what God had informed them. The Book of Daniel predicted the end of the history, yet events did not turn out as envisioned. Daniel was considered more of a wise man or seer than a classic prophet. Bandstra, *Reading the Old Testament*, 471–72.

74. When the apocalyptic writers referenced how the end of history would occur, they placed a heavy emphasis on God's initiative. It would be God breaking into history in a cataclysmic way to bring an end to things. In contrast, the prophets anticipated God's use of human influences and historical processes to bring about the final culmination. Bandstra, *Reading the Old Testament*, 395.

75. In Christianity a similar vision was part of St. John's experience. In the book of Revelation (11:19) it is written: "Then God's temple in heaven was laid open, and within the temple was seen the ark of his covenant. There came flashes of lightning and peals of thunder, an earthquake, and a storm of hail."

76. In his Autobiography Josephus reported that in a dream God told him great success awaited him. In his account of Vesparian's successful conquest of Galilee in 67 C.E. Josephus told of his hiding from the Romans in a cave for several days with 40 prominent citizens. While there Josephus had a series of dreams, one of which predicted Vesparian's success over the Jews. In another dream Josephus was told by God Vesparian would one day become Caesar. These dreams apparently convinced Josephus that he was called by God to be his messenger. The information about Josephus came from the following sources: Jan Willem van Henten, "The Two Dreams"; James A. Montgomery, "The Religion of Flavius Josephus"; G. J. Goldberg, "The Galilean Campaign, 67 CE.";"The Life of Flavius Josephus". Another important reference is Robert Karl Gnuse, *Dreams and Dream Reports in the Writings of Josephus*." Dr. Gnuse argued Josephus aspired to be regarded as a prophet by his readers and used his dreams as his most important evidence that he was indeed inspired by God, 270.

77. Another scholar who believed dreams come from God was the Spanish rabbi, Solomon Almoli, who lived in Constantiople and functioned as the sultan's physician. Almoli's first dream book, *Mefasher Chelmin* (Dream Mediator), was published in 1515. Three years later it was republished as *Pitron Chalomot* (The Interpretation of Dreams) and then again in 1551. The book was a success and republished in Cracow in 1576. It continued to be republished until the beginning of the twentieth century. Freud mentions the book in a footnote of his dream book by the same name. Joel Covitz, *Visions in the Night*, 83–84.

Rabbi Menachem di Lonzano was another scholar who believed dreams come from God. Rabbi Lonzano was well respected because he helped to correct the biblical text of the *Mikroat Gedolot*, a famous commentary on the Torah. In 1572 Rabbi Lonzano wrote a book about Talmudic subjects that was based on his dreams. This information was taken from Rabbi Aaron Parry's column; "Ask the Rabbi."

78. Rabbi Louis Jacobs notes that Jewish Law is found mainly in the first five books of the Hebrew Bible, known as the Pentateuch or Torah. Here there are three codes: Exodus 21–23; Leviticus 19; and Deuteronomy 21–25. There are also laws found in other parts of the Torah. While the prophets refer to laws not found in the Torah, rabbis have determined that these laws were also given to Moses either at Mt. Sinai or later during the journey in the wilderness because prophets were not "authorized" to introduce new laws. "About Jewish Daily Life: Halakhah: Sources and Development."

79. Observant Jews do not "read' their sacred texts, they "study" them. Studying is a process "that involves tracking the thread of ideas across and back through generations of texts, as if the footnotes and connections can retrace and uncover the sanctity of God's own speech in the text." "About Jewish Texts".

80. This information is from Dr. Jacob Neusner's article, "Talmudic Thinking."

81. Each of the Mishnah's six divisions is divided into parts called tractates, which in turn have chapters and paragraphs. The six divisions are Seeds (agricultural laws); Festivals; Women (marriage laws); Injuries (civil and criminal law); Holy Things (ritual law); and Purifications.

82. Of the two collections, the Babylonian Talmud is the larger and more studied. The Babylonian Talmud influenced the halakhah tradition more than the Jerusalem Talmud

did. With the founding of the modern State of Israel however, the Jerusalem Talmud, with its emphasis on the Torah's agricultural laws, has experienced a renewed popularity and relevance. Whereas the scholars of the Jerusalem Talmud are identified as "rabbi," most of the distinguished scholars connected with the Babylonian Talmud have the lesser title of "rav." Only in Israel was the title "rabbi" conferred.

83. There are three main codes. A Jew who was born in Spain created each. The three are the "Secondary Torah" created by Maimonides (1135–1204); the "Four Columns" often abbreviated as *Tur*, created by Jacob ben Asher (1270–1340); and the "Set Table" of Yosef Karo (1488–1575). Rabbi Karo's code is generally considered the standard for the *halakhah*. Each of these three codes had opponents who offered different interpretations. This information comes from Rabbi Louis Jacobs' article "About Jewish Daily Life." Rabbi Parry in his article, "The Talmud & dreams," wrote that Rabbi Karo "discussed legal problems with a teacher in his dreams." Rabbi Parry goes on to say that Rabbi Yeshayahu Horowitz wrote that he had a dream of Rabbi Karo thirty years after Rabbi Karo's death. In his dream, Rabbi Horowitz saw Rabbi Karo "sitting on a very majestic throne in the presence of innumerable world-renown rabbis. His face was shining like the brightness of the sky . . . and he taught the meditations applicable to *kedusha*.

84. Parry, "The Talmud & dreams."

85. Italics added for emphasis.

86. This prayer is included in the prayer books and recited in some congregations between each of the three blessings constituting the priestly benediction, whether they have dreamt or not.

87. Parry, "The Talmud & dreams."

88. "Babylonian Talmud: Tractate Berakoth." Rabbi Joel Covitz notes that while the Talmud records the presence of 24 dream interpreters in Jerusalem, there never developed a religious significance for dreams or dream interpretation in mainstream Judaism following the end of the prophetic period. "If the only dreams that are significant are the prophetic dreams," Covitz wrote, "then dreams in our unprophetic world must be insignificant." 13.

89. Orthodoxy emphasizes the study of scripture, the observance of correct religious and ethical practices, and worship. It is the largest of the three movements. Mysticism emphasizes the importance of a personal experience of God. The creation of the Kabbalah is the significant achievement of Jewish mysticism. Zionism developed during the nineteenth century when many intellectual Jews were intrigued with secular nationalism, with the desire to return to the land that they believed God gave them. The desire to return to the Homeland grew as other ancient peoples (Greeks and Italians) formed nations of their own. The establishment of the state of Israel on May 14, 1948 is the most significant achievement of Zionism.

3

Christian Perspectives

Suddenly I was caught up in the spirit and dragged up to the tribunal of a judge. . . . Asked about my identity, I replied, "I am a Christian." And he who sat [behind the tribunal] said, "You are lying; you are a Ciceronian, not a Christian; for where your treasure is, there is where your heart is also." Immediately I became mute, and, amid the floggings—for he had ordered that I be beaten—I was tortured more strongly by the fire of conscience, pondering within myself that verse, "In hell who shall acknowledge you?" Nevertheless I began to cry out and woefully to say: "Have mercy on me, Lord, have mercy on me." Amid the lashings this sound rang out. Finally those who were standing around, falling down on their knees before the one who was presiding, begged that he have mercy on my youth and give me the opportunity for penitence. There would be more torture at a later point if I were ever again to read pagan literary books. . . . I began to make an oath and, calling on his name as witness, I said, "Lord, if at any time [in the future] I possess pagan writings or read them, I will have denied you." Dismissed after this oath, I returned to the upper room. . . . This was not an idle dream. . . . My shoulders were black and blue, and I felt the bruises after I awoke from sleeping. Thenceforth I read the divine books with much more eagerness than I had read the books of human beings.[90]—Jerome, 374 C.E.

INTRODUCTION

The connection between God and dreams was vital for the early Christians. Like their ancestors and contemporaries, the early Christians believed God used dreams to convey his messages. Examples are found in the New Testament, particularly in the Gospel of Matthew and in the book of Acts. The early Church Fathers also taught that God communicates through dreams. Jerome's translation of the Bible into Latin (Vulgate) appears to have been influenced by both Deuteronomy's and Jeremiah's concern that dreams can lead people astray and Cicero's negative opinion of dreams and divination. Following Jerome fewer people regarded dreams as the usual way God reveals himself. During the Middle Ages visions replaced dreams as the accepted medium of revelation. During the centuries that followed, some Christian thinkers kept alive the belief God that communicated through dreams, but they were the minority point of view. In the twentieth century with the birth of psychology, a renewed interest in God's role in dreams developed.

THE NEW TESTAMENT USE OF DREAMS

In the New Testament we find a return to the attitudes of the Hebrew Bible: God uses dreams as a medium to convey His will. As in the Hebrew Bible, hard lines were not drawn between the various altered states of consciousness in which dreams occur or visions are received. There is fluidity among these experiences. On several occasions two or three different names are used to refer to the same occurrence, making it difficult to know which state of consciousness the writer had in mind.

While none of Jesus' dreams were recorded in the New Testament, there are accounts of the frequent visionary experiences Jesus had that surrounded the important events of his life. His baptism experience and the following temptations, his transfiguration and his vision of an angel in the Garden of Gethsemane are especially noteworthy.

The Gospel of Matthew and the book of Acts contain nearly all of the dream incidents recorded in the New Testament. For example, dreams played an essential role in the birth of Jesus as recorded in the first two chapters of Matthew. There was a dream that told Joseph to take Mary as his wife (1:20); dreams that enabled the magi, Joseph, Mary and Jesus to avoid Herod's brutality (2:12-14); dreams that told Joseph when it was safe to return to Israel (2:19-23). As Matthew described it, the birth of Jesus would have been vastly different (if at all) had Joseph not believed his dreams came from God.

Matthew (27:19) reports a dream from near the end of Jesus' life. Matthew wrote that Pilate's wife was warned in a dream that her husband should have nothing to do with Jesus. Pilate's wife told her husband, "Have nothing to do with that innocent man; for today I have suffered a great deal because of a dream about him."

The book of Acts needs to be studied in conjunction with the Gospel of Luke since Luke wrote them as a unit. Dr. Bart Koet observed that with regard to God's use of dreams and visions, Luke made an important distinction between the Gospel and the book of Acts. Dr. Koet observed:

> In the Gospel Jesus is so near to God that he, like Moses, does not need dreams and visions.... In Acts the disciples, like the prophets from the [Hebrew] Scripture, do need dreams and visions. After Jesus' resurrection dreams and visions tell the disciples how Jesus' mission is to be followed by their mission and especially the mission among the Gentiles. Dreams and visions in Acts are a proof that the mission to the Gentiles comes from God.[91]

In the book of Acts (chapter 10) Luke recorded one of the major events in the history of Christianity: Peter's conversion of Cornelius. It marked the first time a non-Jew, a Gentile, was admitted into the fellowship of the church. With Peter's action and the church's approval of it, Christianity changed from being one of many parties within Judaism into being an independent religion of its own.[92] Luke's account of this dramatic event contains a mixture of God speaking through a dream, a vision, an angel, a trance, and the Holy Spirit.

Luke began his report of the event by saying God took the initiative through a dream. Cornelius, a Gentile and high-ranking officer in the Roman army, was the recipient of this dream. In the dream Cornelius was told he should seek out Peter and have Peter come speak to him. The day after Cornelius' dream, Peter had a vision. In the vision God made clear to Peter that Gentiles were no longer to be regarded as unclean. When Cornelius' invitation arrived, Peter trusted the message of his vision and chose to violate the Jewish prohibition against associating with Gentiles. Peter traveled to Cornelius' home to meet with him. During his visit with Cornelius, Peter articulated a new understanding of what it means to be a Christian. "I truly understand," Peter said, "that God shows no partiality, but in every nation anyone who fears him and does what is right is acceptable to him." 10:34[93]

When church leaders in Jerusalem criticized Peter for defying tradition by converting a Gentile like Cornelius, Peter recounted point by point what occurred that led him to do it. Upon learning of the dream, the vision and all the rest, Peter's critics were convinced he'd done the correct thing by bringing non-Jews into the church. "Then God has given even to the Gentiles the repentance that leads to life." 11:18

Paul, too, was deeply influenced by dreams and visions. He believed God communicated through dreams. Paul's vision on the road to Damascus changed his life. Acts 9:3-9 Part of Paul's transforming experience involved a healing dream, 9:10-19a, which came to Ananias. According to Luke, it was a vision/dream from God that instructed Paul not to go to Asia, but to Europe.16:6-10 When Paul was in Corinth, the opposition he encountered discouraged him. He wanted to leave. It was a vision/dream that told Paul to stay. Paul obeyed his vision/dream and stayed in Corinth for another year and a half. 18:1-11

It was also a vision/dream, 23:11, that directed Paul to go to Rome. The last of Paul's recorded vision/dreams in Acts 27:21-26 came while he was a prisoner on a grain boat that was taking him to Rome. A harsh storm arose. Violent winds and heavy seas put the vessel in peril. Even after the cargo and ship's gear was tossed overboard, fear overwhelmed the crew and passengers. The hope of being saved was gone. Although Paul was a prisoner, he addressed the others aboard. He told them the night before an angel sent by God assured him all of them would be saved, but the boat would not survive. "So keep up your courage, men", Paul said, "for I have faith in God that it will be exactly as I have been told." Not long after, the boat ran ashore where the surf pounded it into pieces. Nevertheless, everyone was saved.

Jude 8 contains the final reference to dreams in the New Testament. It warns dreamers not to treat their bodies, or the powers above them, dishonorably.

The New Testament closes with an entire book, The Revelation to John, devoted to describing visions John had while on the island of Patmos. When the writings that form the New Testament were fixed, 367-405 C.E., a book of visions, regarded as the inspired word of God, was included.

EARLY CHURCH PERSPECTIVES

The writings of the early church Fathers up to 150 C.E. were directed to groups within the Christian community. Their attitudes are similar to those found in the New Testament: Dreams are messages from God.

38   GOD AND DREAMS

During the period 150–325 the writers were known as Apologists. Their writings were aimed at non-Christians, hoping to convert them. This was the time of Christian persecution. Believers who were discovered were condemned to death, their families sold into slavery and all their property confiscated for the government. These writers, willing to die for their beliefs, wrote of dreams as a way of maintaining a living connection with God. Leaders such as Justin Martyr in Rome, Irenaeus in Gaul, Origen and Clement in Alexandria and Tertullian in Carthage all believed dreams were a way that God communicated to men and women. Tertullian in Carthage summarized the prevailing attitude when he wrote: "Is it not known to all people that the dream is the most usual way that God reveals himself to man?"[94]

According to the Christian account given by Eusebius,[95] in the year 312 Constantine had a vision. In the vision Constantine saw a cross appear in the sky with the words, "by this sign you shall conquer." Constantine had no idea what this meant, but the vision touched him deeply. That night Christ appeared to Constantine in a dream. The dream, following the vision, convinced Constantine that the Christian God was his protector. Lactantius, a Christian writer close to Constantine, reported Constantine had the sign he saw in his vision put on his soldiers' shields. With the inspiration that the Christian God was protecting his troops and himself, Constantine engaged his rival Maxentius at the Milvian Bridge and won a decisive victory. As a result of the vision, dream and Constantine's victory, history changed. With Constantine as the new Roman Emperor, Christians were no longer persecuted and the state became the church's ally.[96]

Other Christian leaders of the early church who used their dreams to receive directives from God include Gregory Nazianzen, Gregory of Nyssa, Basil the Great, Synesius of Cyrene (who also wrote a treatise on dreams), Ambrose, Augustine, Gregory the Great and even Jerome. Athanasius assumed God communicated with people through dreams, but that one should not boast of it. Gregory Thaumaturgus received his inspiration for the first real Trinitarian creed through a dream.[97]

In the late fourth century the Latin grammarian Macrobius wrote *Commentary on the Dream of Scipio*. Macrobius classified dreams into five types, two of which he asserted came from God. The first type Macrobius identified were common dreams that are hard to understand. These dreams are ambiguous and contain strange imagery. The second type he distinguished was the nightmare. Macrobius suggested that these dreams arise from conditions the dreamer experienced during the previous day. The third type represented those dreams that come immediately after falling asleep. In them specters appear that are either delightful or disturbing. The fourth type was the prophetic dream. These dreams foretell the future accurately. The fifth type was a variation of the fourth. In these dreams a figure appears who reveals what will or will not occur and what action the dreamer should take. It was these last two types Macrobius believed come from God. Again for Macrobius, like those before him, it was the predictive quality of a dream that indicated its divine origins.[98]

The earliest known recorded reference to a lucid dream was found in a letter dated 415 written by Augustine of Hippo (354–430).[99] Augustine wrote extensively about the importance of dreams. According to Morton T. Kelsey, it was Augustine's belief that dreams and visions come from God as gifts, as examples of God's providential care. For example, referring to a dream that brought him conviction about life after death, Augustine wrote, "By whom was he taught this but by the merciful, providential care of God?"[100]

THE INFLUENCE OF JEROME

The Christian scholar Jerome (342?–420) was a contemporary of Macrobius and Augustine. Jerome, whose given name was Eusebius Hieronymous Sophronius, was born into a wealthy Christian family living in the small town of Stridonius in what is today Bosnia/Herzegovina. Pope Liberius baptized Jerome when he was 18. As a boy, the famous grammarian, Donatus, who was not a Christian, was Jerome's teacher. Donatus believed it was important that Jerome study non-Christian scholars like Cicero and Plautus. Donatus' instruction enabled Jerome to become an expert in Greek and Latin and exposed him to Cicero's attitudes that were so critical of dreams and divination. In spite of the piety he'd learned at home, Jerome grew up to become a man of the world, enjoying his pleasure-loving instincts.

Jerome's worldly ways ended abruptly in 374. His transformation was brought about by a dream, the one quoted at the opening to this chapter. Jerome's response to the dream included turning away from his dedicated reading of the classics to wholeheartedly studying the Christian Bible. So motivated was Jerome that he sought out a Jewish scholar to teach him Hebrew until Jerome became an expert in that language too. Six years after his life-changing dream, Jerome was ordained to the priesthood. Two years after his ordination Jerome became Pope Damasus' secretary and began his translation of the Bible from Greek into Latin.[101]

As Jerome made his translation, he appears to have been influenced by Cicero's attitudes about dreams as well as by the cautionary concerns found in Deuteronomy and Jeremiah. According to the Rev. Morton T. Kelsey, even though Jerome returned to the study of Christianity because of a dream, he mistranslated the Hebrew word *'anan* in Leviticus 19:26, Deuteronomy 18:10–11, and II Chronicles 33:6. Jerome translated *'anan* when it occurs elsewhere as "to augur or soothsay." Yet when he came to Leviticus, Deuteronomy, and II Chronicles, Jerome changed the translation from "to augur or soothsay" (*auguror*) to "observe dreams" (*observo somnia*). Instead of reading "there shall not be found among you any one who burns his son or his daughter as an offering, any one who practices divination, a soothsayer, or an auger, or a sorcerer" Jerome's translation read, "there shall not be found among you. . . any one who practices dream interpretation. . . ." This mistranslation, which lumped listening to dreams with superstitious activities like soothsaying, became the authorative text for the Roman Catholic Church for the next fifteen-hundred years.[102] After Jerome fewer people agreed with Tertullian that dreams are "the usual way God reveals himself to man."

MEDIEVAL TO CONTEMPORARY ATTITUDES ABOUT GOD AND DREAMS

Christian thinking in the period following Jerome until the middle of the ninth century was consumed with doctrinal disputes. There were few discussions of dreams because visions had replaced dreams as the primary medium of revelation. Nevertheless, in the centuries that followed there continued to be some Christians who regarded dreams as communications from God.

In the middle of the ninth century in the monasteries of France a new piety awakened that sought certainty with regard to salvation. This quest for certainty traveled two paths.

Thinkers known as Scholastics developed one path.[103] Scholastics sought to be objective in their pursuit and favored an intellectual approach to certainty, utilizing logical considerations. Thomas Aquinas

(1225?-1274) was the giant of Scholasticism.[104] When asked, "Is divination through dreams lawful?"Aquinas replied:

> The whole question consists in determining the cause of dreams, and examining whether the same may be the cause of future events, or at least come to the actual knowledge of them. Dreams come sometimes from internal, and sometimes from external, causes. Two kinds of internal causes influence our dreams: one animal, inasmuch as such images remain in a sleeping man's fantasy as were dwelt upon by him while awake; the other found in the body: it is indeed a well-known fact that the actual disposition of the body causes a reaction on the fantasy. Now it is self-evidence that neither of these causes has any influence on individual future events. Our dreams may likewise be the effects of a twofold external cause. This is corporeal when exterior agencies, such as the atmospheric conditions or others, act on the imagination of the sleeper. *Finally dreams may be caused by spiritual agents, such as God,* directly, or indirectly through his angels, and the devil. It is easy to conclude thence what chances there are to know the future from dreams, and when divination will be lawful or unlawful.[105]

The Christian mystics of the tenth, eleventh and twelfth centuries developed a second path to certainty about salvation. Among the impressive Christian mystics were Hildegard von Bingen (1098-1179) and Juliana of Norwich (1342-1413). Mysticism sought certainty not through objective, rational activities but through direct spiritual experience. The mystics' path was a subjective one with their personal visionary experience providing immediate knowledge about God.[106]

Scholastic rationalism prevailed over the mystical experience to become the mainstream Christian way to God. The victory of Scholasticism can be seen in the shift in power away from monasteries, where mysticism prospered, to schools of learning, universities, where scholasticism thrived. Orthodoxy followed the Scholastic path.

King William II (1056-1100) of England, the favorite son of William the Conqueror, exemplifies the twelfth century Christian attitude about God and dreams. On the night of August 1, 1100, King William II had a dream that disturbed him enough to mention it the next day to a group of friends and relatives with whom he was to go hunting. In his summertime dream, the King dreamed an extremely cold wind passes through his sides. Some accounts report that the King saw himself going to heaven. When King William shared the dream, a few in the hunting party advised him not to go with them that day. The King's reply was: "They are not good Christians that regard dreams." Off on the hunt they went. As the sun was setting, the King chased a stag he'd wounded. He raised his hand to keep the sun out of his eyes. Just then a poorly shot arrow missed the stag, hit the King in the chest, and killed him.[107]

King William's thoughts were in keeping with the Christian attitudes of the time that emphasized God as transcendent, distant, and unknowable. This emphasis left people hungering for a personal connection with God, yet doubting their experience if they had one. It also encouraged the development of a humanism that sought to reform Christianity by removing its dogmas and stripping it of its supernatural features. This humanism cared about the tangible, physical world more than it did the unseen, spiritual world.

Not everyone in the twelfth century shared King William II's perspective on dreams. For example, dreams and visions were important in the life of Francis of Assisi (1182–1226). In 1205 Francis had a series of dreams while going off to war. These dreams stopped him from going. He returned home and gave up his ambition to be a soldier. An auditory vision instructed him to "Go, repair God's house that was falling into ruin." A dream that Pope Innocent III had in 1209 led the Pope to approve the new religious order Francis proposed. The Pope's approval was given even though the Pope's advisors suggested he not give it. In 1224 Francis undertook a forty-day fast. Toward the end of his retreat, while in prayer on a mountainside, Francis had a vision of an angel. While viewing the seraph, Francis' body manifested the same five wounds suffered by Jesus during his crucifixion, the stigmata.

Albertus Magnus (1193–1280), a German Dominican friar and bishop, was a contemporary of St. Francis and a teacher of Thomas Aquinas. A Scholastic scholar, Albertus wrote eight books on physics, six on psychology, eight on astronomy, twenty-six on zoology, seven on botany, five on minerals, one on geography and three on life in general. His interest in the nature led him in 1250 to isolate arsenic. Albertus was known to have had a series of visions that began in childhood. Albertus encouraged the use of potions to stimulate visions and advocated dream interpretation.[108] He is one of the few who is recognized by Rome as a Doctor of the Church. In 1931 he was canonized.

Heinrich Cornelius Agrippa von Nettesheim (1486–1535) was a German mystic and alchemist. As a boy he became well known when he refused to speak any language but Latin. In 1510 he wrote *De Occulta Philosophiae* to defend alchemy, the hidden philosophy. His writings sought to systematize everything from tastes, smells and colors to herbs, charms, spirits and dreams in order to find connections between consciousness and the external world. His early lectures on theology angered the church, as did his defence of a woman accused of witchcraft in 1520. He was forced to leave Cologne by the Inquisition.

The fifteenth through seventeenth centuries were a very creative period for Christian thought, especially in Spain. Ignatius Loyola (1491-1556), Sister Teresa of Avila (1515-1582), and St. John of the Cross (1542-1591) had visions that profoundly influenced their lives.[109]

During the sixteenth century a Saxon court physician, Kasper Peucer (1525-1602), the son-in-law of Melanchthon, wrote about dreams. He concluded:

> Finally, to consider whether the dreams which ofttimes disturb us and move us to evil courses are put before us by the devil, as likewise on the good hand to ponder whether by which we are aroused and incited to good, as for example to celibacy, almsgiving, and entering the religious life, are sent to us by God, is the part not of a superstitious mind, but of one that is religious, prudent and careful and solicitous for its salvation.[110]

Peucer advised that no one should or could interpret dreams "unless he be divinely inspired and instructed."[111]

Benedictus Pererius (1535-1610) was a Jesuit scholar and Peucer's contemporary. Pererius wrote a book in which he investigated God's involvement with dreams.[112] His attitudes, like Peucer's, are consistent with biblical perceptions of dreams. Pererius found, 147: "For God is not constrained by such laws of time, nor does he await opportune moments for his operation; for he inspires dreams where he will, when he will, and in whomever he will." Pererius proposed that dreams have a variety of origins: Many are natural, some are of human origin and some are from God. He wrote:

> In the dream, those things made known to a man . . . are those things which in the schools of the theologies are called contingent future events; further, the secrets of the heart which are wholly hidden from all men's understanding; and lastly, those highest mysteries of our faith which are known to no man unless he is taught them by God. . . . that this [is divine] is especially declared

by certain enlightenment and moving of the spirits, whereby God so illumines the mind, so acts upon the will, and so assures the dreamer of the credibility and authority of his dream that he so clearly recognizes and so certainly judges God to be its author that he not only desires to believe it, but must believe it without any doubt whatsoever.[113]

The split between physical and spiritual, this world and otherworld realities, increased during the eighteenth century. However the Swedish mystic, Emanuel Swedenborg (1688–1772), minimized these differences. Trained as a scientist as a young man, Swedenborg recorded and studied his dreams when he was in his mid-fifties. On Easter weekend of 1744, he had a vision of Christ that changed his life. A year later he had a second vision that indicated to him that he should leave science and work on disclosing the inner, spiritual meaning of the Bible. He said he could make contact with spirits as easily as he could with humans. Swedenborg published a great deal of information about the spirit world based on his contacts with it.

John Wesley (1703–1791), the English cleric who founded Methodism, valued dreams too. He preached that God on occasion revealed himself in dreams. One of Wesley's good friends was the Anglican priest David Simpson. In 1791 Fr. Simpson published *Discourse on Dreams and Night Visions* in which he stated: ". . . has not the experience that many men have of significant dreams and night visions a more powerful effect on their minds than the most pure and refined concepts?" Fr. Simpson believed that "dreams are . . . of equal authority with the Bible. . . . "[114]

During the second half of the eighteenth century, the German philosopher Immanuel Kant (1724–1804) argued that Swedenborg was wrong. Kant taught that it is not possible to know spiritual reality directly. We can speculate about metaphysical matters, but we can't prove them.

Kant's thinking was highly influential in secular and Christian circles. His reasoning convinced people that God is not directly knowable and that spiritual reality is speculative and not verifiable. In Kant's thinking there was no place for dreams being messages from God. Following Kant, science replaced theology as the discipline by which things are reliably known.

Christian thinkers after Kant differed regarding how rationalism should be used. Some wanted to exclude new applications of it in order to protect traditional beliefs. Others wanted to exclude rationalism altogether because it isn't a useful path to God—mystical means are. A third

Christian Perspectives 45

group embraced rationalism bringing its methods to the study of scripture. These differing attitudes have conflicted ever since.

Joseph Smith, Jr. (1805-1844) was not inspired by traditional Christian teachings. Visions guided his religious life and he spoke of them. A vision he had on an early spring morning in 1820, he said, instructed him not to join any of the existing churches but to restore the church on earth. At seventeen Joseph Smith had another vision. In it he was visited by the angel Moroni, who told him of an ancient record of God's dealings with former inhabitants of the American continent. The retrieved manuscript became the *Book of Mormon*, first published in 1830.[115]

Rationalism increased in popularity during the nineteenth century. Its influence can be seen in the life of Don Giovanni (1815-1888). At age nine he had a dream in which God revealed His will for Giovanni's life: to work with poor and neglected boys. Yet when the young boy shared his dream with his family, his brothers laughed at him. His grandmother advised him "not to pay any attention to dreams."[116] He tried to ignore the dream but he could not forget it. Don Giovanni went on to devote his life to ministering to unwanted Italian children. Throughout his adult years Giovanni paid attention to his dreams and used them in his work. So unconventional was this behavior that two of his friends sought to have him committed to an institution for the mentally ill. After his death Don Giovanni was canonized as St. John Bosco.

Nineteenth century rationalism peaked during the century's final decades. In 1885 Friedrich Nietzsche (1844-1900) wrote in his journals that God was dead. In 1901 his sister published these reflections as a book, *The Will to Power*. If God is dead, then immediate, personal experiences of God are not possible.[117]

On November 18, 1965, toward the end of the fourth and last session of Vatican II, Pope Paul VI promulgated *Dei Verbum* to address the issue of revelation. This proclamation asserts that Christians "now await no further new public revelations" before the Second Coming of Christ. Chapter 1, #4 It also declared "the task of authentically interpreting the word of God, whither written or handed on, has been entrusted exclusively to the living teaching office of the Church. . . . " chapter 2, #10

According to Dr. Gerard Condon, revelation, as defined in Roman Church theology, has a public character, is normally accompanied by a suspension of the laws of nature, and happens in and through Christ.[118] Private revelations such as a dream might offer, are measured against the public standard and the messages are typically relevant to the Church. For this reason, Dr. Condon noted, the possibility of God speaking through dreams is quite limited. When revelation through dreams does occur, Dr. Condon emphasized, it can add nothing new to our knowledge of God.[119]

Not all twentieth century writers followed the path authorized by rationalism. Influenced by psychology, individuals like the English Dominican priest, Victor White, OP (1902-1960) and the American Episcopal priests Morton T. Kelsey (1917-2000) and John A. Sanford (1929-2005) reaffirmed the biblical perspective that God does indeed communicate through dreams.

SUMMARY

Christian scripture and beliefs that helped to form the church regarded dreams as a medium God uses to convey His will. Dreams played a central role in the birth of Jesus, the conversion of Cornelius, in the history of Paul, and the Fathers of the early church.

Jerome, whose life was changed by a dream, appears suspicious of how others might use them. His mistranslation of certain biblical texts created an authoritive source that discouraged others from looking to dreams as a source for God's revelation. During the centuries that followed Jerome, Christian attitudes shifted from Tertullian's observation that dreams are "the usual way God reveals himself to man" to King William II's observation that "they are not good Christians that regard dreams." The biblical perception that a direct, personal, immediate experience of God is possible was replaced by the perception that God is distant, unknowable and disconnected from everyday reality. The reasoning of Emmanuel Kant convinced people that spiritual reality is speculative and not verifiable.

Nevertheless, throughout each century there have been Christians whose experience affirms the biblical teaching that God communicates directly through dreams.

ENDNOTES

90. Miller, Dreams in Late Antiquity, 210-11.

91. Bart J. Koet, "*Why Does Jesus Not Dream?* p 745-58. Numbers 12:6-8a reads: "And he [God] said, 'Hear my words: When there are prophets among you, I, the Lord make myself known to them in visions; I speak to them in dreams. Not so with my servant Moses; he is entrusted with all my house. With him I speak face to face—clearly, not in riddles; and he beholds the form of the Lord.' "

92. Judaism was not homogenous at this time. There was a rich division of opinion about how Jewish life was to be practiced within a Greco-Roman culture. Differences of opinion existed among the various groups which included Sadducees, Essences, Zealots, Pharisees and perhaps as many as 28 other groups. Of the traditional groups, only the Pharisees survived the disasters of the first and second Jewish Revolts (66–73 C.E. and 132–135 C.E.). For a brief discussion of the influence of Hellenism on Judaism see Dr. Bandstra, *Reading the Old Testament*, 467–68.

93. Luke reports that while Peter was speaking with Cornelius "the Holy Spirit fell upon all who heard the word. The circumcised believers who had come with Peter were astonished that the gift of the Holy Spirit had been poured out even on the Gentiles, for they heard them speaking in tongues and extolling God. Then Peter said, 'Can anyone withhold the water for baptizing these people who have received the Holy Spirit just as we have?' So he ordered them to be baptized in the name of Jesus Christ." Acts 10:44–48a.

94. Morton T. Kelsey, Dreams, A Way to Listen to God.

95. Eusebius (275–339 C.E.) was Bishop of Caesarea in Palestine. He is considered by many as the "father" of church history. His account of Constantine's vision is found in his Church History, IX.9.

96. Morton T. Kelsey. God, Dreams and Revelation. 123–126.

97. Kelsey, God, Dreams and Revelation, 92–120.

98. Kelsey, God, Dreams and Revelation, 156.

99. Stephen LaBerge. "The Origins and History of Lucid Dreaming," *Lucid Dreaming*, chapter 2.

100. Kelsey, *God, Dreams and Revelation*, 148–51.

101. In Jerome's time, Greek, the language of the New Testament, was widely known throughout the Roman Empire. The Old Testament was also available in Greek in the Septuagint. So anyone who knew Greek could read the entire Bible. But there were people in the Roman Empire who did not know Greek. For these non-Greek reading people there were a variety of translations available but the translations were not always in agreement. Jerome's effort was to correct these conflicting versions and create one, authoritative, non-Greek translation of the Christian Bible. As Jerome made his translation, he followed the arrangement of the Hebrew canon instead of the Septuagint's.

102. Kelsey, *God, Dreams and Revelation*, 153–55, 159. Kelsey referenced S. Eusebius Hieronymus, *Divinae Bibliothecae: Pars Prima*, J. P. Migne, *Patrologiae Latinae*, Paris, 1889, Vol. 28, Cols. 361, 479, 567, 815, 830, 890, 944, 1105, and 1466 as the source for his assertion. J. P. Migne was a nineteenth century French Roman Catholic priest. Dr. Gerard Condon, a Roman Catholic psychologist, agrees with Dr. Kelsey. Dr. Condon noted in a 2001 presentation: "Scripture and tradition occasionally condemned spiritual dreamwork.... Central to a negative stance was St. Jerome's Vulgate reading of Deuteronomy 18:10 as 'you must not practice dream interpretation.' The original text is now translated as: "You must not practice divination." Dr. Condon at the time of his presentation was the Spiritual Director at the Pontifical Irish College in Rome. The presentation was entitled, "Dreams: A Way of Listening to God?"

The Fourth Session of the Council of Trent (1546) reiterated the Vulgate's authority as the official Latin version of the Bible to be used "in public lectures, disputations, sermons and expositions . . . and so no one dare or presume under any pretext whatsoever to reject it." Pope Pius XII, in a 1943 encyclical letter (*Divino Afflante Spiritu*), stated that the Vulgate is "free from any error whatsoever in matters of faith and morals."

The Douay-Rheims edition of the Bible, completed in 1609, is an English translation based on a faithful rendering of the Jerome's Vulgate. It became the standard Bible for English-speaking Roman Catholics for over three hundred years. A 1961 version still retained Jerome's mistranslations. Leviticus 19:26 reads: "You shall not eat with blood. You shall not divine nor observe dreams." Deuteronomy 18:10 reads: "Neither let there be found among any one that shall expiate his son or daughter, making them to pass through the fire: or that consulteth soothsayers, or observeth dreams and omens, neither let there be any wizard." 2 Paralipomenon (Chronicles) 33:6: "And he [Manasses] made his sons to pass through the fire in the valley of Benennonom: he observed dreams, followed divinations, gave himself up to magic arts, had with him magicians and enchanters: and he wrought many evils before the Lord, to provoke him to anger."

Just a few years later new translations of the Bible, like the New American Bible, the Jerusalem Bible, the New Jerusalem Bible, and the Revised Standard Edition—Catholic Edition, corrected Jerome's mistranslations.

What is curious about Jerome's translations is that Jerome wrote extensively about how God communicates through dreams. Jerome acknowledged he was a prolific dreamer and wrote about other people's dreams too. In his *Life of Paul the Hermit*, Jerome recounts how the monk Anthony was inspired by a dream from God to seek the eremite Paul, Anthony's predecessor in the desert. According to Patricia Cox Miller, Jerome was most interested in dreams he interpreted to be about virginity or ascetic life-styles. She wrote: "Jerome's tendency was to use [dream] images of the body that he thought were negative—the withered hands, the naked women and dancing girls—to argue positively for a remaking of the body in ascetic terms." Miller, *Dreams in Late Antiquity*, 209. For Miller's full discussion of Jerome and his dreams, see 208–231.

103. Men like Anselm, Archbishop of Canterbury; Abelard, the brilliant Frenchman who was bitterly opposed by Bernard of Clairvaux; Hugo, a German systematic thinker along with his countryman, the Dominican Albertus Magnus; and Peter Lombard, the Italian who became Bishop of Paris, led the way. Lombard wrote *Sentences*, which became the medieval textbook on dogmatics.

104. Aquinas' lasting impact on the thinking of the Roman Catholic Church is seen in his canonization just fifty years after his death; being declared a Doctor of the Church three hundred years following his death, and; proclaimed "patron of all Catholic schools" six hundred years after he died.

105. Italics emphasis added. Charles L. Souvay, "Interpretation of Dreams" with the citation II–II: 95:6.

106. Men like John Scotus Eriugena, Bernard of Clairvaux, Meister Eckhart, and Richard Rolle craved out the mystical path along with the vastly influential women mystics, Birgitta of Sweden, Catherine of Siena and Margery Kempe.

Hildegard von Bingen's (1098–1179) visions began in childhood and lasted throughout her life. She frequently pointed out how limited her formal education was and said any wisdom she had was divinely inspired. In spite of doubting she was equal to the task and fearing the reactions of her male contemporaries, Hildegard wrote three books of visions. Kings, queens and popes sought her out because of her acknowledged gift of prophecy in the sense of having access to God's secrets. Flanagan, "Hildegard von Bingen."

Juliana of Norwich was an English religious writer and hermit. On May 13, 1373 at the age of 31 she received sixteen visions of Jesus. Like Hildegard, she wrote a description of them and a brief analysis of their content that culminated in her book, *Revelations of Divine Love*, in which Juliana testifies that it is possible to have a direct, immediate, personal experience of God.

107. King William II was also known as "Rufus" for his red face. William of Malmesbury (1128) wrote that King William, besides his red face, had "yellow hair, different colored eyes, astonishing strength. . . was not very tall and his belly [was] rather projecting." He also stuttered, especially when he was angry. Rufus was an effective soldier who was loved by his troops but was an angry, ruthless ruler of everyone else. Chroniclers at the time indicated that he was "hated by almost all his people," especially church leaders from whom he stole money. In the *Orderic Vitalis* account of his death it states that the King was presented with six arrows prior to the hunt, but kept only four. The other two he gave to Walter Tyrrel saying, "It is only right that the sharpest be given to the man who knows how to shoot the deadliest shots." It was Walter Tyrrel, Lord of Poix, well known for his skill as a bowman, that shot the arrow that killed the King. Even though King William II's younger brother, Henry, who was also on the hunt, assumed the throne and rewarded Walter Tyrrel's family generously for their loyalty to him, there is no clear evidence that William's death was an assassination. Bluestone, *The World Dream Book*, 162; "William II"; and "William II of England".

108. Dr. Jeff Mishlove, "ESP and Ceremonial Magic". For the information about Albertus' attitudes about visions and dreams, Dr. Mishlove references Lynn Thorndike's *The History of Magic and Experimental Science, Vol. 5*.

109. Ignatius Loyola was a handsome young Spaniard, born of a noble family, consumed with a competitive desire for glory, obsessed with his hair and clothes, who joined the military and fully enjoyed what life offered him. In 1521, at age 30, his leg was severely injured in a battle with the French. Ignatius wrote in his autobiography that while convalescing he had a vision in which "he saw clearly" the Virgin Mary and Jesus. This vision led him to renounce his previous carnal lifestyle and to begin a spiritually focused one. After making a confession, he lived in a cave in Manressa. There he prayed, fasted and contemplated God's will for his life. Many visions came to him during this time and he began to make notes about the spiritual experiences that he was having. These experiences became the inspiration for his book, *The Spiritual Exercises* (1541). During the winter of 1537 Ignatius had another vision while on a trip to Rome. Ignatius saw God the Father associating him with Jesus, who promised him he would be successful in Rome. Three years later, Pope Paul III sanctioned the "Society of Jesus." Pollen, "St. Ignatius Loyola."

Sister Teresa of Avila had visions that played a significant role in her life also. St. Teresa, a Carmelite nun, taught that when someone has a vision that person "is perfectly certain" that God is the source. "When it is the Lord and He speaks, it is natural that He should be easily recognized," she explains in her book, *Interior Castle*. Peers, *St. Teresa's Complete Works, Volume II*, Chapter 9. While St. Teresa believed God communicates directly with people—her own experience confirmed it—she was cautious when it came to encouraging others to seek visions. Among her reasons for playing down visionary experiences were the following: The desire for a vision from God shows a lack of humility; that you can be deceived by the devil; that your imagination may think it is seeing something that isn't really there; that you may not be able to bear the trials such an experience can bring with it. The safest approach according to St. Teresa is to put yourself in God's hands so that His will may be done. If you do this, she taught, you will not go astray.

St. John of the Cross amplified Teresa's cautionary theme. He argued that while visions occur, and he was the recipient of many, we should "pay no attention to those representations." "With this attitude," he continued, "individuals take from these apprehensions only what God wants them to take, that is, the spirit of devotion, since God gives these experiences for no other principal reason." Kavanaugh and Rodriguez, *The Collected Works of St. John of the Cross*, 209.

110. *Commentaries de praecipius generibus devinationum*, 1560.

111. The Peucer quotes were found in the *Collected Works of C .G. Jung*, Volume 11, footnote 12, 19–21.

112. *De Magia, De Observatione Somniorum et de Divinatione Astrologica libri tres*, 1598. The Pererius quotes were found in the *Collected Works of C.G. Jung*, Volume 11, footnote 12.

113. Kelsey, *God, Dreams, and Revelation*, 180–81.

114. Smith, Handy, and Loetscher, *"The Pearl of Great Price: Being a Choice Selection from the Revelations, Translations, and Narratives of Joseph Smith, First Prophet, Seer, and Revelator to the Church of Latter-day Saints,"* 37–39, 40–41, 43–44, American Christianity, 81–84.

115. Public Broadcasting Service (PBS), "American Prophet: The Story of Joseph Smith."

116. Terry Matz, "St. John Bosco."

117. Twentieth century Christianity struggled with rationalism too. Christian Neo-Orthodoxy under the influence of Karl Barth (1886–1968) and Rudolf Bultmann (1884–1976) applied reason to theology. Barth believed the crisis of the modern world was in part a symptom of an alliance between Christianity and modern culture. He stressed the discontinuity between the Christian message and the world. God is totally transcendent, unknowable except in His revelation of Himself in Jesus. Barth rejected the possibility of all contact between God and man in feeling, consciousness or rationality. Dreams, not surprisingly, were not of interest to him. Perhaps they should have been. Thomas Merton wrote about a dream Barth had about Mozart. In his dream, Barth is appointed to examine Mozart in theology. Barth was obviously troubled by the dream. Merton comments: "The dream concerns his salvation, and Barth perhaps is striving to admit that he will be saved more by the Mozart in himself than by his theology." 11–12

Rudolf Bultmann believed the gospels are not history but theology in story form. The New Testament, he argued, is full of mythological material and needs to be "demythologized." God is wholly other and sin keeps man from connecting with God. "The invisibility of God excludes every myth which tries to make him and his acts visible.... God withdraws himself from the objective view: he can only be believed upon in defiance of all outward appearance." Rudolf Bultmann, "Kerygma and Myth by Rudolf Bultmann and Five Critics." Bultmann sparked such a controversy with his call to demythologize the Bible that heresy trials were instituted in Germany and the United States against those who used Bultmann's thinking in their preaching. Dreams were not one of Bultmann's interests.

118. Dr. Gerard Condon, "Dreams: A Way of Listening to God?" In the lecture Dr. Condon noted that when a private revelation does occur, it is typically one of three types: *visio sensibilis, visio imaginativa,* or *visio intellectualis. Visio sensibilis* is a revelation received through the senses. *Visio imaginativa* is a revelation that is transmitted through interior images while *visio intellectualis* is an infusion of knowledge that does not affect the senses. Dream communication falls into the second category. However, Dr. Condon noted, "the Church would tend to be very critical of someone who would come out with some preaching about their visions or mystical experiences."

In Pope Paul VI's *Dei Verbum* (11/18/1965), revelation is described as God choosing to reveal Himself out of his goodness and wisdom to make known the hidden purpose of His will. This revelation happened through Christ so that people might have access to God the Father and share in the divine nature as friends. "By this revelation then, the deepest truth about God and the salvation of man shines out for the sake of Christ, who is both the mediator and the fullness of all revelation." Chapter 1, #2.

119. Charles L. Souvay in his 2003 article, "Interpretation of Dreams" takes Dr. Condon's attitudes a step further. In the article Mr. Souvay reviews attitudes about God and dreams from antiquity, the Bible, and the early church Fathers. He concludes: "As a matter of fact dreams are now—we speak of civilized peoples—seldom heeded; only very ignorant and superstitious persons ponder over the 'dictionaries of dreams' and the 'keys to the interpretation of dreams' once so much in favour. 'As idle as a dream' has become a proverb expressive of the popular mind on the subject, and indicating sufficiently that there is little need nowadays to revive the laws and canons enacted in the past ages against divination through dreams."

4

Islamic Perspectives

> God, wishing to render intelligible to men the idea of inspiration, has given them a kind of glimpse of it in sleep. In fact, man perceives while asleep the things of the invisible world either clearly manifest or under the veil of allegory to be subsequently lifted by divination.
> —Abu Hamid al-Ghazali[120]

INTRODUCTION

THE CONNECTION BETWEEN GOD and dreams in Islam is strong. If Judaism can be characterized by a continuing conversation with God, then Islam can be characterized as being the final word of God. For Muslims, God's conversation started with Adam, the first person to whom God revealed himself, and continued with Abraham, Moses, the prophets, Jesus and ultimately Muhammad. God sent His final, authorative revelation to Muhammad. The definitive Word of God is contained in the Qur'ān,[121] the holy book of Islam. When the Qur'ān speaks of how God communicates, dreams are one of the ways identified.

DREAMS, MUHAMMAD, AND THE EARLY YEARS OF ISLAM

Muhammad's family members were among those who believed God speaks through dreams. Before Muhammad was born in 570, 'Abdel Muttalib, Muhammad's grandfather, had a series of dreams that told him to look for the hidden Well of Zamzam. This important well had been buried for generations. Its rediscovery would shorten significantly the distance water needed to be carried. 'Abdel Muṭṭalib's fourth dream told him where the well was located. He dug there and found the well.[122]

Aminah, Muhammad's mother, early in her pregnancy with him, had a dream in which she saw "lights coming from my womb, lighting up the mountains, the hills, and the valleys all around Mecca!" Aminah's teenage African servant girl interpreted the dream. "You will give birth to a blessed child who will bring goodness."[123]

Later in the same pregnancy Aminah heard a voice tell her in a dream, "You carry in your womb the lord of this nation. When he is born say, 'I place him under the protection of the One, from the evil of every envier,' then give him the name Highly Praised." When her baby boy was born Aminah named him *Muhammad*, which is Arabic for "highly praised."[124]

When Muhammad grew to be a man, he too had dreams that came from God. At first the dreams seemed strange and disturbing. He did not know what to make of their voices and images. With time Muhammad realized the dreams depicted events that had not yet happened. When they did occur, Muhammad responded by taking more time to be alone to pray and meditate. He went to a favorite cave outside Mecca that had a sweeping view of the desert. It was there, in the year 610, that Muhammad had a very intense spiritual experience. The Archangel Gabriel[125] appeared to him and told him he was the messenger of God. It is unclear whether the visitation by Gabriel occurred in a dream, as a vision, or as an actual presence.[126]

Because of the Prophet's experience, sleep in Islam is regarded as a window opening on the world of the Unseen.[127] Dreams are a way of receiving information about the Unseen. Muhammad is quoted in a hadīth as saying, "The worst lie is that a person claims to have seen a dream which he had not seen."[128]

Because Muhammad was illiterate, he recited verbatim to his family and friends what God revealed to him. These individuals either memorized what he told them or wrote it down. Muhammad received God's revelations the rest of his life.

THE PROPHET'S NIGHT JOURNEY AND ASCENSION

Muhammad's famous Night Journey[129] occurred perhaps a year or two before he left Mecca in 622 C.E. It was one of his most intense and important mystical experiences.[130]

The journey consisted of two parts. The first part, known as *isra'*, describes Muhammad's journey from Mecca to Jerusalem. It is said that Gabriel came to Muhammad while he slept, awoke and cleansed him within, and then took him through the air on the back of the winged mare Al-Buraq to Jerusalem.[131] When he arrived, Muhammad led all the prophets of the past in prayer. Sūrah 17:1 says, "Glory to Him Who took His servant by night from the sacred temple [at Mecca] to the more remote temple [at Jerusalem], whose precincts We have blessed, to show him some of Our signs."

The second part of Muhammad's journey that night is called the *mi'raj*. It describes Muhammad's ascension to heaven and the meetings that took place there. After Muhammad led the previous prophets in prayer, Gabriel took him to the sacred rock (now known as the Temple Mount) from which he ascended to Heaven. When Muhammad and Gabriel reached heaven, Gabriel asked the guardian angel to open the door of heaven to them. It was opened and Muhammad saw Adam. Muhammad saluted Adam who in turn welcomed Muhammad and expressed faith in his prophethood. Muhammad saw the souls of martyrs on his right and the souls of the wretched on his left.

Gabriel then ascended with Muhammad to the second heaven. Gabriel asked for the gate to be opened, and they entered. Here Muhammad saw John the Baptist and Jesus. They returned Muhammad's salute, welcomed him and like Adam before them, expressed faith in his prophethood. Gabriel and Muhammad moved on to the third heaven where they met Joseph, who also welcomed him and expressed faith in his prophethood. In the fourth heaven Enoch was met. Enoch saluted Muhammad and expressed faith in his prophethood as did Aaron, whom they met in the fifth heaven and Moses whom they met in the sixth heaven. It is reported that upon their leaving, Moses began to weep because he'd met the prophet who would lead more people to Paradise than he did. In the seventh heaven, Muhammad met Abraham who, like the others before him, saluted Muhammad and expressed faith in his prophethood.

Gabriel could travel no further into the depths of heaven, so Muhammad continued his journey unaccompanied. Muhammad was carried into the great space beyond the seventh heaven to the remotest lote tree. Here Muhammad was shown the sacred house to which the angels will return upon the Resurrection. Muhammad was now in the very presence of Allah. Among the many things that Allah spoke about with Muhammad was the importance of prayer. Out of these discussions came the instruction that all Muslims would pray five times each day. At the conclusion of their discussions, Muhammad returned to Gabriel.

Together they went back through the seven levels of heaven to the Temple Mount and then returned to Mecca.

For Muslims, it was during Muhammad's night journey that prayer was ordained. It is believed that through prayer Muslims can ascend to Allah. During the earliest years of Islam, when believers prayed, they faced the holy city of Jerusalem. Then, after four and a half years of observing this custom, the practice shifted to facing Mecca, as Mecca is the holiest of all cities in Islam.

This mystical journey demonstrates to Muslims that Muhammad is at least the equal of all other prophets in the sight of God. It also indicates to believers that Islam is not a new religion but the continuation of the same divine message that was preached by the previous prophets.

MUHAMMAD'S FINAL YEARS

Because Muhammad's teachings stirred up trouble in Mecca in 622,[132] he moved 200 miles north to a community that came to be known as Medinat al-Nabi, the City of the Prophet. A constitution was written and became the basis for all future Islamic governance. In 630 the spread of Islam moved beyond Medina with a successful attack on Mecca. In particular, Muhammad was victorious over his own clansmen, the Quraysh. Following his victory, Muhammad forgave all of his enemies.

Muhammad died in 632 at the age of 63. His death created a problem as no provision had been made for identifying a successor. Those who had been closest to Muhammad devised a process for selecting a successor that worked successfully for the first four caliphs.[133] However, following the death of the fourth caliph, the Islamic world split between those who wanted total authority to remain within the Prophet's family (Shi'a) and those who did not believe political and religious authority needed to be limited to the Prophet's clan (Sunnī). The Sunnī perspective prevailed.

QUR'AN AND HADĪTH

Islam means "submission" to God's will.[134] God's will, made explicit in the Qur'ān, is knowable. Studying the Qur'ān in its fullness, as a whole rather than by abstracting or paraphrasing its parts, is the way Muslims discern God's will.[135]

Many issues, however, were not addressed in the Qur'ān. These unaddressed matters caused controversy. The resolutions to those conflicts were found both in the manner the Prophet lived his life and in the way he governed Medina. These became the foundation on which Islamic law, *Sharīa'* ("Way") was built.[136]

A record of the Prophet's words and deeds, policies and judgments, were collected into a series of books which are known as *hadīth*.[137] From the start, some hadīth have been regarded as being more reliable than others. Therefore strict rules developed that separated the true traditions from the false ones. Sunnī Muslims regard six as authoritative with *Sahih Bukhari's* (810–870) being the most important. Shiite Muslims have their own collection[138] and regard many of the Sunnī editions to be forged.

Although collecting the contents of the hadīth and codifying the *Sharīa'* were the main activities of scholars during this early period of Islam, interest in dreams, especially because of Muhammad's experience, remained high. Even though the hadīth contains many references to dream interpretation[139] and provides principles for how to interpret a dream, secular Islamic culture took up the study of dreams as a scientific endeavor, not as a religious one. A vast amount of dream material was produced through their efforts. Catalogues of thousands of dream images were created, as were carefully developed detailed methods for interpreting dreams. Most books on Islamic dream interpretation have been attributed to Muhammad ibn Seereen (653–729) or attribute much of their material and methodology to him.

A theological difference of opinion about revelation occurred following the death of Muhammad. The Sunnī tradition considered God's revelations finished and complete. They taught that dreams occurring after Muhammad were not religiously important. All the guidance a person needed is to be found in the Qur'ān.[140]

Shiites and Sufis shared the minority attitude about revelation. They believed that prophecy continued rather than ceasing with Muhammad. Dreams remained a part of their religious practices. The same is true of the Lahore Ahmadiyya Movement in India.

Those who believed revelation continued divided dreams into three groups. The first two groups were regarded as "jumbled" or "false" dreams. One group of jumbled dreams originates inside the body or mind of the dreamer. These are dreams in which a person's imagination plays with his or her moods or the actual events of that person's life to create images and stories.

The second group of jumbled dreams originates in Shaytān (Satan).[141] These are frightening dreams or an expression of suppressed bodily desires. Jumbled dreams, because they are not from Allah, are false. They are not to be repeated or interpreted, for when they are interpreted that is the moment the event foretold in the dream will transpire.[142]

The third group of dreams consisted of "true" dreams. These originate in Allah. True dreams were of two kinds. Some were "pleasing." These are dreams after which a person feels satisfied and refreshed and can *feel* that his or her soul senses happiness. The second kind of "true" dream was regarded as being a higher stage. These dreams inform the recipient about the future. In these dreams Allah reveals to the dreamer some of His knowledge. Both kinds of true dreams are very clear and unforgettable. Having a true dream was seen as a confirmation that the dreamer was on the right path with his or her life. The more a person resembled a prophet in character, actions, speech, knowledge and piety, the more likely it was that the individual's dreams would be true ones.[143]

Muhammad instructed that dreams should not be shared with just anyone, but only with a beloved and intelligent person. Interpreting dreams is a gift from Allah to those who deserve it because of their moral and spiritual purity.[144] If a dreamer does not know such a person, then a prayer to Allah for understanding of the dream is advised.[145]

GOD AND DREAMS IN LATER ISLAMIC THOUGHT

At the end of the tenth century, innovative interpretations of the Qur'ān gave way to one literal interpretation. This understanding of the Qur'ān became and remains the official doctrine of Islam. Nevertheless, important Muslim thinkers continued to teach that God uses dreams to communicate His messages. Included in this distinguished group is Abu Hamid al-Ghazali, Ibn 'Arabi, Julalu'd-Din Rumi, and Ibn Khaldun.

Abu Hamid al-Ghazali (1058–1111) was a Sunnī theologian, logician, jurist and mystic. al-Ghazali is considered to be the greatest scholar of Islam. He possessed such an expansive knowledge that he was known as "The Proof of Islam" and he became the prototype for Muslim intellectuals. al-Ghazali taught true knowledge is the consequence of divine illumination. One way divine illumination can be received, al-Ghazali believed, is through a dream.

58 GOD AND DREAMS

Ibn 'Arabi (1165–1240) was a Sufi intellectual who was given the title "the greatest master" because of his brilliance. Ibn 'Arabi challenged the legalism of Islamic orthodoxy.[146] He stressed that each individual comes to know God in a unique and personal way established through a private, intimate dialogue with God. One way this dialogue happens is through dreams.

Ibn 'Arabi also offered a new way of thinking about dreams. He identified three types. First is an ordinary dream. An ordinary dream originates in the sleeper's imagination and uses images that are drawn from the dreamer's life. The images are magnified in order to depict the dreamer's desires, but the desires are presented in a distorted way.

The second type of dream is more significant in that it originates in the "universal soul" and reveals fundamental truths about reality. Ibn 'Arabi found a problem with this kind of dream too. The human imagination distorts the images that have come from the "universal soul." To understand the dream's message, an interpretation is needed.

The third type of dream is a direct revelation from God. It is so clear that there is no distortion or need for interpretation.[147]

Ibn 'Arabi also encouraged people to practice lucid dreaming. "The training of this alertness will produce great benefits for the individual. Everyone should apply himself to the attainment of this ability of such great value."[148]

A third inspired and influential Islamic thinker was Jalalu'd-Din Rumi (1207–1273), a contemporary of Thomas Aquinas. Rumi, who founded the Mevlevi Order of Dervishes, was also a Sufi. Like his father, Rumi was a distinguished jurist and preacher. As a younger man Rumi was staid. All that changed when at 37 he had a life-altering vision of God. "I was the country's sober ascetic," he wrote. "I used to teach from the pulpit—but destiny made me one of Thy hand-clapping lovers."[149] Rumi brought music and dance to worship ceremonies at a time when music and dance were not approved worship activities. Because Mevlevi worshippers liked to spin and move freely as they worshipped God, they came to be known as Whirling Dervishes.

Rumi taught the way to divine knowledge is not by means of the physical senses or the intellect as Aquinas and Sunnī theology were teaching, but by turning inward where the soul can hear God's call.[150] Rumi believed God enters dreams so individuals can have a direct experience of Him. Divine knowledge is knowledge that arises out of spiritual experience or mystical illumination. "Sell intelligence and buy bewilderment," Rumi advised. "Intelligence is conjecture and bewilderment is vision. Sacrifice understanding and say: God is sufficient for me."[151]

For his work in the social sciences, Abd al-Rahman Abu Zaid ibn Khaldun (1332–1395) was regarded as one of the intellectual giants of the fourteenth century. Khaldun was not afraid to acknowledge he used dreams to guide his development. In his book on world history, *Muqaddimah*, Khaldun taught that God created people so that when we sleep we are freed from "the veil of our senses." This allows our rational souls to "learn the things it desires to know in the world of Truth." Khaldun identified three types of dreams. First there is the "clear dream [that comes] from God." A second kind, allegorical dreams, come from angels and requires interpretation. A third type of dream Khaldun called "confused." These come from Satan. Their messages are utterly futile to understand, just "as Satan is the source of futility."[152]

More recently, in 1992 Muhammad Al-Akili's book, *Ibn Seerin's Dictionary of Dreams: According to Islamic Inner Traditions* sparked a renewed interest in dreams and dream interpretation among Muslims in the West. What is an authentic Islamic approach to dreams and what is not has again become a topic for debate.[153]

Valerie J. Hoffman, in her study of late twentieth century Egyptian Muslims, wrote that Muslims "believe that the ability to receive visions through dreams and in the waking state is a faculty that is latent in human beings, whose attachment to material things clouds their receptivity to impulses from the spiritual realm."[154]

SUMMARY

Islam teaches there is a connection between God and dreams. This is because the Prophet Muhammad received some of his revelations from God through dreams. God's revelation is considered to have been completed with the passing of the Prophet. Although dreams continue to occur, the mainstream Muslim perspective evolved into believing dreams no longer have any religious value. The only significance dreams have is the private meaning the dreamer takes from them.

ENDNOTES

120. Abu Hamid al-Ghazali, Confessions, or Deliverance from Error, 1100 c.e.
121. Qur'ān is Arabic for "recitation."
122. Yahiya Emerick, *The Life and Work of Muhammad*, 17.
123. Emerick, *Muhammad*, 21–22.
124. Emerick, *Muhammad*, 29.
125. Gabriel is the same angel that appeared to Mary, the mother of Jesus. The cave is now sealed and closed to visitors. The mountain where the cave is, is called "the mountain of light" (Jabal an-Nur). Muhammad was forty when Gabriel first appeared to him.
126. See Qur'ān 96:1–5. According to a hadīth written by Muhammad ibn Ishāq (d.768), perhaps the earliest biographer of the Prophet, Muhammad was asleep when Gabriel first appeared to him in the cave. Muhammad's first revelation was thus a dream experience. The information about Ishāq comes from Williams, editor, *Islam*, 61–62 who relied on Guillaume, 105–7.

Muhammad ibn Ishāq wrote *Sirat Rasul Allah* (*The Life of the Apostle of God*). His reports survived only through the writings of others. In 1955 Guillaume gathered all of the material into one source and published it as *The Life of Muhammad*. In his own day, Ishāq was accused of transmitting false hadīths. It appears that Ishāq's reports were uneven with regard to historical accuracy. Some of Ishāq's accounts were more historically authentic than others.

127. A prayer to be read when awakening from sleep is this: "All praise to Allah Almighty who gave me life (consciousness) after death (sleep) and towards Him in our rising again (at the time of the resurrection)."
128. *Sahih Bukhari*, Volume 9, Book 87, "Interpretation of Dreams." Number 167. Another mention of telling a dream that one did not actually have also comes from this same source and is Number 165. "The Prophet said, "Whoever claims to have seen a dream which he did not see, will be ordered [in Hell] to make a knot between two barley grains which he will not be able to do. . . . ."
129. For Muslims, the Journey shows that Mohammed is the fulfillment of what spiritual development can be and therefore Muhammad is God's greatest prophet.
130. It has long been the subject of debate within and outside of Islam whether this journey was another of Muhammad's revelatory dreams, or occurred in a vision, or perhaps was an out-of-body experience, or actually happened as recorded. However the journey occurred, the experience was tremendously significant.

In the Christian tradition, the Gnostic *Gospel of Mary*, contained in a fifth century manuscript, describes a vision Mary had in which she is shown an enlightened soul traveling through seven planetary spheres. James, *The Apocryphal New Testament*, xxii.

131. It is noteworthy that Jerusalem is Muhammad's destination. It is this experience that makes Jerusalem a holy city within Islam and why Muslims, along with Jews and Christians, have an equal claim upon the holy city. It also indicates to Muslims that Muhammad was sent as a prophet to not only his own people, but to all people. This international out-reach distinguishes Muhammad from previous prophets.
132. 622 is year one of the Islamic calendar. Islam is dated from the year of the founding of the community of Believers, not from the year of Muhammad's birth or from the year of his first revelation. The month in which Muhammad received his first revelation was Ramadan.
133. A single leader, a caliph, was determined to be the sole legitimate Muslim au-

thority. All other authority in the Muslim community is a delegation of power from the caliph. The first elected leader after Muhammad's death was Abu Bakr. He was the first to have the title of caliph (successor) to the Messenger of God. His leadership was 632–634. After Caliph Bakr came Caliph 'Umar (634–644), Caliph Uthman (644–656), and Caliph Ali (656–661). Each of these men was close to Muhammad.

134. *Muslim* is Arabic for "submitter."

135. The Qur'ān had not been collected into one book when Muhammad died. This was not a high priority; defending, strengthening and spreading the Faith were. A number of fierce battles were fought with rebellious Arab tribes and with the Roman Empire. In these battles many of Muhammad's closest associates were killed. With them died valuable knowledge of the Prophet's revelations that they had personally preserved or memorized. Consequently Caliph Bakr collected and compiled the verses of the Qur'ān.

136. All the Prophet did is considered worthy of study and emulation. Indeed, it is dogma that everything the Prophet did after the initial revelation, even his slightest behavior, was preserved by God from error. Thus Islamic law is understood to be divine in origin. A devout Muslim observes the "five pillars" of faith: profession of faith, prayer, fasting, almsgiving, and pilgrimage. Ritual purity is also vital since without it the prayers of the worshipper are rendered invalid and the Qur'ān may not be touched.

137. A hadīth has two parts: One lists the names of the individuals handing down the traditions (the chain of transmission), and the other part consists of the actual information. The great compilers of hadīth were al-Bukhari, Abu Dawood, al-Tirmidhi, Ibn Maja and al-Nasai. These men published their books between the years 751–800.

138. The most important Shi'a collection are two of Mohammad Ibne Yaqoob Abu Jafar Kulaini's: *Usool al Kafi* and *Forroh al Kafi*. Others also considered important include Muhammad ibn Babuya's *Man la yahduruhu al Faqih* and Shaykhut-Fa'ifa's *Tahdhib al-Akhkam*.

139. Some of the references describe the Prophet's interpretation of a particular image from the dream of one of his followers while other references describe Muhammad's own dreams and his understanding of them.

140. This attitude is still held. See "Understanding Islam." Answering a question submitted from Pakistan in February, 1999 (What is the position and significance of dreams in Islam?) the site replies, "Dreams, normally, do not have any religious significance. The only exception is the dreams of a prophet of God. A person may dream about something, which on the basis of his subsequent experience, is found to be true. But even in this case, the importance or significance of such dreams is not religious."

141. *Shaytān's* etymology means "he was or became remote." It refers to the evil impulses in the heart of those who deny the truth and oppose what is true and good. In the Qur'ān, Sūrah 15:16 teaches that it is a satanic force that would lead someone to divine the future by stealth means (i.e., by using an occult science). The hadīth *Sahih Bukhari*, Vol. 9, Book 95, no. 113 says, "True dreams are from Allah and bad dreams are from Satan." "Tara's World of Islam: Dreams."

142. When an evil dream occurs the appropriate response is threefold. First, spit lightly three times to the left side. Next, sleep on the other side of the bed. Finally, perform two Rakaats of Salaat. A rakaat is a unit or time of Salaat. A Salaat is a spiritual communication performed with mental concentration, verbal communication, vocal recitation and physical movement. Cleansing of the body, clothes and place precede a Salaat. A devout Muslim performs a Salaat five times a day: dawn, noon, afternoon, sunset, and late night.

62   GOD AND DREAMS

143. Islamic scholars have determined dreams are most potent during the latter part of the night, during siesta, and during fruit ripening season. Information about these three types of dreams comes from Discover Islam, "Dreams, Their Truth and Meaning."

144. Interpreters are cautioned not to rush to interpret dreams nor should they make people believe their interpretation is a fact.

145. Information about Islamic attitudes about dreams was found in the articles, "Dreams in Islam." and "Tara's World of Islam: Dreams."

146. Ibn 'Arabi was so upset with the orthodox leaders in Cairo that he called them stupid, ignorant and depraved. These leaders did not take kindly to his challenges and 'Arabi had to flee to Mecca to save his life.

147. Bulkeley, *Overview: Reflections on the Dream Traditions of Islam.*

148. LaBerge: *Lucid Dreaming*, 13. There he references I. Shah, *The Sufis*, 141.

149. Chittick, *The Sufi Path of Love*, 3.

150. Rumi taught in ecstatic moments an immediate meeting with God can occur. Ecstasy sweeps away personal consciousness so the spiritually elevated individual may be intoxicated by the Love of God. Holy men clap when freed from ego constraints and dance when freed from their own imperfection.

151. Khosla, *The Sufism of Rumi*, 184.

152. This information was found in Dr. Bulkeley's article, *Overview*, in which he cites Rosenthal's translation of *The Muqaddimah*, 80–81, 83.

153. In 1996 Abu Ameenah Bilal Philips argued against the historic perception when he wrote that "without a shadow of a doubt [Ibn Seereen] did not write any book on dream interpretation. He did, however, write a compilation of Aboo Hurayrah's narrations from the Prophet along wit the opinions of Aboo Hurayrah. . . . The Arabic text, *Muntakhab al-Kalaam fee Tafseer al-Ahlaam*, which is in wide circulation today, is also falsely attributed to Ibn Seereen. Consequently, English translations based on it as well as other books, like *Ibn Seerin's Dictionary of Dreams* and *Dreams and Interpretations*, are all unauthentic." Philips, "Dream Interpretation."

154. Hoffman, "The Role of Visions in Contemporary Egyptian Religious Life," 53 as found in Bulkeley, *Overview*.

5

A Few Other Religious Perspectives

> There is a Spirit who is awake in our sleep and creates the wonder of dreams.
> He is the Spirit of Light, who in truth is called the Immortal.
> All the worlds rest on that Spirit and beyond him no one can go.
> —Upanishads (ninth century, B.C.E.)[155]

INTRODUCTION

THE BELIEF THAT DREAMS come from God is not limited to the Middle East and Europe. It is not exclusive to Judaism, Christianity and Islam. People throughout the world, with their own faith traditions, share the belief that dreams are a communication between the spiritual realm and individuals. It is such a strongly held belief that many of these people structure their communal lives so that they can take advantage of the guidance and healing their dreams provide. The survey that follows is a sampling of these other religious perspectives.

AFRICA

William Howells, a Christian missionary among the Dyak people of Borneo at the beginning of the twentieth century, wrote:

> The Dyak revelation is communicated by means of dreams or visions, they therefore consider dreams as oracles from the gods; they read their dreams and pretend to understand them as we do the Holy Writ. In all their pursuits they are guided by their dreams.[156]

Mandaza Kandemwa, a Bantu healer of both the Shona and Ndebela peoples in Zimbabwe, reported that each day in Bulawayo, Zimbabwe's second largest city, starts with people gathering to share their dreams.

Dreams for the Shona and the Ndebela are a channel between the living and the world of the invisibles.[157]

Among other African tribes who value dreams [158] are the Ashanti of Ghana; the Bambara of Mali; the Dogon of Sudan; the Konde and Nyakyusa of Tanzania; the Northern Yaka of Zaire; the Rif of Morocco; the Tiv of Nigeria; and the Zulu of South Africa.

ASIA

In the Hindu Vedic writings from 1500–1000 B.C.E., dreaming is understood to be an intermediate state between this world and another. While asleep, the soul can leave the body to experience both realms.

In the Himalayas the Chamar and the Lepcha pay attention to their dreams.

The Lepcha live in the thick forests of southwestern Bhutan,[159] a small country between India and Tibet. On a daily basis it is important for the Lepcha to be in rapport with the spiritual forces that are in nature. While shamans are the community's principal source for contact with spiritual forces, the Lepcha regard dreams as a visual manifestation of the mystical universe that surrounds them.

> There is widespread belief [among the Lepcha] that while dreaming the soul can detach from the body and wander from village to village in the empirical reality of night, or, by going through the appropriate gates, can travel to the underworld, generally thought to be inhabited by the deceased. In the underworld, as well as on the earth's surface, the individual may meet, communicate with and have visions of, the spirits of the deceased, deities and demons. However, while normal people's dreams are often not remembered or are confused and difficult to interpret, shamans' dreams are of an entirely different nature.
>
> It seems, in fact, that shamans are somehow able to control their own oneiric activity, weaving a kind of logical thread from one dream to another. So shamans often think in terms of an oneiric continuum, causing them to live double lives.[160]

Long ago in China, the Miao believe, their people could meet with spirits and talk with them. When the physical world and the spiritual world separated, a new way of communicating with the spirits became necessary. Ancestors became mediators and sent dreams to communicate with the living.[161]

A Few Other Religious Perspectives   65

The members of the Kol tribe in central India also are sensitive to the separation between the physical and spiritual realms. Dr. Sarvananda Bluestone has researched their dream experience.

> [There is] a very thin and fragile thread [that] connects the dreamer with his waking soul. A kind of bio-spiritual telephone wire, this thread allows the soul to remain in constant contact with the dreamer, no matter how far it wanders. If, on its nightly journey, the soul is attacked by an evil spirit, the ensuing struggle is communicated to the sleeper through this thread. Nightmares are this communication of the soul's struggle at some distant place. The sleeper shouts or groans or thrashes about, depending on the severity of the attack upon the soul. At such times the sleeper should be gently wakened to force the soul to return to the body and out of harm's way.[162]

CANADA

The Naskapi Indians live in the forests of the Labrador Peninsula. In the 1960s the Swiss psychologist Dr. Marie-Louise von Franz wrote about their use of dreams.

> These simple people are hunters who live in isolated family groups, so far from one another that they have not been able to evolve tribal customs or collective religious beliefs and ceremonies. In his lifelong solitude the Naskapi hunter has to rely on his own inner voices and unconscious revelations; he has no religious teachers who tell him what he should believe, no rituals, festivals, or customs to help him along.
>
> Those Naskapi who pay attention to their dreams and who try to find their meaning and test their truth can enter into a deeper connection with the Great Man [their inner spiritual center]. He favors such people and sends them more and better dreams. Thus the major obligation of an individual Naskapi is to follow the instructions given by his dreams, and then to give permanent form to their contents in art. . . . Dreams give the Naskapi complete ability to find his way in life, not only in the inner world but also in the outer world of nature. They help him to foretell the weather and give him invaluable guidance in his hunting, upon which his life depends.[163]

According to Ojibwe legend,[164] Asibikaashi (Spider Woman) gave the dream catcher to people to protect them from bad dreams. Good dreams know their way through the hole in the center of the web and float along the sacred feathers to the person sleeping below. Bad dreams, on the other hand, are caught on the web and rinsed away by the morning dew. Other tribes share the same legend (or slight variations of it) and make use of dream catchers also.

The Nootka and Kaska tribes in Canada also pay careful attention to their dreams.

CENTRAL AND SOUTH AMERICA

In Mexico the Mayan people regard their dreams as being so important that one out of every four people is designated to be a dream interpreter.[165]

The Cuna Indians on the San Blas Islands near Panama also have a high regard for dreams. Dreams for the Cuna have social implications and prophetic power, so they are shared collectively and their warnings are heeded. For example, if an ominous dream causes a person not to report for a community work project, the social censure and large fine that normally accompanies not fulfilling these responsibilities is waived. Important dreams are reported at town council meetings without hesitation.[166]

The Araucanos and Yama people of Chile also pay attention to their dreams, as do the Mapuches. The Mapuches (People of the Earth) view dreams as providing them a path to follow, especially when seeking advice about health concerns or premonitions about present or future events. *Machi* are holy, wise Mapuches who interpret dreams, especially ones that contain images of deceased friends or relatives. *Machi* are usually women.

> The Mapuches believe that he who dreams is not the person, but rather his spirit (or pullu). . . . If dreams are good, then they must not be told. The belief is that the envy of the ones who hear it would make it unfeasible. If dreams, however, are bad or nightmares, they should be told around a bonfire, because the fire with the smoke will take them away, thus expelling the evil spirit that sent the dream.[167]

The Kagwahiv and Kalapalo tribes in the central part of Brazil also pay attention to their dreams.[168] The Kagwahiv report their dreams daily to one another with lots of intense discussion regarding their dreams' meaning. The Kagwahiv believe dreams foretell the future. Dreams offer a special kind of perception that accesses a reality beyond the one known to the senses. Nightmares, for example, can be experienced as a direct encounter with a ghost or demon.

The Kalapalo tribe also has a great interest in dreams, but unlike their neighbors the Kagwahiv, the Kalapalo do not report their dreams publicly. Dream interpretation is a valued skill among them because they understand dreams as helping them with problem solving and with forming new roles and relationships.

In Macas, Ecuador the first European explorers gave several different tribes a common name, Jivaro.[169] A small Jivaroan tribe, the Achuar, live in the Ecuadoran/Peruvian lowlands along the Pastaza River. The Achuar rely heavily on their dreams to help them plan what they will do during the day, especially with regard to that day's hunt. The Achuar identify three types of dreams (in addition to visions): *kuntuknar*, which prefigures success in hunting; *mesekramprar*, which indicates misfortune, especially death; and *karamprar*, which is a dialogue of souls between a dreamer and someone living or dead, or a supernatural being. They believe these last dreams provide literal, not metaphorical, messages. *Kuntuknar* and *mesekramprar* dreams are understood metaphorically. The Achuar recognize that some dreams need interpretation, but they have no set rules for how to do so.

The members of the Guajiro tribe live in northern Colombia and Venezuela on the peninsula that juts into the Caribbean. The Guajiro are part of the Wayú ethnic group, which has identified five kinds of dreams. There are ordinary dreams that are neutral or positive in nature and have clear meanings. There are bad dreams that warn of unfavorable events. These dreams are more often symbolic than literal. There are trivial dreams that have no meaning whatsoever. A fourth kind of dream is the nightmare, which is much worse than a "bad dream." A nightmare represents a direct attack on the sleeper from a spirit of a known dead person or from some generalized evil spirit. Nasty bodily symptoms accompany nightmares. The fifth kind of Guajiro dream is called a *contra*, meaning a fetish-like power object. These dreams are associated with the Spirit Master, who appears in the dream to show the sleeper how to acquire or make a *contra* and how to harness its powers.[170]

NATIVE AMERICAN TRADITIONS

Native Americans teach that dreams are like a guiding light given by the Great Spirit to souls that otherwise would wander in darkness. Among the Iroquois of the Great Lakes as early as 1390, and perhaps as early as the twelfth century, dreams were regarded with complete seriousness. Tracy Marks, in her writings about the Iroquois, noted that dreams guide their lives, especially with regard to "fishing, hunting, war, dancing, marriage and other significant life events. The Iroquois especially listened carefully to dreams their people had prior to war and hunting—a war party would even turn back if one of its members dreamed of failure immediately before or during the hunt."[171]

The seventeenth century French Jesuit missionary Paul Ragueneau (1608–1680) watched the Iroquois of the Great Lakes closely and made notes about their spiritual practices. He wrote:

> The Iroquois believe that our souls have other desires, which are, as it were, inborn and concealed. These, they say, come from the depths of the soul, not through any knowledge. . . .They have no divinity but the dream. They submit themselves to it and follow its order with the utmost exactness. Whatever they see themselves doing in dreams they believe they are absolutely obliged to execute at the earliest possible moment. Iroquois would think themselves guilty of a great crime if they failed to obey a single dream.[172]

Dreams, as the Iroquois understand them, have the power to cure disease and disorders of the mind. Through dreaming and sharing dreams, the Iroquois believe that they can contact the sacred power, *Orenda*. Dream quests are part of a boy's initiation into manhood.

Among the Iroquois, sharing dreams is often done in a communal setting. They find it eases tensions experienced in the dream. The Midwinter Dream Festival is an annual six-day sacred festival of renewal that has been observed for centuries. The festival brings the previous year to a close and opens the new one. Dreams of healing from the previous year are recalled, their lessons expressed and renewed through song and dance. Prayers of thanksgiving are offered. Dreams that were helpful from the past are recalled and reaffirmed. New dreams are shared with those in attendance. If the dream is not already understood, then a kind of competition follows among the dream "experts" and others offering interpretations to see who can come closest to getting it right. Whoever is most helpful with the interpretation is obliged to help the dreamer satisfy or fulfill the dream, literally or symbolically, depending on the dream's content. The responsibility to help with the dream is viewed as an honor.

Among the Delaware tribe dreams are also considered to be of spiritual significance. Delaware priests are of two kinds: those who interpret dreams and divine the future, and those who heal.[173]

The Lakota tribe utilizes dreams to connect with the Great Spirit. When a Lakota seeks a vision, he/she goes through a long preparatory ceremony. This ceremony is the Lakota version of dream incubation. In the evening the seeker, called a "lamenter," may use a pillow of sage while sleeping to keep evil spirits away. Often it is during this sleep that the vision will come from WakanTanka (the Great Spirit).

For the Utes, guidance from dreams has taken the form of new songs and dances. Their Bear Dance originated in a dream, and the songs, costumes and paintings worn by the performers of the Sun Dance also came from dreams.[174]

Among the other Native American tribes who have utilized their dreams for guidance and healing are the Apache (White Mountain and Jicarilla), Bella Coola, Blackfoot, Cherokee, Crow, Gras Ventres, Hare Indian Nation, Hopi, Klamath, Maricopa, Mohave, Paviotso, Piute, Plateau, River Yuman, Sinkyone, Yurok, Western Shoshone, and Wintu.

PACIFIC REGION

In Malaysia the Temiar, Iban and Mantia tribes use their dreams for guidance and healing. The Iban, who live on the northwestern tip of Indonesia, have long constructed *meligai* (spiritual dream houses). It is to the meligai that the Iban people go to await the appearance of their guardian spirit in a dream.[175]

In the Philippines the Mayawyaw are guided and healed by their dreams, as are the Kiwai people of Papua, New Guinea and the Tikopia of the Solomon Islands.

In Australia, the Aranda tribe of Aborigines has an outlook on the universe, which they refer to as "the Dreaming" or "Dreamtime." "Dreamtime" is a mythological reference to the period before the Earth came into being, when everything was spirit and nothing was physical. The Aranda believe the "Dreaming" still exists and can be accessed to communicate with spirits, acquire knowledge, and be healed. It is in the "Dreaming" that the sacred dimensions of the Earth can be found. Dreams are a way of accessing the "Dreamtime."[176]

SUMMARY

Judaism, Christianity and Islam are not the only faith traditions that affirm God communicates through dreams. Scattered throughout the world are other faith traditions that also affirm this reality. Indeed, the belief is so profoundly held by some tribes that they have a long history of structuring their communal lives so that they can take advantage of the messages their dreams provide.

ENDNOTES

155. "Upanishad" means inner or mystic teaching. The Sage Yajnavalkye is credited with most of the later Hindu teachings.
156. Sarvananda Bluestone, Ph.D., The World Dream Book, 159.
157. Maryam Henein, "Shamanic Healing Quest," Whole Life Times.
158. Some African alphabets were inspired by dreams. Momolu Duwalu Bukele had a dream in 1830 that inspired him to devise a syllabary for the Vai language. A standardized version of his writing system still is used in Liberia by about 75,000 people. [Simon Ager, "Vai Syllabary"] At the end of the nineteenth century, Sultan Ibrahim Njoya, King of Bamoun (Cameroon) for more than forty years, had a dream that led to an independent system of writing for his own language and for a secret "court language." [Saki Mafundikwa, "Afrikan Alphabets"] Chief Gbili of Sonoyea is said to have had a dream that resulted in the Kpelle writing system. The Kpelle are found in Liberia. They believe that humans have two brains or spirits. One is used for waking life and one is used for dreaming. For the Kpelle, dreams are as real as waking reality. [Bluestone, The World Dream Book, 21] Also in Liberia the Bassa Vah came from a dream of Di Widah and the Bond Lorma script came from a dream of Widoh Zobo. ["The Liberian Post"]
159. Bhutan is the world's only Buddhist kingdom.
160. Mario Giampà, Stefano Beggiora, Luca Caldironi, "Dreams and Shamans in sub-Himalayan Tribal Groups."
161. There are more than 7,000,000 Miao people living in China. They are China's fourth-largest nationality. Their religion is animistic and emphasizes ancestor worship. The Miao believe it is important to interpret dreams. The Chu'un Miano, another nationality within China, also believes it is important to interpret dreams.
162. Bluestone, The World Dream Book, 97.
163. von Franz, Man and His Symbols, 162.
164. This tribe goes by two names. In Canada they are called Ojibwe while in the United States they are called Chippewa.
165. Marc Ian Barasch, Healing Dreams.
166. Robert L. Van de Castle, Our Dreaming Mind, xvi–xvii.
167. Anwandter, "Dreams of the Mapuches." The Mapuches constitute approximately ten percent of the population of Chile and are the only people originating in Latin America who was not overcome by the Spanish colonization.

A Few Other Religious Perspectives   71

168. Gordon Ingram, "Dreaming as Precognition in Lowland South America."

169. Jivaro's etymology is "savage." The name is still in use to identify the Amazon tribes Shuar, Aguaruna, Huambisa, Huaorani, Achuar, and Shiviar who share a common language but with variations in dialect. The Spanish forced the Jivaro south from Macas into the jungle along the Peru-Ecuador border. The Jivaro gained notoriety for their practice of headhunting and ability over a six-day period to shrink a head to the size of a man's fist. It is estimated that about 7,000 Achuar live in Ecuador and 4,800 live in Peru. Eric Schniter, "The Jivaro and Shuar of the NorthWest Amazon."

170. Guajiro dreams are interpreted by their shamans. Ingram, "Dreaming."

171. Tracy Marks, "Iroquois Dreamwork and Spirituality." I have drawn on her article for much of the information presented about the Iroquois.

172. Marks, "Iroquois Dreamwork and Spirituality."

173. Information about the Delaware comes from Lee Sultzman, "Delaware History."

174. Bluestone, *The World Dream Book*, 79.

6

Some Non-Religious Perspectives

> We are so captivated by and entangled in our subjective consciousness that we have forgotten the age-old fact that God speaks chiefly through dreams and visions.
> —C. G. Jung[175]

INTRODUCTION

THE EXPLORATION OF THE connection between God and dreams next surveys several non-religious perspectives. This chapter first highlights the philosophical background of the last 300 years. What evolved during this period was a struggle between a rationalistic perception that claims all ideas are grounded in human consciousness and a spiritual perception that argues communication to and from God is possible. These attitudes influenced the thinking in other disciplines too, including psychology, research psychology, parapsychology, anthropology, theoretical physics and the philosophy of science. These other disciplines are also surveyed for how they perceive the connection between God and dreams.

PHILOSOPHICAL PERSPECTIVES

The seventeenth and eighteenth centuries were the time of the Enlightenment.[176] This period began with René Descartes (1596–1650) who threw out all previous knowledge and started anew. Descartes' thinking was built on the foundation of the one certainty: "I think, therefore I am." All of Western philosophical thought following Descartes takes its grounding in human consciousness (not God) and emphasizes the ideas present in consciousness.

What started Descartes on his efforts to find certainty in thought—which led to the revolutionary change in Western thinking,—was a dream that Descartes believed came from God.[177] On the night of November 10, 1619, when Descartes was 23, he dreamed of two books: one a dictionary, the other a compendium of poetry. Descartes interpreted the dream himself. The dictionary, he reasoned, represented all the specialties in science gathered together in a disconnected, sterile way. Consequently, these specialties had no sense of what wisdom is. The collection of poetry, Descartes concluded, represented the union of philosophy with wisdom. Descartes believed the dream was a sign from God that he was to establish an all-encompassing science of human wisdom. In response to the dream, Descartes made a pilgrimage to Loreto to give thanks for God's favor.

The intellectuals who led the Enlightenment believed logic and philosophy were superior to mystical experiences. When dreams became popular among European commoners, intellectuals such as Thomas Hobbes (1588–1679) and John Locke (1632–1704) were horrified. As prominent leaders of the educated class Hobbes and Locke regarded dreams as an irrational orientation to reality. Hobbes,[178] who feared dreams would make people believe they were prophets, wrote, "where all is but dream, reasoning and arguments are of no use, truth and knowledge nothing."

Philosophers of the Enlightenment developed two schools of thought to explain the origins of knowledge: Rationalism and Empiricism. The Rationalists were mostly French and German thinkers[179] who assumed knowledge begins with certain innate ideas. The Empiricists[180] held that knowledge begins not with innate ideas but with sensory experience. In the eighteenth century Immanuel Kant sought to bring unity to Rationalism and Empiricism by showing that both answer the wrong question. The crucial question is not whether the origin of knowledge is innate or empirical, but how the world is understood. In *Critique of Pure Reason* (1781, 1789), Kant showed how the structure of our concepts shape our experience.

Another significant influence on Western thinking was the scientific method of Sir Isaac Newton (1643–1727). His simple and analytical approach to the exploration of mathematics and physics became a model for all thought. Following Newton, order and regularity were expected from the proper analysis of observed facts.

Newton's mechanical vision of the universe allowed deism to flourish, especially in England. Deism emphasized God as impersonal and distant. Man had to save himself. Society became the place where salvation was sought. For many people establishing social justice on earth replaced

74   GOD AND DREAMS

seeking salvation from God as the meaning of life. Democracy took hold during the late eighteenth century as an idea worth dying for, as many did in the American and French revolutions.

Denis Diderot (1713–1784), the most famous of the French encyclopedists, created a book that was more than a summary of contemporary knowledge; it was a manifesto for new ways of looking at things.[181] Diderot's *Encyclopédie* highlighted innovations occurring in mechanical processes. His focus helped to make natural science much more interesting than theology.

Three nineteenth century philosophers who offered a spiritually oriented perspective were Hegel, Schopenhauer and Kierkegaard. Georg Wilhelm Hegel (1770–1831) distinguished three types of religion: nature, art, and revealed; with revealed religions considered to be the highest kind. Hegel believed that God's presence dwells inside everyone and that oneness between the believer and God is possible.

Arthur Schopenhauer (1788–1860) was one of the philosophers who disagreed with Kant's thinking. He expressed his concerns at two different moments in his life. As a young man, Schopenhauer expressed his differences in *The World as Will and Representation* (1819). Twenty-five years later, after being exposed to the Upanishads and Buddhism, Schopenhauer wrote a second edition of the book. In it he pointed out the possibility of a mystical consciousness being the means by which "things-in-themselves" are known.

Søren Aabye Kierkegaard (1813–1855) made a distinction between subjective and objective truth, between existence and essence. When Kierkegaard chose passionate, subjective existence; "existentialism" was born. For Kierkegaard the moment, the individual, the subjective, the contextual situation was more significant than eternal truths and absolute values.

Friedrich Wilhelm Nietzsche (1844–1900), the son of a Lutheran pastor in Röcken, Saxony, grew up to reject the idea of God, absolute truth and all systematic philosophy. Nietzsche rejected any thinking that purported to transcend the individual. Nietzsche's belief that God is just an idea transformed God from a theological question into a psychological problem. "Is man one of God's blunders, or is God one of man's?" Nietzsche asked.[182]

The next development in the philosophical struggle between the rational and spiritual perspectives came with the Frenchman, Henri Bergson

(1859–1941). In *Creative Evolution* (1907) Bergson argued that *élan vital* ("creative impulse"), not natural selection, is at the heart of evolution and that *élan vital* continues to shape all of life. Man's future, according to Bergson, lies in a mystical union with God.[183]

John Dewey (1859–1952) became the pre-eminent American philosopher of the early twentieth century. Dewey had no need for God. He regarded the idea of God as being hostile to culture. His philosophy differed from Nietzsche's in that Dewey saw power as residing in the community; not the individual.[184] Dewey marked an important turning away from metaphysics and toward logic.[185]

Early in his career Ludwig Wittgenstein (1889–1951) turned his attention to the study of language (*Tractatus Logico-Philosophicus*, 1922). He argued that language, thought and reality all share a common structure that logic can express. Later in life Wittgenstein saw that this idea was not right. Instead, he taught that philosophical problems arise from intellectual bewilderment that is induced by the misuse of language. The only way to resolve philosophical problems, Wittgenstein reasoned, is by paying careful attention to the actual usage of ordinary language. Wittgenstein's focus on language and logic influenced several generations of philosophers.[186]

As philosophy moved away from perceiving God as a reality, the possibility of a direct, personal experience of God diminished. With philosophy's focus on the study of logic and language, the consideration of God's role in dreams disappeared.

PSYCHOLOGY AND DREAMS

Unlike philosophy, psychology has paid a great deal of attention to dreams. Among the initial findings in psychology was that part of the psyche is unconscious. Awareness of the unconscious changed the way dreams were understood. Stirrings in the unconscious joined with environmental and bodily factors as causes of dreams. Dream images were no longer interpreted exclusively as literal representations of an outer reality, but also as symbolic representations of an inner reality. These psychological insights into the nature of dreams stimulated a renewed interest in them clinically, academically, and religiously.

William James (1842–1910) was one of the first psychologists in the United States. He used his psychological orientation to examine the nature of personal religious experience in his groundbreaking book, *Varieties of Religious Experience* (1902). In the book, Dr. James described dreaming as one of the most common experiences of the "subconscious" realm of the mind where religion and psychology come together. Dr. James believed in the reality of mystical experience.

> This overcoming of all the usual barriers between the individual and the Absolute is the great mystic achievement. In mystic states we both become one with the Absolute and we become aware of our oneness. This is the everlasting and triumphant mystical tradition, hardly altered by differences of clime or creed. In Hinduism, in Neoplatonism, in Sufism, in Christian mystical tradition, in Whitmanism, we find the same recurring note, so that there is about mystical utterances an eternal unanimity which ought to make a critic stop and think, and which brings it about that the mystical classics have, as has been said, neither birthday nor native land. Perpetually telling of the unity of man with God, their speech antedates languages, and they do not grow old.[187]

Sigmund Freud (1856–1939) was a contemporary of William James. Dr. Freud's thinking focused on the structure of the human personality and what he believed to be psychosexual stages of development. One technique Dr. Freud favored for inquiring into a person's psyche was the use of dreams. Dreams for Dr. Freud represented repressed desires, fears, and conflicts in disguised or symbolic form. By having a person freely associate to his or her dream images, important repressed memories could be identified. Dr. Freud spoke of two kinds of dream content: the actual events of a person's life that found their way into a dream (manifest content) and the hidden symbolic meaning of dreams (latent content). His work with dreams led him to conclude some dream images signified the same thing for nearly every individual: an internal conflict, usually sexual. Dr. Freud stressed that dreams needed to be understood in the context of the individual's conflict so that the same image could mean different things to different people. Among other findings of Dr. Freud's were that dreams reveal conflicts only in a condensed and intensified form, and; that there are many different causes for a dream. The causes range from mundane environmental factors such as a breeze blowing over the sleeper, to contact with one's partner or internal unresolved issues. Dr. Freud did not believe God caused dreams.

Karen Horney (1885–1952), after having her own psychoanalysis from a disciple of Freud's, developed theories about how a child's personality is formed.[188] Like Freud, Dr. Horney used dream analysis in her exploration of the psyche, believing dreams reveal a person's true personality. She, too, saw dreams as the psyche's attempt to resolve conflict and believed that they represent a more accurate picture of the personality than the illusory one a person may prefer to believe is true. She thought that to get to the real meaning of a dream it had to be interpreted by an analyst within the context of that person's problem. Although Dr. Horney did not speak of God and dreams, at the end of her life she did become interested in Zen Buddhism.

Harry Stack Sullivan (1892–1949)[189] also worked with patients' dreams, though his primary focus was on how the psyche is affected by human interactions. He did not believe there are hidden meanings to be discovered in a dream's content. Dreams, Dr. Sullivan argued, are an attempt to gain some satisfaction not attained while awake. Dr. Sullivan did not believe God is involved with dreams.

Freud's analyst and heir apparent was C.G. Jung (1875–1961)[190] Dr. Jung, a psychiatrist, did detailed research into dreams. He studied more than 67,000 dreams before he wrote about them. Dr. Jung believed dreams are both prospective (helping an individual prepare for the future) and compensatory (functioning to bring a balance between opposites in the psyche).

Dr. Jung believed God does play a role in dreams. He wrote:

> We are so captivated by and entangled in our subjective consciousness that we have forgotten the age-old fact that God speaks chiefly through dreams and visions.
>
> Dreams were the original guidance of man in the great darkness. . . . When a man is in the wilderness, the darkness brings the dreams—*somnia a Deo missa* [dreams sent by God]—that guide him. It has always been so. When you are in the darkness you take the next thing, that is a dream. And you can be sure that the dream is your nearest friend; the dream is the friend of those who are not guided any more by the traditional truth and in consequence are isolated . . . So, you see, the one who is going alone and has no guidance, he has the *somnia a Deo missa*. . . .[177]

Since the time of Dr. Jung, interest in dreams continues to grow within and outside the religious community. Writers such as John

Dourley, Russell Holmes, Murray Stein, Robert Johnson, Reb Yakov Leib HaKohain; scholar/therapists such as Dr. Max Zeller and Edward Edinger, M.D., J. Marvin Spiegelman, Ph.D., Mokusen Miyuki, Ph.D., and others have written about the religious role of dreams.

Research Psychology and Dreams

Research psychology has focused primarily on the biological and quantative aspects of dreams. These are measurable, while God's influence is not.

The scientific study of dreams began in 1953, when University of Chicago professor Dr. Nathaniel Kleitman (1895–1999) and his student, Eugene Aserinsky (1921–1998), published their work on rapid eye movement. Prior to their discovery of REMs, it was believed there was just one sleep state. Other early researchers[192] built on their work, exploring especially the neurophysiological and neurochemical aspects of REM sleep.

That same year Glenn V. Ramsey systematically reviewed the studies of dreaming compiled before Kleitman's and Aserinsky's discovery. Dr. Ramsey concluded little had been reliably established by the previous dream research other than what an unsophisticated self-observer might have suspected. In Dr. Ramsey's view there was no possibility that dreams come from God.

Dr. Calvin Hall, also in 1953, published his thoughts on dreams and dream symbols from a strictly cognitive perspective. Dr. Hall, a professor at Case Western Reserve University, was one of the first to use a "cognitive" approach to psychological functioning and he did so at a time when the Freudian perspective was the commonly accepted understanding. Dr. Hall's research led him to believe that dreaming is the product of the same mental processes as waking consciousness. This belief led dream researchers in a different direction from their clinical colleagues. While clinicians continued to focus on the meaning of dream content, researchers focused on the process of dreaming.

William C. Dement (1928–) took Aserinsky's position as Dr. Kleitman's graduate assistant when Aserinsky left to finish his medical studies. Dr. Dement identified that there are four other stages of sleep besides REM. Dreaming, he revealed, is connected only to the REM phase of sleep. Dr. Dement also was able to answer such questions as, "How often do we dream?" "How long do dreams last?" and "Is dream time the same as waking time?"

Dr. Dement's success spawned such a vast amount of new laboratory research that in 1961 a new specialty organization was formed so research could be presented and discussed. It was named the Association for the Psychophysiological Study of Sleep (APSS). By 1983 however, interest in dream research had diminished so much that the APSS changed its name to the "Sleep Research Society." Its primary focus became sleep and sleep disorders.

Interest in dream research, and the money that supported it, diminished when it was found that Dr. Dement's research was flawed.[193] For example, other researchers discovered dreams occur during other sleep stages, even during the level of deepest sleep, as well as during the REM stage.

Dr. Harry T. Hunt, a psychologist at Brock University in Ontario, Canada, also investigated the function of REM sleep. He speculated that REM sleep is less advanced than non-REM and someday will simply disappear. He went on to suggest that there are a variety of dream types: ordinary dreams; prophetic-telepathic dreams; mythical or archetypal dreams; nightmares; and lucid dreams. He found that dreams serve a multiplicity of purposes that influence memory, imagination and consciousness. For Dr. Hunt, dreams appear to reside at the intersection of the mind, body, and spirit.[194]

Cognitive Theories of Dreaming

There has been a variety of theories advanced for understanding dreams from a cognitive perspective. Agreement among them has not yet been achieved.

The first significant finding in cognitive theory after Dr. Hall came in 1970 when Dr. Fred Snyder published *The Phenomenon of Dreaming*. In his research Dr. Snyder studied the normative characteristics of adult dreams and concluded dreaming is not a bizarre or crazy process, but both content and form of dreams "have a texture not so vastly different from, or unfamiliar to, waking experience."[195] During the 1980s, Dr. David Foulkes, along with Dr. John S. Antrobus, developed a model that suggested dreaming "is a symbolic process with strong cognitive prerequisites and with a developmental history much like that of waking symbolic thought."[196]

Dr. Mark Solms, a University of Cape Town neuropsychologist and psychoanalyst, explored the physiological aspect of dreams. In 1997 he outlined what he believed to be the neural network that underlies dreaming.[197] Dreams are stimulated, Dr. Solms asserted, by impulses received from the same frontal region of the brain that also regulates motivation, emotion and memory. Drs. Claudio Bassetti and Matthias Bischof of the University of Bern (Switzerland) found a different neural network from the one Dr. Solms advanced. In 2004 they studied a 73-year old woman that had suffered a stroke and stopped dreaming. A magnetic resonance imaging confirmed damage had occurred, not in the forebrain, but deep in the back of the brain. Over time her dreams did return.[198]

Dr. G. William Domhoff of the University of California, Santa Cruz, built on Drs. Hall's and Dr. Van de Castle's findings and argued in 2001 for a neurocognitive theory of dreaming. Based on research findings, he asserted,

> Dreaming is best understood as a developmental cognitive achievement that depends upon the maturation and maintenance of a specific network of forebrain structures. The output of this neural network for dreaming is guided by a "continuity principle" linked to current personal concerns on the one hand and a "repetition principle" rooted in past emotional preoccupations on the other.[199]

Dr. Domhoff also said that since we recall so few of our dreams, they have no purpose. Since a dream's only meaning is that it reveals what is on our minds, dreams aren't worth the trouble of remembering. Don't bother with them, Dr. Domhoff advised.[200]

Dr. Gordon Globus investigated the functioning of the mind, not the functioning of the brain. Dr. Globus regarded dreams as vital to understanding how consciousness operates. He believed that in sleep we continue to produce models of the world (as we do when we are awake) only there are different rules for the sleep models than for the ones when we are awake. Understanding these different rules, Dr. Globus proposed, can help explain how the mind functions.[201]

Dr. Ernest Hartmann, M.D., a professor at Tufts University, also has studied the connection between dreaming and consciousness. He proposed what he called the contemporary theory of dreaming. "We consider a possible (though certainly not proven) function of a dream to be weaving new material into the memory system in a way that both reduces emotional arousal and is adaptive in helping us cope with further trauma or stressful events."[202]

Some Non-Religious Perspectives 81

Lucid Dreaming

In the late 1960s Dr. Charles T. Tart (1937-) brought attention to the fact that some people are aware that they are dreaming while still asleep and that some voluntary direction of dream content is possible. In the late 1970s Dr. Hearne in England and Dr. Stephen LaBerge at Stanford each independently demonstrated Dr. Tart was correct.[203]

Dr. LaBerge believes the imagination, not God, is where dreams originate. "I would suggest that the dream is not so much a communication as a creation," Dr. LaBerge wrote. "In essence, dreaming is more like world-making than like letter-writing ... an uninterpreted dream is [more] like an uninterpreted poem [than an uninterpreted letter]."[204]

On the other hand, it is possible to experience God while having a lucid dream. Dr. Van de Castle quotes George Gillespie, a minister and Sanskrit scholar, when he offered this example.

> It did not occur to me at first, during waking analysis, to consider the God of my lucid dream experiences to be the God I pray to and worship when awake. But I did eventually accept on faith that the experiences of the fullness of light were what they seemed to be—experiences of the God who transcends body, mind, dream imagery, dreamless sleep imagery, unconscious processes and God archetype.[205]

Parapsychology[192]

Weserman (1819) is the first person to publish experiments that used dreams for telepathy. Weserman "attempted to project his 'animal magnetism' into the dreams of friends who later reported their dreams to him. Weserman claimed to have been successful on five occasions."[206] His efforts, however, failed to motivate his contemporaries to do more research on dreams and telepathy.

By 1882, however, the intellectual climate had changed. Interest in paranormal phenomena in general and dream telepathy in particular was sufficiently strong that a distinguished group of scholars in Cambridge, England formed the Society for Psychical Research.[208]

Forty-five years later Dr. Joseph Banks Rhine (1895-1980) and his wife, Dr. Louisa E. Rhine (1891-1983) arrived at Duke University to investigate unexplained powers of the mind.[209] Dr. J. B. Rhine carried out experiments on telepathy, clairvoyance and precognition using Zener cards and dice. He did not use dreams, but his wife did.

Dr. Louisa Rhine (*Hidden Channels of the Mind*, 1961) became the leading researcher of spontaneous psychic experiences. She studied more than 45,000 unsolicited letters from adults worldwide who told her of their personal psychic experiences that puzzled and concerned them.[210] In one of her studies Dr. Rhine found that sixty-five percent of the anecdotes reported consisted of dreams. Unexpectedly, the dreams contained more complete information about an event in question than did reports of the event that occurred while the individual was awake.

In the 1950s, psychiatrist and psychoanalyst Dr. Montague Ullman conducted experiments to see whether he could correlate dreaming with experiences of telepathy or precognition. The experience motivated him in 1962 to found the Dream Laboratory at Maimonides Medical Center in Brooklyn, New York.[211] Working with Dr. Stanley Krippner on some of the research, the investigators found that an individual, while dreaming, could receive information from someone else.[212]

Although Drs. Ullman's and Krippner's psi findings were disputed by other authorities, there was another, unanticipated outcome. The research showed that dreams help to solve problems. Dr. Krippner and Dr. Robert Van de Castle and later Dr. Henry Reed developed a group strategy for problem solving. They called their approach "the dream helper ceremony." All the members of a small group would go to sleep focusing on one member's problem. In the morning the collected dreams typically would weave together something that addressed the selected person's problem.[213]

Dr. Charles T. Tart[214] sought to bring scientific method to the study of spirituality. His goal was twofold: to separate the sense from the nonsense within spirituality and to build a bridge between the scientific and spiritual communities. About dreams he wrote: "Some dreams are idle chatter, some nonsense, some express our craziness and psychopathology, some express intelligent thought (although sometimes of a different nature between dreaming and waking), some express our highest nature and some may be contacts with higher or lower realms outside ourselves."[215]

ANTHROPOLOGY[216]

When early anthropologists studied religion in general and dreams in particular, there was uncertainty about what their focus should be. For example, in the latter part of the nineteenth century, anthropologists[217] regarded religion as an archaic mode of thought that one day would just disappear. When they did study dreams, they studied the dreams of "primitives" for their religious content. When Dr. Freud personalized dreams, anthropologists stopped studying them for their social significance.[218]

During the last part of the twentieth century, anthropologists again studied the connection between God and dreams, especially in Western culture.[219] One of those who paid attention to the connection was Mircea Eliade (1907–1986). In his 1974 writings on shamanism, Dr. Eliade noted that to become a shaman involved an initiation into the spirit world. One method of initiation was through dreams.

> If a candidate does not follow the instructions received in his dreams, or the traditional patterns, he is doomed to fail.[220] In some cases the spirit of the dead shaman appears in his heir's first dream, but in the following dreams the higher spirits that grant him the "power" make their appearance. If the heir does not take the "power," he falls ill.[221] We have found the same situation, it will be remembered, almost everywhere.[222]

David Shulman and Guy G. Stroumsa, editors of *Dream Cultures: Explorations in the Comparative History of Dreaming* (1999), also studied the connection between God and dreams. After reviewing fifteen essays on dreams from leading scholars in the field, they offered this observation.

> The gates of revelation can never become hermetically closed. Here dreams play a central role. It should be emphasized that since dreaming is usually, in some sense, a personal phenomenon, the individual can develop a direct link to the divinity through dreams—hence the great danger of dreams for religious hierarchies and orthodoxies. Dreams are often the direct path to heresy. Indeed, the hallmark of a heretic is often the revelatory dreams, which set him apart from the traditional religious hierarchy. It is in this context that we can understand the constant shying away from—indeed, often fierce opposition to—dreams on the part of religious authorities, who are motivated by a wish to contain, as much as possible, the power of divination.[223]

THEORETICAL PHYSICS

Theoretical physicists made discoveries during the twentieth century that changed the way science understands how nature functions.[224] These findings point to a possible explanation of how the link between God and dreams occurs.

Quantum physics began in the 1920s as an effort to explain the interaction of light with atoms. Now it is used to explain the interaction of anything with anything. It is how physicists understand reality.

In February, 1927 Dr. Werner Heisenberg (1901–1976) presented what has come to be known as the "uncertainty principle."[225] Dr. Heisenberg's thinking showed that Newtonian premises about reality were not correct. Dr. Newton believed that a "real world" exists independently, regardless of whether or not it is observed. Dr. Heisenberg showed that concepts such as the orbit of electrons do not exist in nature independently, but only when they are observed.[226]

Dr. Heisenberg went on to challenge the concept of causality. He wrote in his paper on the uncertainty principle that "In the sharp formulation of the law of causality—'if we know the present exactly, we can calculate the future'—it is not the conclusion that is wrong but the premise." Dr. Heisenberg's discovery changed how physicists think about determining past and future events.

In 1931 Dr. Wolfgang Pauli (1900–1958) predicted mathematically the existence of the "neutron." In 1945 he was awarded the Nobel Prize for Physics[227] for his 1925 description of the exclusion principle, called the Pauli Principle ever since. He spent the last ten to fifteen years of his life studying and lecturing on the philosophy of science with a particular emphasis on the intersection between physics and psychology. In a letter written in the 1950s, Dr. Pauli wrote:

> It is my personal opinion that in the science of the future reality will neither be "psychic" nor "physical" but somehow both and somehow neither.[228]

In 1964 Dr. John Stewart Bell (1928–1990) published his theorem that like Dr. Heisenberg before him, contradicted what previously had been two basic principles of orthodox physics. Dr. Bell showed *realism*[229] and *determinism*[230] are wrong. The American physicist Dr. Henry Stapp in 1975 called Bell's theorem "the most profound discovery of science." Empirical evidence that confirmed Dr. Bell's theorem was found in 1982.

Dr. Bell's theorem shows quantum interconnectedness exists, that when two objects briefly interact and then separate, they are bound together for ever even though they may never interact again. Physicist Dr. Nick Herbert explains:

> Bell's theorem shows this connection must exist, but it also says that in some sense it's an invisible connection, it's an inner connection. There are two aspects to quantum physics; in a sense it's a little bit like dice. There are the individual dice events that occur, and then there are the statistical patterns—like lots of sevens will occur and not many twelves. So there's the overall pattern, and the individual events. Now what quantum theory talks about are the patterns; quantum theory predicts patterns. And what Bell's theorem shows is that none of these patterns are ever connected faster than light; you will never see a faster-than-light pattern. But the individual events, the dice falls themselves, must be tied together faster than light. One could say, "Well, everything is connected faster than light, instantaneously," but that's not so, because the patterns don't connect, but individual dots do.
>
> All the patterns are perfectly ordinary; they preserve space and time, and they're separated at light speed. Yet the bricks that make up these patterns are not that way at all. They don't know anything about space and time, and they're connected spontaneously.
>
> Local is a term used by people involved with Bell's theorem. A local connection is an ordinary connection that obeys the speed of light and a non-local connection is like voodoo—that when you do something here, instantly it affects someone over there. What Bell proved was that no model of the world that used only local connections would work. Everything is non-local.[231]

Further, non-local influences do not diminish with distance and are not affected by any amount of matter between entities. A non-local interaction links one location with another without crossing space, without decay, and without delay.

Quantum mechanics and Dr. Einstein's theory of general relativity proved difficult to reconcile. Each offers a valuable, yet limited explanation of nature's behavior. To close the gap between the two, string theory was proposed in 1974 by Dr. Joel Scherk and Dr. John Schwarz. String theory has two basic types. One speaks of "strings" that are closed loops that can break open, while the second type says "strings" remain closed loops. An assumption among string theorists is that there exists one unified theory (M) that is yet to be identified.

Using mathematics, string theory shows that at the depths of reality are patterns of vibrations. Three-dimensions of space plus one of time is not adequate to account for all the possible variations these patterns of vibrations can assume. At least nine dimensions of space and one of time—some physicists argue more—are necessary. These dimensions are not fixed, as once believed, but fluid. They shift when an observer watches. String theory indicates that there are uncontrollable effects the observer has on the system observed.[232]

Another interesting development is that physicists have identified 20 basic numbers that are in a delicate balance and which make the universe work the way it does. If any of these numbers differed from what it is, the universe would not only be changed, it would disappear. String theory is attempting to understand and explain why this is.[233]

Dr. Alan Wolf is a theoretical physicist who believes quantum mechanics points to the reality that there are spiritual underpinnings to all existence. His book *Dreaming Universe* (1994) combines anthropology, psychology and physics to explain the links between the physical act of dreaming and consciousness. Dreams, Dr. Wolf suggests, are a vital aspect of evolution that enable a person to develop self-awareness and a sense of self. He goes on to suggest that an "imaginal realm" is found between material and mental reality. It is here, he suggests, that lucid dreaming occurs.

> I feel like we're on the verge of a gigantic discovery—maybe the nature of God, maybe the nature of the human spirit. Something of that sort is going to emerge . . . because our normal notions . . . of space and time and matter—they are just breaking down, they're just falling apart . . . in classical physics the idea . . . that the past influences the present is pretty normal. . . . But there is another notion. What about the future influencing the present? Quantum physics says . . . there is a real mathematical basis for saying actions in the future can have an effect on the probability patterns that exist in the present. In other words what takes place now, what choices are being made right now, may not be as free to you as you think they are.[234]

PHILOSOPHY OF SCIENCE

Reconciling science and spirituality is an area of interest for some of those in the field of the philosophy of science. This endeavor grows out of the quest to understand the meaning of the reality that theoretical physics describes.

Dr. David Bohm (1917–1992) began his career as a research physicist (*Wholeness and the Implicate Order*, 1980) and ended it as a professor of theoretical physics at Birkbeck College, University of London. Dr. Bohm's research on subatomic particles led him to believe that behind the visible world lies an implicate order of undivided wholeness. In Dr. Bohm's perception, reality is a seamless whole in which interconnectedness is primary and discreteness is secondary.

> Bohm suggests that the whole universe can be thought of as a kind of giant, flowing hologram, or *holomovement*, in which a total order is contained, in some implicit sense, in each region of space and time. The explicate order is a projection from higher dimensional levels of reality, and the apparent stability and solidity of the objects and entities composing it are generated and sustained by a ceaseless process of enfoldment and unfoldment, for subatomic particles are constantly dissolving into the implicate order and then recrystallizing.
>
> [Bohm] proposes that there may be an infinite series, and perhaps hierarchies, of implicate (or "generative") orders, some of which form relatively closed loops and some of which do not. Higher implicate orders organize the lower ones, which in turn influence the higher."[235]

For Dr. Bohm, the separation of matter and spirit is an abstraction. Dr. Bohm's thinking has implications not only for physics, but also for parapsychology and for the understanding of prayer, revelation and dreams.

Dr. Holmes Rolston III, a philosopher of science at Colorado State University, has attempted to reconcile the views of science with those of religion. Dr. Rolston (1932–) suggested that

> Science and religion share the conviction that the world is intelligible, susceptible to being logically understood, but they delineate this under different paradigms. In the cleanest cases we say that science operates with the presumption that there are causes to things, religion with the presumption that there are meanings to things.[236]

The conflict between the two different interpretations, he believes, is due to the boundary between causality and meaning being semipermeable. Dr. Rolston wrote:

> To believe in the *supernatural* is to believe that there are forces at work that transcend the physical, the biological, the sociocultural. These spiritual forces sway the future because they are already breaking through and infusing what is now going on. To term these *supernatural* forces, transcending *natural* ones, is not to make an absolute bifurcation between the secular, natural, and the sacred, spiritual, realms. It is not to posit forces antinatural, unnatural, or foreign. It is only to speak from our present vantage point and believe in a fourth dimension (spirit) when three dimensions (matter, life, mind) are already incontestably evident and the fourth is secretly and impressively also at work.[237]

Dr. Rolston observed that when measuring science and religion, one's findings must be evaluated on two criteria: Is what the data are saying true? And what is its value?

> In the end we turn to *truth* for *worth*, on the axiom that we should get some clues about truth from the worth of a teaching ... a truth that is nonilluminating about values cannot be the final word in a world that willy-nilly we must evaluate. . . . Unless a doctrine can tell us something about what the story is worth, and show us how to be worthy actors in the story, it has not yet achieved salient truth-value. Here science proves to lack ultimacy, while religion offers the pearl of great price.[238]

Because of the advances that have occurred in the natural sciences and in the study of consciousness, the thinking about matter, life and mind is undergoing major revisions. Dr. Ervin Laszlo (1932–), founder of systems philosophy, wrote in 1996:

> The astonishing psi-phenomena that come to light in controlled experiments and the equally astonishing findings of expert psychotherapists cannot be dismissed as mere chimera, figments of a fertile but undisciplined imagination. The findings are part and parcel of the manifestation of human consciousness: an entity whose subconscious domains extend far beyond the confines of the subject's brain and organism.[239]

Dreams, he goes on to say,[240] are one way the human mind is able to penetrate beyond the limits of personal sensory experience to make contact and communicate with another.

Dr. Laszlo suggested the new reality described by quantum physics changes the most fundamental notions of life.

Life evolves, as does the universe itself, in a "sacred dance" with an underlying field. This makes living beings into elements in a vast network of intimate relations that embraces the entire biosphere itself an interconnected element within the wider connections that reach into the cosmos.

In the on going co-evolutions of matter with the vacuum's zero-point field, life emerges out of nonlife, and mind and consciousness emerge out of the higher domains of life. . . . Matter as well as mind evolved out of a common cosmic womb: the energy-field of the quantum vacuum. The interaction of our mind and consciousness with the quantum vacuum links us with other minds around us, as well as with the biosphere of the planet. It "opens" our mind to society, nature, and the universe. This openness has been known to mystics and sensitives, prophets and meta-physicians through the ages . . . it is as if something like an antenna were picking up signals from a transmitter that contains the experience of the entire human race.

It seems likely that world and brain—cosmos and consciousness—are interconnected by a continuous information—*conserving and transmitting field*.[241]

SUMMARY

Non-religious traditions, especially in the nineteenth and twentieth centuries, struggling with the conflict between rational and spiritual perceptions of reality, increasingly moved away from the concept of God and, therefore, of God's influence in life. In philosophy, for example, the intellectual trend was toward rationalism, then logic and finally word analysis as the true reflection of reality. Following Nietzsche, the idea of God was dismissed from intellectual discussion in Europe. Dreams were of little interest to philosophy.

In contrast, religious experience was one of the first things psychology studied. It also affirmed the importance of dreams in healing and personal growth. Currently psychology studies the brain, seeking to understand the function and meaning of dreams. Research psychologists rejected the notion that God is the origin of dreams even though some clinicians maintain that dreams are communications from God. Cognitive theorists maintain dream images reflect waking consciousness while some clinicians believe many dream images are symbols that point beyond themselves to a greater reality.

90 GOD AND DREAMS

Anthropologists have documented that people throughout the world believe their dreams are communications from God. They also noted that organized religion is uncomfortable with the idea that God still communicates through dreams.

Theoretical physics has shown that Newtonian perceptions of reality, including causality, no longer adequately explains the reality that quantum physics describes. Discreteness is being replaced by interconnectedness; multiplicity by wholeness; three-dimensional materialism by multi-dimensional orders that influence one another. Direct, spontaneous connections that are not restricted by space-and-time are part of this new understanding of how reality functions.

Some scholars in the philosophy of science, in their thinking about the implications of quantum physics, suggest that dreaming is one way interconnectedness between individuals and the entire cosmos occurs.

ENDNOTES

175. Jung, "Symbols and the Interpretation of Dreams," (1961), *Collected Works* Vol. 18:601, 674.

176. The Enlightenment critically examined previously accepted doctrines and institutions from the perspective of rationalism. It was the time of the Counter-Reformation, when the Roman Catholic Church in Europe felt threatened by the rise of Protestantism. The Roman Church asserted its power over all the areas of life that it could through censorship and indoctrination. In particular the Church used the arts to spread its message. Any creation that was not appropriately religious was regarded as heretical, and its artist was not supported financially. The motto of the Enlightenment, according to Immanuel Kant in his 1784 essay, "What is Enlightenment?" was, "Have courage to use your own intelligence." Enlightenment thinkers stressed the autonomy of reason; perfectibility; progress; and confidence in the ability to discover causality.

177. Chojnowski, "Descartes' Dream: From Method to Madness."

178. Hobbes, who rejected Descartes, Aristotelian and Scholastic thinking, believed we could only view the world in a material way. This was very much in keeping with his friend, Galileo Galilei (1564–1642) who regarded the world as matter in motion. At age 86 Hobbes translated the *Iliad* and the *Odyssey* into English verse and at 91 he was working on yet another book when he died, reportedly with pen in hand. His final written words are said to be: "I am about to take my last voyage, a great leap in the dark." O'Connor and Robertson, "Thomas Hobbes."

179. Men such as Descartes, Benedict De Spinoza (1632–1677), and Gottfried Wilhelm von Leibniz (1646–1716) were Rationalists.

180. Locke, George Berkeley (1685–1753), and David Hume (1711–1776) represent Empiricism. Scottish philosopher David Hume used skepticism to attack theological doctrines such as miracles. Hume argued that it is impossible to violate the laws of nature and any claim to have done so (resurrection of Jesus) requires extraordinarily strong evidence to prove it happened. The utilitarians, John Stuart Mill (1806–1873) and analytic

philosophy are sometimes regarded as extensions of empiricism.

181. Voltaire, the pen name for Francois-Marie Arouet (1715–1750), and Jean Jacques Rousseau (1712–1778) were among the contributors. Diderot was one of the first to be regarded as a humanist, secular, modern and scientific.

182. In *Thus Spoke Zarathustra* Nietzsche argued for a reappraisal of nineteenth century cultural values that he felt were pulling society down. Nietzsche believed Darwin got it wrong, that evolution is not toward the general elevation of the species (the mediocre flock) but toward the production of distinctive specimens or geniuses (supermen). He believed these superior individuals would demonstrate that the nature of the world is ceaseless development and progress.

One reaction to Nietzsche can be seen in the poems of Rainer Maria Rilke (1875–1926). Rilke wrote a series of poems to God that expressed his intense spiritual yearnings.

> You see, I want a lot.
> Maybe I want it all:
> the darkness of each endless fall,
> the shimmering light of each ascent.
> So many are alive who don't seem to care.
> Casual, easy, they move in the world
> as though untouched.
> But you take pleasure in the faces
> of those who know they thirst.
> You cherish those
> who grip you for survival.
> You are not dead yet, it's not too late
> to open your depths by plunging into them
> and drink in the life
> that reveals itself quietly there.

"Du siehst, ich will viel . . . /You see, I want a . . . ," from RILKE'S BOOK OF HOURS: LOVE POEMS TO GOD by Rainer Maria Rilke, translated by Anita Barrows and Joanna Macy, copyright © 1996 by Anita Barrows and Joanna Macy. Used by permission of Riverhead Books, an imprint of Penguin Group (USA) Inc., p. 61.

183. Bergson was awarded the Nobel Prize for Literature in 1927 for his efforts to challenge Newton's (static) mechanistic view of nature with his own dynamic, vital view. Bergson used the concepts of "static" and "vital" to differentiate his views from others. Newton's worldview and the world of the intellect were "static" for Bergson. In contrast, he argued, there exists in the world a creative spirit, a living force (élan vital) that keeps life from being static. The élan vital is best apprehended through intuition. Bergson maintained that intuition, the direct apprehension of process, reveals the world in a way that rational analysis does not. "Henri Bergson."

184. Dewey adopted fallibilism as a guiding principle: Something was true for him only if it agreed with reality and, if and only if, it were successfully employed in the resolution of a problematic situation. Richard Field, 'John Dewey."

185. During the twentieth century at Cambridge two philosophers of a similar orientation to Dewey were Bertrand Russell (1872–1970) and George Edward Moore (1873–1958). Their thinking came to be known as analytical philosophy. Bertrand Russell regarded logical analysis as the only method for doing philosophy; as a tool for resolving all human disputes, and; as the resource that could provide an explanation for all human

experience. Moore was an advocate of common sense (*A Defence of Common Sense*, 1925). Russell's colleague, Alfred North Whitehead (1861–1947), joined him in the pursuit of a logical foundation for mathematics (*Principia Mathematica*, 3 vols., 1910–1913). Garth Kemerling. Analytical philosophy's counterpart in Germany and Austria was logical positivism. Friedrich Ludwig Gottlob Frege (1848–1925) was one of the first to try showing that mathematics could be reduced to logic. One of his concerns was to insulate logic from ambiguities. At the end of his life Frege changed his mind. He began writing that geometry, not logic, is the basis of mathematics.

The Vienna Circle built on Frege's thinking. Moritz Schlick (1882–1936) founded the Vienna Circle, which included Otto Neurath (1882–1945), and Rudolf Carnap (1891–1970). They moved away from metaphysics and focused on empiricism. Schlick was murdered by a mentally ill student in a disagreement over the student's class paper.

Between World War I and World War II, a complex set of ideas grouped under the name "phenomenology" was debated. Edmund Husserl (1859–1938) was the first to develop this approach. He would examine a phenomenon, say geometry, and ask whether it is true or not. Those strongly influenced by Husserl included Martin Heidegger (1889–1976), Georg Lukács (1885–1971), Jean-Paul Sartre (1905–1980), and Hannah Arendt (1906–1975).

186. Those influenced by Wittgenstein included John Wisdom (1904–1993), Gilbert Ryle (1900–1976), J. L. Austin (1911–1960) and Sir Peter Strawson (1919–2006). After World War II, Sir Alfred Julius Ayer (1910–1989) in England and Willard Van Orman Quine (1908–2000) in the United States focused on formal logic and semantics. Dr. George Lakoff (1941–), an American linguistics professor at the University of California, Berkeley, argued that the entire development of thought has been the process of developing better metaphors. The greater the level of abstraction in thought, he observed, the more layers of metaphor are required. Kemerling.

187. James, *The Varieties of Religious Experience*, 419. Other scholars of this field that addressed religion were Wilhelm Stekel (1868–1940), Alfred Adler (1870–1937), Gordon Allport (1897–1967), Abraham Maslow (1908–1970) and Erik Erikson (1902–1986). Other academics of note include the German Indologist Heinrich Zimmer (1890–1943); the Hungarian mythologist Carl Kerenyi (1897–1973). Non-religious theorists of dreams include Fritz Perls (1893–1970), Medard Boss (1903–1990), and Eugene Gendlin (1926–).

188. Dr. Horney focused on children's needs for security and freedom from fear. Dr. Horney looked at the role of the parents to see how much warmth and affection the parents provided their children. She believed a child could withstand traumatic experiences if he or she felt wanted and loved and, therefore, secure.

189. Dr. Sullivan worked as a psychiatrist after being trained as a Freudian analyst. He developed an interest in public health and helped create the World Federation for Mental Health. He believed that one's personality is determined by tensions that arise from both within (physiological) and without (psychosocial). The primary aim of behavior, according to Dr. Sullivan, is to reduce these tensions. One of the important contributions he made to psychology was his technique for obtaining information from a patient: the interview.

190. Dr. Jung and Dr. Freud had a parting of the ways in 1913 when Dr. Jung refused to accept Dr. Freud's theories and authority about the development of personality.

191. Jung, "Symbols and the Interpretation of Dreams," Vol. 18:601, 674. When an immediate, personal experience of God occurs, it frequently is referred to today as a spiritual "rebirth" experience. Dr. Jung described the experience psychologically this way: "The ego becomes the stable in which the Christ child is born." Dreams, Dr. Jung believed, are one way God influences lives.

192. Shapiro, Snyder, Antrobus, Roffwarg, Whitman, Kramer, Lewis, Fiss, Foulkes, Kamiya, Orlinsky, Stoyva, Rechtschaffen, Monroe, Verdone and Zepelin were the early leaders. Foulkes, *Sleep,* 611.

Other researchers into the physiological dimensions of dreams during the 1970s included Dr. Fred Snyder at the National Institute of Mental Health; Dr. J. Allan Hobson and Dr. Robert McCarley of Harvard University; Sir Francis Crick at the Salk Institute and Dr. Graeme Mitchison of Cambridge University; and Dr. Christopher Evans and Dr. Kenneth Atchity.

193. Another reason for the 1970s shift in interest away from dreams to the study of sleep is the emergence of treating psychiatric disorders with a biological/pharmaceutical approach rather than a strictly psychological one. Dreams could not be demonstrated scientifically to be helpful in understanding mental illness. Consequently, funding for laboratory dream research stopped in the early 1980s.

194. A couple of years after Dr. Hunt published his thinking, Dr. Donald R. Goodenough (1991) sought to identify the function of REMs by depriving sleepers of this phase of rest. His controversial finding was that a lack of REM appears to impair cognitive functioning. Wilkerson, "Dream Science and Dreamwork."

Recent research by Dr. David Maurice, a professor of physiology at Columbia University, suggests REM activity exists to stir the eye so it can obtain the much-needed oxygen the cornea needs while we sleep with our eyes closed.

195. Foulkes, "Sleep and Dreams. Dream Research: 1953–1993," 615.

196. Foulkes, "Sleep and Dreams," 619. Dr. Foulkes, a clinical psychologist, directed the dream research laboratories at the University of Wyoming and the Georgia Mental Health Institute, Atlanta, Georgia. He was a critic of neurological dream theories like those advocated by Drs. Solms and Domhoff. Dr. Foulkes regarded them as being too reductionistic and as denying dream content has meaning. He was critical also of Dr. Freud for having a theory that lacked an empirical basis and that was contradicted by empirical findings. Dr. Jung, too, was criticized for inflating the meaning found in dreams into a connection with God. In 1995, Dr. Foulkes argued that, "If dreaming is to continue to be studied, it will have to be studied for what it is—a distinctive human cognitive process—rather than for what it can tell us about personality or mind-body relationships." Foulkes, "Sleep and Dreams," 621.

Dr. Foulkes had no use for the unconscious or for the content of dreams. In his book *Children's Dreaming and the Development of Consciousness* (1999), Dr. Foulkes argued that by studying children's dreaming it is possible to observe the development of consciousness. Dream imagery has meaning, he asserted, that is not bizarre, but merely the mundane workings of the mind. His primary concern was with *how* we are thinking when we are dreaming, rather than with *what* we are thinking when we are dreaming.

197. These findings are presented in Dr. Solms' book, The Neuropsychology of Dreams: A Clinico-Anatomical Study. The research to outline the neural network that underlies dreaming had not been done before; Dr. Solms hypothesizes, in part because dreams have been associated with questionable metaphysics. That association has caused many scientists to avoid dream research, since they might not be taken seriously or not considered respectable.

198. "Studying a stroke patient, researchers zero in on where dreams unfold," The Sacramento Bee, Sept. 2004.

199. Domhoff, "A New Neurocognitive Theory of Dreams,"13–33. Dr. Domhoff's remarks about dreams having no purpose were found in his paper, "The 'Purpose' of

Dreams." Other late twentieth century dream researchers include Dr. Gayle Delaney (Breakthrough Dreaming); Dr. Robert Bosnack (A Little Course on Dreams); Dr. Jeremy Taylor (Where People Fly and Water Runs Uphill, Using Dreams to Tap the Wisdom of the Unconscious); Dr. Alan Moffitt (a professor at Carleton University, Ottawa, Canada); Dr. Tore Nielsen (at the University of Montreal); Linda Lane Magallon (Mutual Dreaming); Dr. Mark Blagrove (at the University of Wales Swansea); Dr. Deidre Barrett (Trauma and Dreams); and Dr. Harry Fiss (at the University of Connecticut).

200. Domhoff, "A New Neurocognitive Theory of Dreams."

201. Wilkerson, "Dream Science and Dreamwork: " In 2000, Dr. Antti Revonsuo at the University of Turku, Finland, suggested an evolutionary hypothesis for the function of dreaming. Dr. Revonsuo suggested the biological function of dreaming is to simulate threatening events, and to rehearse threat perception and threat avoidance. Revonsuo, "The Reinterpretation of Dreams."

202. This quotation was a July 14, 2003, response to the question, "Why do we dream?" Scientific America.com. (June 13, 2004). When working with a dream, Dr. Hartmann starts by identifying what he calls the "contextual" [central] image. By looking at the feelings that are connected with this image the dreamer can quickly access the dream's meaning, Dr. Hartmann taught.

203. Actually, lucid dreams have been referenced since at least the fifth century, Christian era. LaBerge, *Lucid Dreaming*, Chapter 2.Lucid dreamers, according to Dr. LaBerge, report being able to freely remember the circumstances of waking life, to think clearly, and to act deliberately upon reflection, all while experiencing a dream world that seems vividly real. They occur most commonly late in the sleep cycle. Most people have only a few of those in a lifetime, but the skills for having a lucid dream can be taught. Lucid dreaming tends to begin when a dreamer experiences something bizarre enough in a dream that the person reflects on what has just occurred while still asleep. In this reflective attitude, the sleeper realizes he/she is still dreaming. Lucid dreaming can also result when a dreamer awakens momentarily and then returns to sleep, re-entering the same dream with no break in consciousness. The working memory necessary for a lucid experience to occur is usually present only during the REM phase.

204. LaBerge, *Lucid Dreaming*, pg. 104. Dr. LaBerge is not without his critics. One of them is Dr. David Foulkes. For those interested in their exchanges, see http://www.sawka.com/spiritwatch/dreaming.htm and http://www.sawka.com/spiritwatch/replyto.htm.

205. Van de Castle, *Our Dreaming Mind*, 465–57. He referenced G. Gillespie, "Light in Lucid Dreaming: A Review," 167–80.

206. Parapsychology is the scientific study of psychic (psi) phenomena. The phenomena studied include telepathy, clairvoyance, remote viewing, precognition and psychokinesis. Those in the field believe there is interconnectedness among all things and that individuals are capable of experiencing that connectedness. They argue the present understanding of the mind, matter, space and time are incomplete.

207. Tolaas, Jon and Montague Ullman, "Extrasensory Communication and Dreams."

208. The Society's mission is to promote the study of reports of paranormal phenomenon in an unbiased, scientific manner. Three of the founders of the Society in 1886 published the results of their investigations in the 1300 page book, *Phantasms of the Living*. The common pattern that emerged from a review of the book's 149 cases of dream telepathy indicated that:

Some Non-Religious Perspectives   95

1. More than half of the dreams concerned the theme of death.

2. Another large group was concerned with the occurrence of an emergency.

3. A smaller group focused on trivial matters.

4. In the majority of cases, the agent-percipient pairs were either related or friends.

The percipients generally had no special psychic experiences or abilities before the dream in question so that these dreams were rare and puzzling experiences. Tolaas and Ullman, "Extrasensory Communication and Dreams."

209. For the next fifty years Dr. J.B.Rhine professionalized the field of parapsychology by conducting experiments in open laboratories, giving the field its concepts, methods and instrumentalities. He gave the name extrasensory perception (ESP) to the ability to acquire information without the use of the five senses.

210. A third of the accounts Dr. Rhine found unusable for her research. She grouped the reported experiences into four categories: intuitions, hallucinations, unrealistic dreams and realistic dreams. Unrealistic dreams are symbolic and require interpretation. Realistic dreams are straightforward in content and do not require interpretation.

211. Dr.Ullman taught dreams have to do with healing disconnections both in individuals and between individuals. He found dreams seek to restore unity where there are disconnections by depicting metaphorically the truth of a person's situation at that moment. "If we allowed them to do so," Dr. Ullman wrote, "our dreams could help us sort out truth from falsehood at both a social and a personal level." Ullman, "Dreams as Exceptional Human Experiences."

212. Building on the research of Dr. Ullman and his associates at Maimonides Medical Center, Dr. Charles Honorton (1946–1992) at the University of Edinburgh in the 1980s developed a new methodology for investigating ESP known as the ganzfelt (total or whole field) technique. His techniques produced results that showed a thirty-five percent rate of success when twenty-five percent would have occurred by chance. His success led others to continue developing his methodology. Dr. Honorton moved away from dreams, instead concentrating his attention on the use of meditation in ESP research. Toward the end of his life, he was working on developing software disguised as computer games that could lead to a more universal form of parapsychological research and that would provide reliable and meaningful testing procedures. The University of Edinburgh, Gothenburg University in Sweden, Cornell University, Princeton University and Rhine Research Center in Durham, North Carolina continued to use ganzfeld techniques. Bem, *Encyclopedia of the Paranormal* and Varvoglis. At the end of the twentieth century, parapsychological research conducted at the Consciousness Research Laboratory under the direction or Dr. Dean Radin, an experimental psychologist. Dr. Radin focused on controlled, laboratory studies of mind-matter interactions, distant healing, clairvoyance and precognition. Dr. Radin's work has shown that some psi experiences are what they appear to be.

213. Dr. Van de Castle wrote in *Our Dreaming Mind*:

In one of our ceremonies, the dream helpers reported a black car driving into the town of White Hall, someone being hesitant to accept an Oreo cookie, someone ordering an ice cream cone with one scoop of chocolate and one of vanilla, someone noticing the black and white keys on a piano keyboard, and Martin Luther King, Jr., preaching in front of the White House. With each successive report, the theme of black and white became more predominant. Several dreams also dealt with family dissension and parental lectures about obedience.

The target person, a white woman, was very surprised by these dreams. Most of the dream helpers were strangers to her and none were aware that she was dating a black man and struggling with the question of how to deal with the negative reaction she anticipated from her family. One of the helpers dreamed that his watch was slow, and another about seeing a movie in slow motion. As the dream helpers discussed these dreams about slow motion, they suggested to the dreamer that she might move slowly in bringing up this relationship to her parents until she was sure she wanted to continue it.

The group was astonished and delighted at what they had accomplished. They felt they had been so successful because they were not attempting to gain anything for themselves; they were engaged in a healing service nourished solely from a sense of love. Everyone benefited and felt energized by their participation. The target person was deeply touched by the obvious sense of caring that the group communicated to her. Although she had not verbalized the problem she sought help with, the dream helpers had been able to comprehend her problem, empathize with her feelings, and reflect on how she might lessen the anguish her conflicts generated. 437-38.

Dr. G. William Domhoff in 2003 disputed that this is possible. He argued that waking reflection on the meaning of a dream that yields insight or direction into problem solving is not evidence that dream processes account for the insight but rather may merely reflect waking cognitive processes. Domhoff, *"The Scientific Study of Dreams."*

214. Dr. Tart devoted his academic career to the study of consciousness, particularly to altered states of consciousness, which for him included spiritual experiences.

215. This quotation comes from an e-mail Dr. Tart sent to the author on 8/12/04. Dr. Tart believed there was more to the brain than its physical functioning. "Something fundamentally different from just material stuff is added to the brain and nervous system, and consciousness is then *mind* interacting with the brain. . . Perhaps some things that, from a materialistic point of view, you'd be totally inclined to dismiss, have something to do with reality." Tart, "Enlightenment and Spiritual Growth."

216. Anthropology focuses on all facets of society and culture to describe the impact that humans have on humans.

217. Early anthropologists of religion were E. B. Taylor (1832-1917); James Frazier (1854-1941); and R. R. Marett (1866-1943). Others who influenced anthropology's study of religion included Karl Marx (1818-1883); Emile Durkheim (1858-1917); Max Weber (1864-1920); Arnold van Gennep (1873-1957); Bronislaw Malinowski (1884-1942); E. E. Evans Pritchard (1902-1920); and Claude Levi-Strauss (1908-2009).

218. In the 1930s a reaction to the Freudian emphasis developed that led researchers to analyze the social function of dreams. The 1960s sparked new ideas in religious anthropology. Religion was perceived as being a set of symbols or structured systems, and the study of ritual was undertaken. A focus on shamanism developed that branched off in a variety of directions. The 1970s and 1980s brought the beginnings of literary criticism to the field. An examination of its own prejudices in the study of religion was undertaken. By the end of the twentieth century, the focus had shifted to the study of urban religion (not tribal) and in particular to the "dark" side of religion: sexism and racism. There was a special emphasis on the importance of "place" in religion as a counterbalance to those who superficially studied "comparative religions."

219. Leaders in the anthropological study of dreams include George Devereux, *Reality*

Some Non-Religious Perspectives 97

and Dream: Psychotherapy of a Plains Indian (1951); G.E. Von Gruenebaum and Roger Caillois, editors, *The Dream and Human Societies* (1966); Carol W. O'Nell, *Dreams, Culture and the Individual* (1976); Géza Ròheim, *The Gates of the Dream* (1979/1952); Barbara Tedlock, *Dreaming: Anthropological and Psychological Interpretations* (1981); Mary-Therese B. Dombeck, *Dreams and Professional Personhood: The Contexts of Dream Telling and Dream Interpretation Among American Psychotherapists* (1991); and Kelly Bulkeley, Ph.D., *Spiritual Dreaming: A Cross-Cultural and Historical Journey* (1995).

Padgett "Anthropology of Religion." and Wilkerson, "Dream Library-Dream Science."

220. Dr. Eliade references Willard Z. Park, *Shamanism in Western North America*, 29.

221. Dr. Eliade references Park's account again, p. 30.

222. Eliade, *Shamanism, Archaic Techniques of Ecstasy*, 101–102.

223. Shulman, David and Guy G. Stroumsa, editors. *Dream Cultures: Explorations in the Comparative History of Dreaming*, 5.

224. Mathematics is the language of theoretical physics. When current mathematical models are insufficient, new ones are invented. Sir Isaac Newton is considered the first theoretical physicist. He created calculus when algebra and geometry proved inadequate for describing objects in motion or those changing in some way. Calculus evolved into classical field theory. Quantum mechanics was developed when an explanation for the activity of particles was needed. In 1905 Dr. Albert Einstein, using Dr. Max Planck's quantum hypothesis, proposed a special theory of relativity. This grew into the relativistic quantum field theory, which is used to describe the behavior of subatomic particles. Several years later Dr. Einstein extended his special theory of relativity into a general theory of relativity. Some of the noteworthy findings that have emerged from the application of Dr. Einstein's thinking include the big bang explanation for the creation of the universe, the awareness that the universe continues to expand, and the existence of black holes in the universe. Dr. Einstein, who never professed belief in a personal God, is quoted as having said: "Everyone who is seriously involved in the pursuit of science becomes convinced that a Spirit is manifest in the laws of the Universe—a Spirit vastly superior to that of man, and one in the face of which we with our modest powers, must feel humble." Beatrix Murrell, "The Imaginal within the Cosmos."

225. Succinctly, the uncertainty principle says: "The more precisely the position is determined, the less precisely the momentum is known in this instance, and vice versa." Dr. Heisenberg's discovery was written to physicist Dr. Wolfgang Pauli in a 14-page letter. Cassidy, "Werner Heisenberg and the Uncertainty Principle."

226. In 1983, physicist Dr. John A. Wheeler (1911–2008) suggested that "observer" is no longer an appropriate term to describe the researcher of subatomic physics. "Participator" is a more apt designation because the mere presence of the scientist changes what is occurring. Dr. Wheeler is professor emeritus from Princeton University. His participatory anthropic principle can be found in "Law without Law." Dr. Wheeler is also known for having said, "A life-giving factor lies at the center of the whole machinery and design of the world."

227. Dr. Albert Einstein nominated Dr. Pauli for the Nobel Prize.

228. "Wolfgang Ernst Pauli." In the 1950s Dr. Pauli wrote:

It is undeniable that the development of 'microphysics' has brought the way in which nature is described in his science very much closer to that of the newer psychology: but whereas the former, on account of the basic 'complementarity' situation, is faced with the impossibility of eliminating the effects of the observer by determinable correctives, and has therefore to abandon in principle any objective understanding of physical phenomena, the latter can supplement the purely subjective psychology of consciousness by postulating the existence of an unconscious that possesses a large measure of objective reality [i.e. Jung's objective unconscious theory]. Jung, "On the Nature of the Psyche," revised, 1954; *Collected Works*, Vol. 8, para. 439n.

In the 1980s David Bohm put it this way:

> Classical physics provided a mirror that reflected only the objective structure of the human being who was the observer. There is no room in this scheme for his mental process, which is thus regarded as separate or as a mere 'epiphenomenon' of the objective process. . . . [Through the] mirror [of quantum physics] the observer sees 'himself' both physically and mentally in the larger setting of the universe as a whole. . . . More broadly one could say that through the human being, the universe is making a mirror to observe itself. Bohm & Hiley, *The Undivided Universe*, 389 in "Bell's Theorem" by David M. Harrison.

229. Realism says a quantity has a value. For example, the physical world has an existence that is independent of the actions of any observer. Whitaker, "John Stewart Bell."

230. Determinism says if we have complete knowledge of the state of a system, we can predict exactly how it will behave. Whitaker, "John Stewart Bell."

231. Mishlove, "Consciousness and Quantum Reality with Nick Herbert, Ph.D."

232. http://superstringtheory.com/basics/basic.html.

233. Physicist Brian Greene spoke of the delicate balance of these 20 numbers at the end of an interview on "Fresh Air with Terry Gross," National Public Radio, 3/16/04.

234. Dr. Alan Wolf, "Physics and Consciousness." Elsewhere Dr. Wolf says,

The key idea to remember . . . is that psi phenomena is an example of human perceptual ability. In many ways it is no different from our normal states of awareness and perceptions. My hunch is that psychic capability may yet be proven to be another human competency akin to emotion. More to the point, psychic awareness is but another way to more richly perceive the very subtle aspects of the world around us. "Global Awareness."

235. David Pratt, "David Bohm and the Implicate Order."

236. Dr. Rolston goes on to write: "science explains but religion reveals; science informs, but religion reforms." *Science and Religion: A Critical Survey*, 24, 29.

237. Rolston, *Science and Religion*," 301.

238. Rolston, *Science and Religion*," 344–45.

239. Ervin Laszlo, "Toward a Physical Foundation for PSI Phenomena."

240. Ervin Laszlo, "Subtle Connections: Psi, Grof, Jung, and the Quantum Vacuum."

241. Ervin Laszlo, "Where No System Is Entirely Closed"; "New Concepts of Matter, Life and Mind"; "Subtle Connections: Psi, Grof, Jung, and the Quantum Vacuum."

7

Another Perspective

> I think what we are looking for is a way of experiencing the world that will open to us the transcendent that informs it, and at the same time forms ourselves within it. That is what people want. That is what the soul asks for.
>
> —Joseph Campbell[242]

INTRODUCTION

WHILE THERE HAS BEEN a long history of people whose experience affirms the connection between God and dreams, we live in a time when most religious thinking ignores the function of dreams and most psychological studies of dreams have a decidedly biological orientation. As a result the spiritual dimension of dreams receives little attention.

In this chapter a different perspective is offered. Problems created by the denial of God's involvement with dreams are identified and solutions are offered. Indications that God and dreams are linked are also discussed. Finally, two things are affirmed: there is a connection between God and dreams; and all dreams, not just some, come from God.

GOD, REVELATION, AND DREAMS

Throughout history, the urge to know and to do God's will has been a part of human experience. The pursuit of God's will grows out of the conviction that it is possible to know what God's will is.[243] That God chooses to reveal His will has been a fundamental premise of most religious traditions. Indeed, in their formative years Judaism, Christianity and Islam[244] accepted as unquestioned that revelations occur[245] and that dreams were one of the more common means of divine disclosure. Non-Western faith traditions also have utilized dreams for receiving divine messages. Some members of these traditions have structured their communal lives and daily activities around the messages provided by their dreams. Secular scholars, like some of those in the philosophy of science, have speculated that dreams penetrate beyond the limits of sensory experience to contact and communicate with another dimension of reality.

Yet, in spite of the long history of experience that affirms God communicates through dreams, most people do not believe it. Even Judaism, Christianity and Islam have evolved from having believers who were open to God disclosing His will directly, to having believers who do not see the need for new revelations. This shift in core beliefs has created problems.

PROBLEMS DUE TO DENIAL

The first problem that arises when a faith tradition no longer sees a need for continuing revelations is that it becomes a closed system of thought that places an emphasis on maintaining the "correct" beliefs it already has. Current orthodoxy within Judaism, Christianity and Islam teaches that all a person needs to know about God is already contained within its scriptures. Orthodoxy's insistence that scripture contains the Truth can lead to religious hubris on one hand and intolerance of those who do not believe "correctly" on another.[246] Persecution and war have emerged from the requirement that everyone believe and behave in accordance with the "correct" dogma. The Medieval Christian church, in particular, sought to control not only what people thought about God but also which scientific findings were acceptable.

The answer to the problems created by being a closed system is simple. It is being open to new messages from God. Openness to new messages from God reestablishes the humility missing from religious systems that are closed. Curiosity about God and God's will is revived. There is always something new to be learned. Being receptive to new revelations encourages the same spirit of discovery that inspires science.[247]

A second problem associated with closed religious systems is that God is perceived as distant, withdrawn, and not involved with life. This perception leaves people hungry for a direct experience of God. Oscar Wilde stated this yearning well.

> I am conscious now that behind all this beauty, satisfying though it may be, there is some spirit hidden of which the painted forms and

shapes are but modes of manifestation, and it is with this spirit that I desire to become in harmony. I have grown tired of the articulate utterances of men and things. The Mystical in Art, the Mystical in Life, the Mystical in Nature—this is what I am looking for. It is absolutely necessary for me to find it somewhere.[248]

Religious orthodoxy tries to protect dreamers from the raw intensity of the dream experience by inserting a preordained interpretation (what is of God and what is not) between the dreamer and the dream. The interpretation makes having a direct experience of God more difficult than necessary. Dreams without preordained interpretations satisfy the hunger for a direct experience of God by providing a fresh connection daily. Awakening to God's presence transforms and regenerates a person's spirit, as those who have experienced being "born again" have found. Being open to receiving God's continuing revelation through dreams makes ongoing transformations and renewal possible.

A third problem that occurs if God is no longer offering revelations is that dreams can no longer be transmitters of messages from God. Disconnecting God from dreams deprives dreams of their historic spiritual roots and leads to the materialistic perspective that reduces dreams to being nothing more than a biological function of the brain.[249] The recent findings of theoretical physics, however, have shown that this materialistic perspective is inadequate for explaining how nature actually functions. The new description of reality that theoretical physicists offer has room for revelations and for the spiritual dimension of dreams.

The way dreams are interpreted is also a problem. The majority of religious and secular authorities still interpret dream images literally. While a small percentage of dreams may be understood this way, it is a mistake to interpret all dream images literally. Clinical psychology has found dreams most often speak a symbolic language, not a literal one. Religious scholars, along with mythologists,[250] have found that symbols are a way a person can penetrate into and connect with the mysterious,[251] transcendent dimensions of life. Because dreams speak a symbolic language it is possible for a person's psyche to receive messages from God in a dream. The primary purpose of dream messages, though not the exclusive one, is to lead each person toward psychic wholeness. The messages conveyed by dreams are one way God calls people to become the unique individuals they were created to be.[252]

Another problem related to faulty dream interpretation occurs when the meaning of a dream is not understood. The religious response has been to deny that such a dream comes from God. Instead it is speculated that the dream has been caused by bodily functions, Satan, or the dream is just nonsense. However, another explanation is more likely: all dreams come from God whether they are understood or not. Not comprehending the message of a dream does not mean the dream does not contain a message or that it does not come from God but indicates the ego of the dream's interpreter is not capable of grasping what the message is. Every dream contains a message whether or not the message is understood.[253] Following the path of literal interpretation increases the likelihood that the dream's message will not be understood. Learning the symbolic language dreams speak increases the likelihood that the dream's message will be comprehended.[254] Because not all dreams are easy to understand and their messages are not of equal significance suggests there remains much to learn about God, revelation and dreams.[255]

Not realizing that dreams speak a symbolic language has contributed to the belief that only a few dreams contain communications from God. As a result, people who have sought God's messages in other kinds of dreams have been considered by some Hebrew scriptures and the Roman Catholic Church to be practicing divination. It appears that many of these seekers' efforts to interpret dreams produced unorthodox interpretations, some of which were used to lead the gullible astray. To protect religious orthodoxy from misguided assertions based on dream messages, dream interpretation was discredited.

The problem of dream interpretation being divination is not really a problem at all. Dreams are revelations since all dreams contain a message from God. The study of a dream to discover the message it contains is an act of spiritual discernment. The study of dreams to understand God's message is no more divination than the study of scripture is.

Dreams have been criticized—and rightly so—when they have been used to authenticate that a person is a consecrated agent of God. For example, during World War I Adolf Hitler was asleep in a trench in a forward German position when he dreamed that he was about to be engulfed in an upheaval of earth and mud. He awoke terrified. He felt as if he was suffocating as he stumbled to get out of the trench. He was just a short distance away from where he had been sleeping when an enemy shell hit the trench and killed all of his companions. Hitler viewed the dream as an act of Providence intervening to save him for a greater destiny.[256] While this dream may indeed have been God intervening to save Hitler's life, it did not mean that God's stamp of approval was on everything that Hitler did following the dream. This is an example of God's action in one moment being used to justify everything that follows. This is a misinterpretation of the dream and illustrates the dangers inherent in dream interpretation.

The possible misinterpretation of a dream however does not mean that dreams should be ignored altogether. Dreams should be studied enthusiastically so what they have to offer can be utilized. While it is not possible to protect the gullible from all false assertions, it is possible to distinguish between a genuine revelation and pathology.

INDICATIONS GOD AND DREAMS ARE LINKED

A) Meaningful Orderedness

One of the ways God's presence in human affairs can be glimpsed is in synchronistic events.[257] When Dr. Jung researched synchronicity what he found matched what theoretical physicist Dr. Wolfgang Pauli was discerning in his own field of study:[258] in the depths of both psychological and physical reality is the influential field of *meaning*. The acausal principle that connects psychic states with physical reality, inner reality with outer reality, is the *meaning* that the conjunction has for the observer.

Dr. Jung argued that synchronicity

> . . . is no more baffling or mysterious than the discontinuities of physics. It is only the ingrained belief in the sovereign power of causality that creates intellectual difficulties and makes it appear unthinkable that causeless events exist or could ever occur. But if they do, then we must regard them as *creative acts*, as the continuous creation[259] of a pattern that exists from all eternity, repeats itself sporadically, and is not derivable from any known antecedents. . . . It is the fact of causeless order, or rather, of meaningful orderedness, that may throw light on psychophysical parallelism.

The presence of synchronistic events shows that there is a level of daily experience that occurs not by cause and effect, but by meaningful orderedness. Meaningful orderedness is a nonreligious, scientific way of describing a reality that appears consistent with what theologians call the will of God.

Dr. Jung and others have found that the particular images that occur in a dream are not random or arbitrary, as they might appear to an untrained observer, but are specific to that person for that moment in time. Meaningful orderedness is an explanation of why the content of dreams is what it is. Meaningful orderedness also explains how it is possible for a dream to contain a message.

B) The Transcendental Background of Reality[260]

Dr. Jung's investigations into the depths of psychophysical reality led him beyond synchronicity. In different essays he wrote:

> Although the first step in the cognitive process is to discriminate and divide, at the second step it will unite what has been divided, and an explanation will be satisfactory only when it achieves a synthesis.[261]

> This much we do know beyond all doubt, that empirical reality has a transcendental background. . . . The common background of microphysics and depth-psychology is as much physical as psychic and therefore neither, but rather a third thing, a neutral nature which can at most be grasped in hints since in essence it is transcendental.[262]

The transcendental background of empirical reality that science is identifying is exciting. It brings people closer to the fundamental workings of reality and thereby closer to God.[263] Dreams appear to provide access to this transcendental realm, connecting the psyche with it. Dr. Jung observed:

> The dream is a little hidden door in the innermost and most secret recesses of the soul, opening into that cosmic night which was psyche long before there was any ego-consciousness, and which will remain psyche no matter how far our ego-consciousness extends. . . . All consciousness separates; but in dreams we put on the likeness of that more universal, truer, more eternal man dwelling in the darkness of primordial night. There he is still the whole, and the whole is in him, indistinguishable from nature and bare of all egohood. It is from these all-uniting depths that the dream arises. . . .[264]

C) Interconnected Universe

Theoretical physics' intriguing speculations about the underlying functioning of reality has implications for understanding how revelation through dreams happens. Theoretical physicists describe a universe that is characterized by profound interconnections. Non-local influences spontaneously link one location with another without the crossing of space. Time moves not only forward; it moves in all directions. The future is as capable of influencing the present as the present is capable of influencing the future.

Revelation through dreams is like the reality theoretical physicists describe in that it functions outside of space-time considerations in a manner that reveals profound interconnections within reality. People dream of solutions to problems that consciously have thwarted them. For example, a dream showed Elias Howe where to put the hole in the needle that made the sewing machine work.

Revelation through dreams is like the reality theoretical physicists describe in a second way. Non-local influences spontaneously link one location with another without the crossing of space. On occasion people dream of events that are actually occurring elsewhere. For example, it is not rare to dream of a clock that is stopped and to discover later that while the dreamer slept, a loved one living elsewhere died at the time shown on the clock in the dream.

A third way revelation through dreams is like the reality theoretical physicists describe is that the future can influence the present as much as the present can influence the future. People dream of circumstances before they occur. For centuries the predictive element of a dream was accepted as proof of a dream's divine origins. The realization that the future can influence the present also calls into question the premise that all ideas are grounded in human consciousness. If something in the future is influencing the present, then something more than the brain is contributing to the message dreams convey.

Revelation through dreams, because of the similarities with the findings of theoretical physics, can be understood as being consistent with the laws of nature rather than being a suspension of them. An implication of this is that God is active in life, nature, and history. Although the hypotheses from theoretical physics do not scientifically prove the reality of revelation through dreams, the reality theoretical physicists describe certainly resonates with that possibility and invites more exploration.

FINAL THOUGHTS

To suggest that God touches our lives and offers meaning and direction to us through our dreams is to acknowledge there is a mysterious, inexhaustible, open-ended, transcendent component to life that communes with and cares about each of us. It suggests that life is active, not static; creatively evolving, not mechanically predictable; becoming, not complete. It resists the temptation to reduce spiritual reality to nothing but natural causes; psychology to nothing but biological functions; biology to nothing but chemical interactions. "We are so captivated by and entangled in our subjective consciousness," Dr. Jung wrote shortly before he died in 1961, "that we have simply forgotten the age-old fact that God speaks chiefly through dreams and visions."[265]

Joseph Campbell was correct when he observed that what people are looking for is a way "of experiencing the world that will open to us the transcendent that informs it, and at the same time forms ourselves within it." Revelation through dreams is one way this happens. Thank God for dreams.

ENDNOTES

241. Campbell, *The Power of Myth*, 53.
243. Appendix A identifies six characteristics of doing the will of God.
244. Appendix B discusses some characteristics of a revelation.
245. Dr. Keith Ward, *Religion and Revelation*, 57, writes:
There are few believers in any religion who would be content to say that their religious truths have been invented as simple imaginative constructs, or that they have been discovered by rational investigation, without the need of some special insight which relates a few humans to a suprasensory realm in a specially privileged way.... The whole idea of a suprasensory realm has two important features. First, it is of a realm which is inaccessible to normal sense-observation or to processes of rational reflection which depend solely on sense-observation. Second, it is of a realm which is greater in value or power than the sensory realm; it is precisely *supra* sensory. Thus arises the idea of persons who develop special powers of nonsensory apprehension, who can be vehicles of relationship with this realm and discern its character.
246. Pope Paul VI's *Dei Verbum* (1965) exemplifies this attitude.
But the task of authentically interpreting the word of God, whether written or handed on, has been entrusted exclusively to the living teaching office of the [Roman Catholic] Church, whose authority is exercised in the name of Jesus Christ.

... It is clear, therefore, that sacred [Roman Catholic] tradition, Sacred [Christian] Scripture and the teaching authority of the [Roman Catholic] Church, in accord with God's most wise design, are so linked and joined together that one cannot stand without the others, and that all together and each in its own way under the action of the one Holy Spirit contribute effectively to the salvation of souls. Chapter II, #10

"With regard to Christianity," Dr. Ward observed, "it might be that the central temptation of Christian faith is the reduction of the mystery of Christ to a set of propositional beliefs; so that faith becomes more a matter of the defence of ancient formulas than a matter of growth into the mystery of Divine Being." *Religion and Revelation*, 34.

247. Writing from a scientist's perspective Dr. Holmes Rolston, III, in 1987 urged an open, curious mind when it comes to understanding what can be expected in nature. He wrote:

> We humans can with considerable success look downward, backward (so to speak) at the matter and life over which we have advanced, making relative sense of these in causal and scientific terms. But the level of mind, at which we stand, and the level of spirit, now incubating and toward which we pass, lie on the frontiers. They may well surpass our capacities for self-referential explanation. We can expect our human-made sciences to stumble over them. Things are going on in our heads that are over our heads, just as things were going on in earlier performers that were over their heads. The emergent steps currently in progress are, and will remain, super-to-the-natural, supernatural from the vantage point at which we stand.... Especially as mind and spirit emerge out of matter and life, our analysis stalls at the cutting edge on which we live historically. Here the category of the supernatural, past the natural, becomes more urgent and inevitable. It is this power in nature to move over our heads toward increased spiritedness that we call supernatural. This inexhaustible open-endedness is greater than we know, or can forseeably know. *Science and Religion: A Critical Survey*, 301.

248. Wilde, Oscar. *De Profundis*. Found in Henry Wei, *The Guiding Light of Lao Tzu*, xii.

249. Marshall McLuhan (1911–1980) noted, "We shape our tools, and thereafter our tools shape us." While contemporary scientific dream research will probably accomplish the significant task of identifying the role of dreams for the functioning of the brain, the materialistic assumptions behind their investigations will limit the meaning of the findings. Harry Fiss (1986) and Harry Hunt (1989) challenged scientific dream research on the basis of ignoring all meaning and value. They noted that to use a method that quantifies but has no way of measuring meaning and then conclude dreams are meaningless is to go beyond what their tools have to offer. James B. Ashbrook and Carol Rausch Albright suggest "A purely biological model of the human person fails to deal with the complexity of human suffering. It equally fails to engage the creativity of human significance." Ashbrook and Albright, *The Humanizing Brain, Where Religion and Neuroscience Meet*, xvi.

250. Mircea Eliade wrote that a symbol "reveals a sacred or cosmological reality which no other manifestation is capable of revealing." "The Structure of Symbols" in *Patterns in Comparative Religion*, 447. The Christian theologian Paul Tillich, in his writings about the "Reality of God" wrote:

> The statement that God is being-itself is a nonsymbolic statement . . . .

However, after this has been said, nothing else can be said about God as God which is not symbolic . . . if anything beyond this bare assertion is said about God, it . . . points to something beyond itself. In a word, it is symbolic. *Systematic Theology,* 239.

In his book about Martin Buber, Maurice S. Friedman noted:

[People grasp] the ineffable through the creation of symbols, in signs and speech which reveal God to men for this age. But in the course of ages these symbols are outgrown and new ones bloom in their place until no symbol performs what is needful and life itself in the wonder of its togetherness becomes a symbol. Religious truth is vital rather than conceptual. "Dialectic of Religion and Culture" as found in *Martin Buber: The Life of Dialogue by Maurice S. Friedman.*

Examples of mythologists include Heinrich Zimmer. In his essay, "The Dilettante Among Symbols" Dr. Zimmer wrote:

"Abundance is scooped from abundance, yet abundance remains." So runs a fine old saying of the Upanishads of India. The original reference was to the idea that the fullness of our universe—vast in space, and with its myriad of whirling, glowing spheres, teeming with the hosts of living things—proceeds from a super-abundant source of transcendent substance and potential energy: the abundance of this world is scooped from that abundance of eternal being, and yet, since the supernatural potential cannot be diminished, no matter how great the donation it pours forth, abundance remains. But all true symbols, all mythological images, refer to this idea, one way or another, and are themselves endowed with the miraculous property of that inexhaustibility. With every draft drawn from them by our imaginative understanding, a universe of meaning is disclosed to the mind; and this is a fullness indeed, yet further fullnesses remain." *The King & the Corpse,* 5–6. See also Joseph Campbell, *The Hero with a Thousand Faces,* 236.

251. The etymology of "mystery" is to be initiated into a reality that can only be known through an experience of it.

252. In Christianity, the Gospel of John (6:38) quotes Jesus as saying: "For I have come down from heaven, not to do my own will, but the will of him who sent me."

253. Dr. C. G. Jung wrote about this:

One will naturally ask what is the point of this function [dreams producing symbols] if its symbols should pass unnoticed or prove to be incomprehensible? But the lack of conscious understanding does not mean that the dream has no effect at all. Even civilized man can occasionally observe that a dream which he cannot remember can slightly alter his mood for better or worse. Dreams can be "understood" to a certain extent in a subliminal way, and that is mostly how they work. Only when a dream is very impressive, or repeats itself often, do interpretation and conscious understanding become desirable. "The Language of Dreams," *The Collected Works of C.G. Jung, Vol. 18, para.* 476.

254. Robert Johnson, *Inner Work,* provides guidelines for determining whether or not a dream has been interpreted correctly.

255. For Christians, this thought is in keeping with John 16:12: "I still have many things to say to you, but you cannot bear them now."

256. Hitler's dream was found in Laurens Van Der Post, *Jung and the Story of Our Time*, 19.

257. Synchronicity is the meaningful coincidence of a subjective psychic state in an observer with a simultaneous, objective, external event that corresponds to the psychic state or content, where there is no causal connection between the psychic state and the external event. Jung, "On Synchronicity" and "Synchronicity: An Acausal Connecting Principle." For a discussion of the psychological background to divination and the connection between synchronicity and divination, see *Marie*-Louise Von Franz, *On Divination and Synchronicity, The Psychology of Meaningful Chance*.

258. Wolfgang Pauli, "The Influence of Archetypal Ideas on the Scientific Theories of Kepler."

259. Jung includes a footnote here that reads in part: "continuous creation is to be thought of not only as a series of successive acts of creation, but also the eternal presence of the *one* creative act, in the sense that God "was always the Father and always generated the Son" (Origen, *De principiis*, I, 2, 3) or that he is the "eternal creator of minds" (Augustine, *Confessions*, XI, 31, trans. F. J. Sheed, p. 232). *Collected Works*, Vol. 8, para. 967 and para. 948.

260. William Blake, in *The Marriage of Heaven and Hell*, wrote:

> "If the doors of perception were cleansed
> everything would appear to man as it is, in-
> —finite—"

261. C. G. Jung, "A Psychological View of Conscience," para. 852.

262. C. G. Jung, "Mysterium Coniunctionis," para. 768. Dr. Jung worked on this article from 1941 until 1954, and it is considered his final major writing and a summation of his later thinking.

263. Jean Shinoda Bolen, M.D., wrote:

> If we are inwardly in a 'really good place,' we seem to be 'humming along'—a common, fitting description for this state. It is interesting that the word 'humming' is vibrationally like 'om-oing,' as in the Sanskrit '*Om mani padme hum,*' which is possibly the most widely used mantra in the Eastern world. (A mantra is a sound or phrase repeated over and over again, and designed to get a person into a certain harmony with the universe.) So when we 'hum along,' it is as if we are aware of being connected with the underlying pattern of oneness in the universe. *The Tao of Psychology, Synchronicity and the Self*, 94.

264. C. G. Jung, "The Meaning of Psychology for Modern Man," para. 304–5.

265. C. G. Jung, "Symbols and the Interpretation of Dreams," para. 601.

Appendix A

SIX CHARACTERISTICS OF DOING GOD'S WILL

Paul's letter to the Ephesians (1:8b–10) states: "With all wisdom and insight he has made known to us the mystery of his will, according to his good pleasure that he set forth in Christ, as a plan for the fullness of time, to gather up all things in him, things in heaven and things on earth." The following circumstances typically exist when we are consciously doing the will of God.

First, there is the sense of being in a relationship, of meeting and engaging with a *Thou*, as Dr. Martin Buber describes it.[266] This meeting between God and an individual is a direct experience that results not from seeking but by grace. Seeking creates openness to God, but does not cause the meeting. God reaches out His hand, as Michelangelo so vividly depicts on the ceiling of the Sistine Chapel, and a person responds.

When meeting the *Thou*, there is the sense of being connected to a life force that is greater than one's own is. The connection is characterized more by surrendering to the *Thou* than it is by the determination to accomplish a specific goal.[267] Surrendering to the *Thou* creates an openness to God's promptings that is stronger than the need to be in control: faith trumps fear. Another aspect of this surrendering experience is an inner peace, a state of being well. Serenity replaces anxiety as a person does what that person is "called" to do.

A second characteristic of doing God's will is finding one's life filled with meaning[268] and purpose. There is an awareness of living the abundant life John's Gospel references (10:10). A person's actions contain a meaning that is more than matter-of-fact and carry more than a commonplace value. A person's essence, that for which a person is particularly intended, becomes increasingly clear.

A third characteristic is that all of life is holy. There is sacredness that is part of each event and encounter. All of life is alive and in dialogue with such a person. Christians describe this as seeing Christ in all people. Seeing God in all things is the height of illumination.

Fourth, there is a conjunction of personal freedom with one's destiny. Of all the choices the ego may select at any given moment, there is only one that gives the person the sense of being in touch with God. Mythologist Joseph Campbell described this experience as "following your bliss." About following your bliss he wrote:

> If you do follow your bliss you put yourself on a kind of track that has been there all the while, waiting for you, and the life that you ought to be living is the one you are living. When you can see that, you begin to meet people who are in the field of your bliss, and they open the doors to you. I say, follow your bliss and don't be afraid, and doors will open where you didn't know there were going to be.[269]

Another way of describing "following your bliss" is to say that a person should follow the interests of theirs about which they are the most enthusiastic.[270]

Potter, poet and professor M. C. Richards described the conjunction of personal freedom with destiny this way.

> When the sense of life in the individual is *in touch with* the life power in the universe, is turning with it, he senses himself as potentially whole. And he senses all his struggles as efforts towards that wholeness. And he senses that wholeness as implicit in every part. When we are working on the potter's wheel, we are touching the clay at only one point: and yet as the pot turns through our fingers, the whole is being affected and we have an experience of this wholeness. The still turning point of the world.[271]

Dr. Buber described the joining of freedom and destiny as being "solemnly promised to one another." Dr. Buber wrote:

> He who forgets all that is caused and makes decisions out of the depths, who rids himself of property and raiment and naked approaches the Face, is a free man, and destiny confronts him as the counterpart of his freedom. It is not his boundary, but his fulfillment; freedom and destiny are linked together in meaning. And in this meaning destiny, with eyes a moment ago so severe now filled with light, looks like grace itself.
>
> The free man is he who wills without arbitrary self-will. . . . He believes in destiny, and believes that it stands in need of him. It does not keep him in leading-strings, it awaits him, he must go to it, yet does not know where it is to be found. But he knows that he

must go out with his whole being . . . He intervenes no more, but at the same time he does not let things merely happen. He listens to what is emerging from reality as it desires. . . . [272]

Free will determines how a person responds to life's circumstances. Free will also determines whether or not a person responds to God's promptings.

A fifth characteristic of being aware of doing God's will is the sense of making a difference with one's life, however big or small. The world is different because you have given in to possibilities that are urged upon you. Unforeseen opportunities present themselves at a moment we are ready and interested in responding. This involves opening the heart to God—as Mary, the mother of Jesus, exemplifies. Gratitude for the difference you have made goes to God, not you, and that adds to the experience instead of diminishing it.

A sixth characteristic of doing God's will is the subjective one of feeling alive, awake (conscious) in the moment. There is a resoluteness that is humble, flexible, tolerant, honest, patient, serene and self-disclosing. Curiosity, compassion, openness and vulnerability are also present. The motivation to do God's will comes not from a desire to be good or dutiful or from the fear of going to hell if it is not done. The motivation is present because at their core this is who that person is and so this is what that person does. It arises from the impulse and courage to be oneself. It means accepting the responsibility of being oneself and the God-given significance of that. As Nietzsche said, "You sought the heaviest burden and found yourself."[273]

ENDNOTES

266. See Buber, *I and Thou*, for a detailed discussion of God's relationship with people. Many of the characteristics identified here come from Dr. Buber.

267. The self-confidence that accompanies the determination to accomplish a specific task often leads to self-will being done more than it does to God's will being served. Religious zealots do not seem to understand this.

268. Meaning is what transforms an event into a conscious experience, an happening into a recognition.

269. Campbell, *The Power of Myth*, 120.

270. The etymology of "enthusiasm" is to be filled with the spirit of God.

271. Mary Caroline Richards, *Centering in Pottery, Poetry and the Person*, 24.

272. Buber, *I and Thou*, 53, 59.

273. Nietzsche, "Between Birds of Prey."

Appendix B

SOME CHARACTERISTICS OF A REVELATION

As discussed in the Introduction, a revelation is a direct, personal experience of God during which a person becomes aware of new information that is beyond normal cognitive capacities. This new information provides clarity with regard to what the will of God is. There is disagreement regarding whether revelations still occur or stopped long ago.

Revelations are not the same as divination or other psychic occurrences. Revelations typically occur through dreams, visions, trances, prayer, meditation, while fasting and in moments of synchronicity. Because of this, a revelation can be confused with other psychic material. It is possible, however, to differentiate a revelation from delusions and hallucinations.

What follows are some other characteristics of a revelation. The first of these has already been touched upon, that it is God who takes the initiative. This is what Judaism, Christianity and Islam all teach. For example, Hebrew scripture uses the image of "uncovering the ear" to describe the process by which a person receives a message from God (I Sam.9: 15; Job 33:16; and others). Balaam's eyes are "uncovered" (Num.22: 31). God comes to Moses in a thick cloud (Exodus 19:9), in the tabernacle, and in the "tent of meeting" [in Greek, tent of testimony] (Exodus 29:42; 33:11 and others). The Greeks add words such as "appearing," "disclose," "make known," and "reveal" to describe the process of revelation.

Christianity affirms that it is the Spirit of God that bestows a revelation by touching the heart, mind or soul of the recipient. Recipients receive an awareness that is beyond the power of unaided consciousness. For Christians, God's revelation of Himself is seen most clearly in Jesus, his ministry and in God's actions in history, particularly with the people of Israel. Romans 1:19–20 asserts that God's revelation also is found in nature. What is revealed for Christians is God Himself—His love, anger, grace, and actions, not statements about Him. Christian scripture indicates revelation is not complete. Only with the Second Coming of Christ will the fullness of God's glory be completely revealed.

Islam teaches revelation is given in words to a selected person or persons with the intention that God's will so conveyed will reach a particular nation or humanity at large. The recipient does not hear the sound of the revealed words through his or her ears, but through a spiritual sense. The revealed words provide an illumination that is both intellectual and emotional, one that changes the recipient. Some revelations in Islam are personal and influence only a limited number of people for a certain moment in time. Other revelations are intended for all people for all time. Some revelations involve a code of conduct; others do not. Those addressing codes of behavior are the most important. The chain of prophets in Islam (Moses, Jesus, and Muhammad) has ended, but revelation has not. Minor revelations called *mubashsharet* continue and assure their recipients of high spiritual attainments. Minor revelations consist of communications of a general nature and their recipients are referred to as "successors of the Prophet."

Three forms of revelation are identified in the Qur'ān. CXL. 51 reads: "And it is not for any mortal that God should speak to him except by inspiring or from behind a veil or by sending a messenger and revealing by His permission what He pleases." The first form of revelation is called *Wahy*. *Wahy* refers to a prophet or righteous man speaking under the influence of God's Spirit. The revelation is an idea coming to that person's mind as if by a flash of lightning and is not the result of meditation. The second form is described as speaking from behind a veil. This refers to sights seen or words heard from an unseen source while the recipient is asleep or in a trance. These are true dreams or visions. In the third form of revelation, a messenger or angel is sent to the recipient and the divine message is delivered in words. The third form is regarded as a major revelation and is called *Wahy Mutluww* (revelation that is recited). The Qur'ān has ended the need for further major revelations.[274]

Secular research offers a second characteristic. A revelation usually involves words, images, sounds and feelings received while the recipient is in an altered state of consciousness. Revelation happens when the ego is weakened: when one's thoughts, emotions and bodily sensations are minimized or excluded from consciousness. This altered state allows other psychological and spiritual influences a chance to be recognized.

Appendix B

Arnold M. Ludwig in his article "Altered States of Consciousness" wrote that similar features tend to be characteristic of altered states of consciousness. He identifies the following:

> ... Alternations in thinking (disturbance in concentration, attention, memory and judgment); disturbed time sense; loss of control (sense of losing a grip on reality); change in emotional expression (sudden and unexpected displays of primitive and intense emotion); body image change (sense of "oneness," expansion of consciousness, schism between body and mind, dissolution of boundaries between self and non-self); perceptual distortions (hallucinations, increased visual imagery, illusions of every kind); change in meaning or significance (increased significance is attached to subjective experiences, ideas or perceptions); sense of the ineffable (inability to communicate the essence of the experience to others); feelings of rejuvenation; hypersuggestibility (propensity to uncritically accept or automatically respond to specific statements of a leader or to misinterpret situations based on the person's fear or wishes).[275]

In the introduction to the first edition of his book, Dr. Tart writes:

> For any given individual, his normal state of consciousness is one in which he spends the major part of his waking hours. That your normal state of consciousness and mine are quite similar and are similar to that of all other normal men is an almost universal assumption, albeit one of questionable validity. An altered state of consciousness, for a given individual is one in which he clearly feels a *qualitative* shift in his pattern of mental functioning, that is, he feels not just a quantitative shift (more or less alert, more or less visual imagery, sharper or duller, etc.) but also that some quality or qualities of his mental processes are different.[276]

A third characteristic of a revelation is that it is experienced as an internal event that on occasion involves some physical sensations. Islamic descriptions of a revelation typically include more physical details about the experience than do the accounts of other religious traditions. For example, the second revelation the Prophet Muhammad received affected his body. His wife, Aisha, reported, "Revelation coming down upon him in the severest cold, and when that condition was over, perspiration ran down his forehead." (Bukhari 1:1) The Prophet also told her that revelation sometimes "comes to me like the ringing of a bell and that is the hardest on me...." (Bukhari 1:1)[277]

In Christian scripture, Zechariah, the husband of Elizabeth, was in the temple functioning as a priest when he had a vision in which he was told Elizabeth was to bear him a son who was to be named John. He left the temple speechless and did not speak again until John was born (Luke 1:5–24). Paul, in his conversion experience, was blinded (Acts 9:1–19).

In Hebrew scripture, Jacob, in his dream of wrestling with an angel, comes away limping from a wound he suffered in the encounter (Gen. 32:26–29).

ENDNOTES

274. Maulana Aftab-ud-Din Sahib, "Phenomenon of Revelation," based on the writings of Hazret Mitza Shahib.
275. Ludwig as found in Tart, *Altered States of Consciousness*, 23–27.
276. *Altered States of Consciousness*, 2–3.
277. "The Lahore Ahmadiyya Movement in Islam."

Bibliography

Ager, Simon. "Vai Syllabary." (1998–2004) Online: http://www.omniglot.com/writing/vai.htm.
Ahlstrom, Sydney E. *A Religious History of the American People.* New Haven: Yale University Press, 1973.
Ahmad, Hassan. "Imam Ahmad ibn Hanbal." Online: http://www.sunnahonline.com/ilm/seerah/0040.htm.
Ahmad, Maulana Aftab-ud-Din, ed. and trans. "Phenomenon of Revelation" (1963) Online: http://www.aaiil.org/text/books/others/aftabdin/phenomenonrevelation/phenomenonrevelationpdf.shtml.
Ahmed, Shaad. "Dreams." Online: http://angelfire.com/mo2/scarves/dreams.html.
Ahmadiyya Muslim Community. "Islamic Schools of Thought." (1995–2004). Online: http://www.alislam.org/library/books/revelation/part_1_section_3.html.
———. "Outline of Differences Between Shi[insert apostrophe after i]ite and Sunni Schools of Thought." Online: http://www.al-islam.org/encyclopedia/chapter9/1.html.
———. "The Nature of Revelation." (1995–2004) Online: http://www.al-islam.org/library/books/revelation/part_4_section_1.html.
Aizenstat, Stephen, Ph.D. "Dream Tending, Techniques for Uncovering the Hidden Intelligence of Your Dreams." Audio Tapes. Boulder, CO: Sounds True, 2001.
à Kempis, Thomas. *The Imitation of Christ.* Garden City, New York: Image Books, 1955.
Alam, M., PhD. and Dr. A Zahoor. "Allama Muhammad Iqbal." (1999) Online: http://www.cyberistan.org/islamic/iqbal.htm.
al-Ghazali, Abu Hamid. *Confessions.* Online: http://www.fordham.edu/halsall/basis/1100ghazali-truth.html.
Al-Islam.org. "Development of History and Hadith Collections." Online: http://www.al-islam.org/encyclopedia/chapter5a/3.html.
———. "Islamic Scientists." Online: http://www.al-islam.org/encyclopedia/chapter11/4/html.
———. "Place of Reason in the Religion." Online: http://www.al-islam.org/encyclopedia/chapter11/2.html.
al-Mahjub, Kashf. "Abu 'Abd Allah Al-Harith Ibn Asad Al-Muhasibi." Online: http://www.naqshbandi.net.
Al-Qaradawi, Sheikh Yusuf. "Al-Israa' and Al-Mi'raj: Everlasting Lessons." (1999–2005) Online: http://www.islamonline.net/English/In_Depth/Al-Israa_Al-Miraj/articles/09/articles08.shtml.
Allison, G. FitzSimmons. *Fear, Love, and Worship.* New York: Seabury Press, 1962.
Alinaam.org. "The Life and Times of Malik ibn Anas (RA). (2003) Online: http://www.alinaam.org.za/library/amaaiki.htm.
al-Mahjub. "Abu 'Abd Allah Al-Harith Ibn Asad al-Mujasibi." Online: http://naqshbandi.net/haqqani/sufi/saints/kashf_al_mahjub/al_harith_ibn_al_muhasib.htm

Bibliography

———. "Abu Ishaq Ibrahim Ibn Adham Ibn Masur." Online: http://www.naqshbandi.net/haqqani/sufi/saints/kashf_al_mahjub/ibrahim_ibn_al_adham.htm.
American Atheist. "Survey Indicates More Americans 'Without Faith'." (2005) Online: http://www.atheists.org/flash.line/atheist4.htm.
"American Prophet: The Story of Joseph Smith." Online: http://www.pbs.org/americanprophet/joseph-smith.html.
Anderson, Bernhard W. *Understanding the Old Testament*. Englewood Cliffs, N.J.: Prentice Hall, 1966.
Anwandter, Rosa. "Dreams of the Mapuches." Online: http://dreamtalk.hypermart.net/international/chile_english.htm.
Aquinas, Thomas. *Summa Theologica*. New York: Benzinger Brothers, 1947.
Aristotle, *On Dreams*. J. I. Beare, trans. The Internet Classics Archive, by Daniel C. Stevenson, Web Atomics. Online: http://classics.mit.edu/Aristotle/dreams.1b.txt.
Armstrong, Karen. *A History of God*. New York: Ballantine Books, 1993.
Ashbrook, James B. and Carol Rausch Albright. *The Humanizing Brain*. Cleveland, OH: The Pilgrim Press, 1997.
Augustine. *City of God*. Vernon J. Bourke, ed. Abridged version, Gerald G. Walsh, Demetrius B. Zema, Grace Monahan and Daniel Honan, trans. Garden City, New York: Image Books, 1958.
Azam, Umar, Ph.D. "Dreams and Islam." (1991) Online: http://www.dr-umar-azam.com/dreams_in_islam/dreams_in_islam_1.htm.
Babylonian Talmud: Tractate Berakoth, Folio 55. Online: http://www.come-and-hear.com/berakoth/berakoth_55.html.
Bacchus, F. J. "Eusebius of Caesarea." Transcribed by WGKofron. (2005) Online: http://www.newadvent.org/cathen/05617b.htm.
Bach, Susan R. *Spontaneous Paintings of Severely Ill Patients, A Contribution to Psychosomatic Medicine*. Basle, Swiss: J.R. Geigy, 1969.
———. *Spontaneous Pictures of Leukemic Children as an Expression of the Total Personality, Mind and Body*. Basel: Schwabe & Co., 1975.
Bachofen, J.J. *Myth, Religion, & Mother Right*. Princeton, N.J.: Princeton University Press, 1967.
Bandstra, Barry L. *Reading the Old Testament, An Introduction to the Hebrew Bible*, second edition. Belmont, CA: Wadsworth Publishing Company, 1999.
Barasch, Marc Ian. *Healing Dreams: Exploring the Dreams That Can Transform Your Life*. New York: Riverhead Books, 2000. Online: http://www.intuitive-connections.net/2004/book-barasch.htm.
Barrett, Deirdre. "The 'Committee of Sleep': A Study of Dream Incubation for Problem Solving." *Dreaming*, Vol. 3, No. 2 (1993) Online: http://www.asdreams.org/journal/articles/barrett3-2.htm.
Bashiri, Iraj. "Jamal al-Din al-Afghani." (2000) Online: http://www.angelfire.com/rnb/bashiri/Afghani/Afghani.html.
Baz, Shaikh Abdul Aziz Ibn Abdullah Ibn. "Imaam Muhammad Ibn Abdul Wahhab, His Life and Mission." (2003) Online: http://www.ahya.org.
Beaudet, Denyse. *Encountering the Monster, Pathways in Children's Dreams*. New York: Continuum, 1990.
Bem, Daryl. J. "Ganzfeld phenomena." (1996) In G. Stein, ed., *Encyclopedia of the Paranormal*, Buffalo, New York: Prometheus Books. Online: http://www.holorressonancia.com/artigo47_pt.html.

Bibliography

———. and Charles Honorton. "Does Psi Exist? Replicable Evidence for an Anomalous Process of Information Transfer." (1994) In *Psychological Bulletin* 115, No. 1. Online: http://sivas.com/beyond/index.php/literature/does_psi_exist_reokucabke _evidence_for_an_anomalous_process_of_information/.
"Henri Bergson." (2000) Online: http://www.kirjasto.sci.fi/bergson.htm.
Bigman, Rabbi David. "Talmud. Critical Talmud Study in an Orthodox Context." Online: http://www.myjewishlearning.com/texts/talmud/Gemara?ModernStudy /BigmanCritical_Prn.htm.
Bingham, John P. *Inner Treasure, Reflections on the Teachings of Jesus.* Pecos, NM: Dove Publications, 1989.
Bohm, David and B.J. Hiley, *The Undivided Universe.* London: Routledge, 1993.
Bolen, Jean Shinoda, M.D. *The Tao of Psychology, Synchronicity and the Self.* San Francisco: Harper & Row, 1979.
Borchert, Bruno. *Mysticism, Its History and Challenge.* York Beach, Maine: Samuel Weiser, 1994.
Bowman, Lee. "Studying a Stroke Patient, Researchers Zero in on Where Dreams Unfold." Scripps Howard News Service, *Sacramento Bee,* 9/04.
Bluestone, Sarvananda, Ph.D. *The World Dream Book.* Rochester, Vermont: Destiny Books, 2002.
Breecher, Maury M., M.P.H., Ph.D. "The biology of dreaming: a controversy that won't go to sleep." Online: http://www.columbia.edu/cu/21stC/issue-3.4/breecher.html.
Brill, Koninklijke. "al-Nazzam." (1999) Online: http://www.muslimphilosophy.com/ei /nazzam.htm.
Brunner, Emil. *The Christian Doctrine of the Church, Faith, and the Consummation.* David Cairns, trans. Philadelphia: The Westminster Press, 1962.
———. *The Christian Doctrine of Creation and Redemption.* Olive Wyon, trans. Philadelphia: The Westminster Press, 1952.
Buber, Martin. *I and Thou.* New York: Charles Scribner's Sons, 1958.
———. *Tales of the Hasidim.* New York: Schocken Books, Inc., 1947.
Bulkeley, Kelly. "A Dreamer's Life: Robert Van de Castle's Our Dreaming Mind." A book review. Online: http://www.asdreams.org/vandeca.htm.
———. "Dreaming: Religious and Scientific Approaches." A course proposal for Santa Clara University (2000) Online: http://kellybulkeley.com/articles/course_dreaminig _religious_scientific.htm.
———. "Overview: Reflections on the Dream Traditions of Islam" Online: http://www .kellybulkeley.com/articles.islam_and_dreams.pdf.
———. "Reflections on the Dream Traditions of Islam." (2001) *Sleep and Hypnosis,* Vol. 4:1, 2002.
———. "Varieties of Religious Dream Experience." Online: http://www.kellybulkeley.com /articles/varieties_of_religious_dream_experience.htm.
———. *The Wilderness of Dreams, Exploring the Religious Meanings of Dreams in Modern Western Culture.* Albany: State University of New York Press, 1994.
Bultmann, Rudolf. "Kerygma and Myth by Rudolf Bultmann and Five Critics." (1953) Online: www.religion-online.org/cgi-bin/relsearchd.dll/showbook?item_id=431.
Burton, Edwin. "Richard Rolle de Hampole." (2002) Transcribed by Herman F. Holbrook. Online: http://www.newadvent.org.
Campbell, Joseph. *Hero With A Thousand Faces.* Cleveland, OH: Meridian Books, 1964.
———. *Myths to Live By.* New York: Bantam Books, 1972.

Bibliography

———. *Renewal Myths and Rites of the Primitive Hunters and Planters*. Eranos Lectures Series, Dallas: Spring Publications, 1960.
———. *Transformations of Myth Through Time*. New York: Harper & Row, 1990.
———. with Bill Moyers. *The Power of Myth*. Betty Sue Flowers, ed. New York: Doubleday, 1988.
Caprio, Betsy and Thomas M. Hedberg. *At A Dream Workshop*. New York/Mahwah, N.J.: Paulist Press, 1987.
Carroll, Robert Todd. "Dreams." (2002) *The Skeptic's Dictionary*. Online: http://skepdic.com/dreams.html
Cassidy, David C. "Werner Heisenberg and the Uncertainty Principle." (1998–2005) Online: http://www.aip.org/history/heisenberg/p01.htm.
———. "The Uncertainty Principle." (1998–2005) Online: http://aip.org/history.heisenberg/p08.htm.
———. "Implications of Uncertainty." (1998–2005) Online: http://aip.org/history/heisenberg/p08c.htm.
Catholic Online Saints. "St. Jerome, Doctor of the Church."(2006) Online: http://www.catholic.org/saints/saint.php?saint_id=10.
Chardin, Teilhard de. *The Phenomenon of Man*. New York: Harper & Row, 1959.
Chittick, William C. *The Sufi Path of Love, The Spiritual Teachings of Rumi*. Albany: State University of New York Press, 1983.
Chojnowski, Peter. "Descartes' Dream: From Method to Madness." (2000–2002) Online: http://www.lifeissues.net/writers/cho/cho_14descartesdream.htm.
Christian History Institute. "Feisty Jerome; His Bible Legacy Lasted over 1,000 Years." (2004) *Glimpses*, Issue #57. Online: http://chi.gospelcom.net/GLIMPSEF/Glimpses/glmps057.shtml.
Chinuch, Merkos L'Inyonei. "The Treasure Hunt," as found in *The Storyteller*. (1996) Online: http://www.tzivos-hashem.org/storytime/storyteller/st1602.htm.
Cicero, Marcus Tullius. *On Divination*. Jeffrey Henderson, ed., W. A. Falconer, trans. Cambridge, Mass.: Harvard University Press, 2001.
Clark, Donald. "Hawthorne Effect." (2000) Online: http://wwwnwlink.com/~donclark/hrd/history/hawthorne.html.
Cohn, Andrew. "From the Many to the One, Enlightenment for the Twenty-First Century." (1998–2004) Moksha Press. Online: http://www.wie.org/j23/andrew.asp.
Collins, James. *A History of Modern European Philosophy*. Milwaukee, WI: The Bruce Publishing Company, 1965.
Condon, Gerard Ph.D. and Harry Fogarty, Ph.D. "Dreams: A Way of Listening to God?" A presentation of the Kristine Mann Library, C. G. Jung Center of New York on 7/19/2001.
Cooper, John. "Mulla Sadra (Sadr al-Din Muhammad al-Shirazi). (1998) Online: http://www.muslimphilosophy.com/ip/rep/H027.htm.
Covitz, Joel. *Visions in the Night, Jungian and Ancient Dream Interpretation*. Toronto: Inner City Press, 2000.
Coxhead, David and Susan Hiller. *Dreams, Visions of the Night*. New York: Thames and Hudson, 1989.
Craig, S. "Why do we dream?" (2003) Online: http://www.sciam.com/askexpert_question.cfm?articleID=00072867-D925-1FOE-97AE80.
Crisp, Tony. "Artemidorus and the First Dream Dictionary." Online: http://www.dreamhawk.com/d-aritem.htm.

D'Orsonnens, Rev. J. I. "Is God Calling?" (1951) Online: http://www.religiouslife.com/a_learn_discern.phtml.
Dan, Joseph. "The Gerona Circle." (1986) Online: http: www.MyJewishLearning.com.
———. "Sefer ha-Bahir: The Book of Brilliance."(2002) Online: http: www.MyJewish Learning.com.
Dei Verbum, Dogmatic Constitution on Divine Revelation Solemnly Promulgated by His Holiness, Pope Paul VI, On November 18, 1965. Online: http://www.vatican.va/archive/hist_councils/ii_vatican_council/documents/vat-ii_const19651118_dei-verb.
Devlin, Mary. "Women Mystics and the New Millennium." Online: http://www.ru.org/92devlin.html
Discover Islam, "Dreams, Their Truth and Meaning." (2000) Online: http://www.dislam.org.
Dobbs, Bryan Griffith. "Sefer Yetzirah." Online: http://www.kheper.net/topics/Kabbalah/SeferYetzirah.htm.
Dodds, E.R. *The Greeks and the Irrational*. Berkeley: University of California Press, 1966.
Dole, George F. "About Emanuel Swedenborg." In *Introduction to a Thoughtful Soul: Reflections from Swedenborg*." Swedenborg Foundation, 1995. Online: http://www.swedenborg.com.
Domhoff, G. William. "The Case Against the Problem-Solving Theory of Dreaming." (2004) Online: http://psych.ucsc.edu/dreams/Library/domhoff_2004b.html.
———. "A New Neurocognitive Theory of Dreams." (2001) *Dreaming*, Vol. 11. Online: http://psych.ucsc.edu/dreams/Articles/domhoff_2001a.html.
———. "The 'Purpose' of Dreams." Online: http://www.ucsc.edu/dreams/Articles/purpose.html.
———. *The Scientific Study of Dreams: Neural Networks, Cognitive Development, and Content Analysis*. Washington, D.C.: The American Psychological Association, 2003.
———. "Why Did Empirical Dream Researchers Reject Freud? A Critique of Historical Claims by Mark Solms." (2004) *Dreaming*, Vol. 14 (1). Online: http//: www.apa.org/journals/drm/304ab.html.
Dossey, Larry, M.D. "The Dream Helper Ceremony." *Reinventing Medicine: Beyond Mind-Body to a New Era of Healing*. New York: HarperCollins, 1999. Online: http://www.creativespirit.net/henryreed/dreamtelepathy/dosseyondreamhelper.htm.
Dougherty, Sarah B. Review of "Children's Dreaming and the Development of Consciousness." by David Foulkes. Online: http://www.theosophy-nw.org/theosnw/science/sc-sbd5.htm.
"Dreams in Islam." Online: http://www.dr.umarazam.com/dreams_in_islam/dreams_in_islam_1.htm.
"Dreamtime." Online: http://www.answers.com/topic/dreamtime.
Drewes, Athena A. "Dr. Louisa Rhine's letters revisited: The Children." The *Journal of Parapsychology* (December 2002). Online: http://www.findarticles.com/p/articles/mi_m2320/is_4_66/ai_97754937.
Dunn, Jimmy. "Ancient Pyramid Legends and Myths." Online: http://www.touregypt.net/featurestories/pyramidlegends.hm.
———. "Piety of the Common Ancient Egyptians." Online: http://www.touregypt.net/featurestories/commonpiety.htm.
Dutton, Blake D. "Benedict De Spinoza" (2004) The Internet Encyclopedia of Philosophy. Online: http://www.utm.edu/research/iep/s/spinoza.htm.
Eckhart, Meister. *Selected Writings*. Selected and trans. by Oliver Davies. New York: Penguin Books, 1994.

Bibliography

Eddy, Mary Baker. *Science and Health, with Keys to the Scriptures*. Boston: The First Church of Christ, Scientist, 1994.

———. "In Her Own Words." Online: http://www.csfirstlessons.com/csfirstlessons_053.htm.

Edinger, Edward F., M.D. *Anatomy of the Psyche, Alchemical Symbolism in Psychotherapy*. La Salle, IL: Open Court Publishing Company, 1985.

———. *Ego and Archetype, Individuation and the Religious Function of the Psyche*. Baltimore, MD: Penguin Books, 1974.

———. *Encounter with the Self, A Jungian Commentary on William Blake's Illustrations of the Book of Job*. Toronto: Inner City Books, 1986.

———. *The Bible and the Psyche, Individuation Symbolism in the Old Testament*. Toronto: Inner City Books, 1986.

———. *The Creation of Consciousness, Jung's Myth for Modern Man*. Toronto: Inner City Books, 1984.

———. *The Mysterium Lectures, A Journey Through C. G. Jung's Mysterium Coniunctionis*. Transcribed and ed. by Joan Dexter Blackmer. Toronto: Inner City Books, 1995.

Edis, Taner. "Why Industrial Caulk is Bad for You." (2004) Online: http://www2.truman.edu/~edis/courses/JINS/papers/antipsi2.html.

Edwards, Denis. *Human Experience of God*. New York/Mahwah, N.J.: Paulist Press, 1983.

Edwards, Mead, Palmer and Simmons. *Spiritual Growth: An Empirical Exploration of Its Meaning, Sources, and Implications*. Washington, D.C.: The Alban Institute, 1974.

Eisen, Robert. "Mysticism Renewed." (2002) Online: http://www.MyJewishLearning.com.

Einstein, Albert. *Science, Philosophy and Religion: A Symposium*, 1941. Online: http://www1.physik.tu-muenchen.de/~ga.,e:/matpack/html/Biographies/Einstein_Quotes.

———. "Famous Quotes." Online: http://www1.physik.tu-muenchen.de/~gammel/matpack/html?Biographies/Einstein_Quotes.

Elaine's Dream Catcher Page. "The Legend of the Dreamcatcher." Online: http://freespace.virgin.net/derek.berger/dreamcatcher.html.

Eliade, Mircea. *Cosmos and History, The Myth of the Eternal Return*. Willard R. Trask, trans. New York: Harper & Row, 1959.

———. *Ordeal by Labyrinth, Conversations with Claude-Henri Rocque*. Chicago: University of Chicago Press, 1984.

———. *Patterns in Comparative Religion*. Rosemary Sheed, trans. New York: New American Library, 1963.

———. *Shamanism, Archaic Techniques of Ecstasy*. Willard R. Trask, trans. Princeton, N.J.: Princeton University Press, 1974.

Emerick, Yahiya. *The Life and Work of Muhammad*, Indianapolis, IN: Alpha Books, 2002.

Ess. "Bohm, Bell – and Boom! The End of Modern Dualism." (1997) Online: http://www.drury.edu/ess/philsci/bell.html.

Eternal Word Television Network. "First Vatican Council." Online: http://www.ewtn.com.

———. "Saint Catherine of Siena, Virgin." *Lives of Saints*, Denver, CO: John J. Crawley & Co. Online: http://www.ewtn.com.

Eusebius, *Church History*. Paul L. Maier, trans. Grand Rapids, MI: Kregel Publications, 2007.

Faraday, Ann. *Dream Power*. New York: Berkley Books, 1984.

Felder, Gary. "Spooky Action at a Distance, An Explanation of Bell's Theorem." (1999) Online: http://www.ncsu.edu/felder-public/kenny/papers/bell.html.

Fidler, Ruth. "A Touch of Support: Ps3, 6 and the Psalmist's Experience." (2005) Online: http://www.bsw.org/project/biblica/bibl86/Comm07m.html.
Field, Richard. "John Dewey." (2001) The Internet Encyclopedia of Philosophy. Online: http://www.utm.edu/research/iep/d/dewey.htm.
Fieser, James, Ph.D., general ed. "Meister Eckhart." (2001) Online: http://www.iep.utm.edu.
Fitzgerald, Robert. "The Soul of Sponsorship." Center City, MN: Hazelden, 1995.
Flanagan, Sabina. "Hildegard von Bingen." (1995) Online: http://www.staff.uni-mainz.de/horst/hildegard/documents/flanagan.html.
Flannery-Dailey, Frances. "Bar, Shaul: A Letter That Has Not Been Read: Dreams in Hebrew Bible." (2004) Online: http://www.bookreviews.org/pdf/1791_4468.pdf.
Forman, Robert K.C. "What Does Mysticism Have to Teach Us About Consciousness?" (1998) Online: http://www.zynet.co.uk/imprint/Forman.html.
Forrest, Jay N. "Dreams and Visions."(2002) Online: http: www.jayforrest.org.
Foulkes, David. "Dreaming: Lucid and Non." Online: http://www.sawka.com/spiritwatch/dreaming.htm.
———. "Sleep and Dreams. Dream Research: 1953–1993." (1996) *Sleep*, Vol.19 (8).
Fowler, James W. *Stages of Faith, The Psychology of Human Development and the Quest for Meaning*. San Francisco: HarperSanFrancisco, 1995.
Friedman, Maurice S. *Martin Buber: The Life of Dialogue*. New York: Harper First Torchbook edition, 1960. Online: http://www.religion-online.org/showchapter.asp?title=459&C=377.
Funk, Robert W.; Roy W. Hoover; and the Jesus Seminar. *The Five Gospels, The Search for the Authentic Words of Jesus*. New York: Scribner, 1993.
Gardner, Edmund. "St. Catherine of Siena."(2002) Transcribed by Lois Tesluk. Online: http://www.newadvent.org.
Garfield, Patricia L., Ph.D. *Creative Dreaming*. New York: Ballantine Books, 1974.
Gaskill, Tom. "al-'Amiri, Abu'l Hasan Muhammad ibn Yusuf." (1998) Online: http://www.muslimphilosophy.com/ip/rep/H041.htm.
Gendlin, Eugene, Ph.D. *Let Your Body Interpret Your Dreams*. Chicago: Chiron Publications, 1986.
Ghirlandaio. "405 Jerome Completes the Vulgate." (1990) Online: http://ctlibrary.com3747.
Ghoniem, Muhammad; Mansur Ahmed; Elias Karim; 'Abd al-Rahman Robert Squires & MSM Saifullah. "The Prophet's Night Journey." (2002) Online: http://www.iman.co.nz/ed/night.htm.
Giampà, Mario; Stefano Beggiora; Luca Caldironi. "Dreams and Shamans in sub-Himalayan Tribal Groups." Online: http://groups.msn.com/Spiritwinds/shamanism.msnw?action=get_message&mview=O&ID_Message=1877&Lastmodified=465437633645507082.
Gillespie, G. "Light in Lucid Dreaming: A Review," *Dreaming* 2, 1997.
Gnuse, Robert Karl. *Dreams and Dream Reports in the Writings of Josephus, A Traditio-Historical Analysis*. Leiden: E. J. Brill, 1996.
Godin, André. *The Psychological Dynamics of Religious Experience*. Birmingham, AL: Religious Education Press, 1985.
Godlas, Alan, Ph.D. "Early Sufi Shaykhs and Shrines." (2001) Online: http://www.uga.edu/islam/sufismearly.html.

Bibliography

Goldberg, G. J. "The Galilean Campaign, 67 C.E." Online: http://hometown.aol.com/fljosephus2/warChronology5Pg2.htm.

Graduate Center of the City University of New York, "American Religious Identification Survey." Online: http://www.gc.cuny.edu/press_information/current_releases/october_2001aris.htm.

Graham, E.P. "Divination." (2004) Transcribed by Joseph P. Thomas. Online: http://www.newadvent.org/cathen/05048b.htm.

Greene, Brian. "Fabric of the Cosmos," *Fresh Air with Terry Gross*. A radio interview conducted on National Public Radio on 3/16/2004.

———. *The Elegant Universe*. New York: Vintage Books, 2000.

———. *The Fabric of the Cosmos: Space, Time and the Texture of Reality*. New York: Alfred A. Knopf, 2004.

Grossman, Cathy, "Charting the Unchurched in America", USA Today, March 7, 2002. Online: http:www.usatoday.com/life/dcovthu.htm. This was found in "Religious Identification in the U.S." Online: http://www.religioustolerance.org/chr_prac2.htm.

Griffith, F. "The Second Story of Khamuas: Prince Khamuas and Si-Osiri." Online: http://nefertiti.iwebland.com/texts/khamuas.htm.

Grube, G.M.A. *Plato's Thought*. Boston: Beacon Press, 1958.

Guillaume, Alfred, trans. "Ibn Ishâq's Life of Muhammad," John Aiden Williams, ed. *Islam*. New York: George Braziller, 1961.

Gurney, E., F.W. H. Myers and F. Podmore. *Phantasms of the Living*. London: Rooms for the Society for psychical research, Trübner and Co., 1886.

Haddad, G.F. "Imam Abu Al-Hasan Al-Ash'Ari." Online: http://www.dartmouth.edu/~alnur/ISLAM/GRMUSLIMS/Al-Ashari.htm.

———. "Imam Al Maturidi." Online: http://www.dartmouth.edu/~alnur/ISLAM/GRMUSLIMS/AL_Maturidi.htm.

———. "Imam Malik." Online: http://www.sunnah.org/publications/khulafa_rashideen/malik.htm.

Haldane, Jane. Washington, D.C.: Alban Institute, 1974?

Hall, James A., M.D. *Jungian Dream Interpretation, A Handbook of Theory and Practice*. Toronto: Inner City Books, 1983.

Halsall, Paul. "Internet Islamic History Sourcebook." (2001) Online: http://www.fordham.edu/halsall/islam/islam/islamsbook.html.

———. "Medieval Sourcebook: Abu Hamid al-Ghazali: The Remembrance of Death and the Afterlife, from *The Revival of the Religious Sciences (Ihya 'ulum al-din)*. (1996) Online: http://www.fordham.edu/halsall/source/alghazali.html.

———. "Medieval Sourcebook: Eusebius of Caesarea, The Life of the Blessed Emperor Constantine." (1997) Online: http://www.fordham.edu/halsall/basis/vita-constantine.html.

———. "Medieval Sourcebook: Ibn Sina (Avicenna): On Medicine." (1998) Online: http://www.fordham.edu/halsall/source/1020Avicenna-Medicine.html.

———. "Medieval Sourcebook: Zamakhshari: The Discoverer of Truth." (1998) Online: http://www.fordham.edu/halsall/source/1130Zamakhshari.html.

———."Modern History Sourcebook: David Hume: On Miracles." (1997) Online: http://www.fordham.edu/halsall/mod/hume-miracles.html.

———. "Modern History Sourcebook: Thomas Paine: Of the Religion of Deism Compared with the Christian Religion." (1998) Online: http://www.fordham.edu/Halsall/mod/paine-deism.html.

Hanh, Thich Nhat. *The Miracle of Mindfulness, A Manual on Meditation*. Boston: Beacon Press, 1976.
Hanson, K.C. *The Epic of Kret*. (2002) Online: http://www.kchanson.com/ANCDOCS /westsem/kret.html.
Harding, M. Esther. *Psychic Energy, Its Source and Its Transformation*. New York, Bollingen Foundation, 1963.
Harris, Virginia. "Spiritual Essence of the Writings of Mary Baker Eddy." (2002) Online: http://www.tfccs.com/spirandheal_vsh_1.jhtml.
Harrison, David. "An Analogy to Bell's Theorem." (2003) Online: http://www.upscale .utoronto.ca/PVB/Harrison?BellsTheorem/Analogy.html.
———. "Bell's Theorem." (Revised, 2004) Online: http://www.upscale.utoronto.ca/PVB /Harrison/BellsTheorem/BellsTheorem.html.
Hartmann, Ernest M.D. "Outline for a Theory on the Nature and Functions of Dreaming." *Dreaming*, Vol. 6, No.2 (1996) Online: http://www.asdreams.org/journal/articles/6 -2hartmann.htm.
Havel, Vaclav. "Address to Forum 2000." (1997) Online: http://cts.cuni.cz?conf98/Procc=x .htm.
Henein, Maryam. "Shamanic Healing Quest." (2003) *Whole Life Times*. Online: http: //www.dragonfly.com/portal/featured_stories/archive/stories_w/t_shamic.html.
Herbert, Nick. "Bell's Interconnectedness Theorem." Online: http://deoxy.org/ire/bell /htm.
Herodotus, "Herodotus' Second Book of Histories, Euterpe." Online: http://www .greektexts.com/library/Herodotus/Euterpe/eng/10.html.
Herzog, Edgar. *Psyche and Death*. David Cox and Eugene Rolfe, trans. New York: G.P. Putnam's Sons for the C.G. Jung Foundation for Analytical Psychology, 1967.
Hillman, James. *Re-Visioning Psychology*. San Francisco: Harper Colophon Books, 1977.
History of the Ancient Near East Electronic Compendium. "Ancient Mari". Online: http: //ancientneareast.tripod.com/Mari_Hariri.html.
Hobson, J.A. and R.W. McCarley. "The Brain as a Dream Generator: An Activation-Synthesis Hypothesis of the Dream Process." *American Journal of Psychiatry*, Vol. 134, 1977.
Hoeber, Karl. "Flavius Josephus." Stephen W. Shackelford, trans. (2003) Online: http: //www.newadvent.org/cathen/08522a.htm.
Hoffer, Eric. *The True Believer*. New York: Perennial Library (Harper & Row), 1966.
Hoffman, Valerie J. "The Role of Visions in Contemporary Egyptian Religious Life," *Religion* (1997) Vol. 27, No. 1.
Holloway, Julia Bolton. "Anchoress and Cardinal: Julian of Norwich and Adam Easton O.S.B." (1998) Lecture at Norwich Cathedral. Online: http://www.umilta.net/.
———."St. Birgitta of Sweden and Her Revelaciones." (2002) Online: http://www.umilta .net/.
Hunnex, Milton D. *Philosophies & Philosophers*. San Francisco: Chandler Publishing Company, 1961.
Hussain, M. Hadi. "Imam Abu Hanifah, His Life and Times." (1995) Online: http://muslim -canada.org/hanifah.htm.
I. Shah, *The Sufis*. London: Octagon Press, 1964.
Ignatian Spiritual Exercises for the Corporate Person. "First Week Rules for Discernment." Online: http://www.isecp.org/chapter_10.html.

Bibliography

Ingram, Gordon. "Dreaming as Precognition in Lowlands South America." Online: http://gordoni.net/Academic/ba_thesis/ba1.htm.

Incigneri, Brian. "Discernment: Recognizing God's Voice." Online: http://www.ccr.org.au/discern.html.

Islamic Awareness. "Prophet Muhammad's Night Journey to Al-Masjid Al-Aqsa — The Farthest Mosque." (2001) Online: http://www.islamic-awareness.org/Quran?Contrad/External/aqsa.html.

Islamic Paths. "Personalities in Islam: Imam ash-Shafi'i." Online: http://www.islamic-paths.org/Home/English/History/Personalities/Content/Shafi'i.htm.

Island of Freedom. "Karl Barth." Online: http://www.island-of-freedom.com/BARTH.HTM.

Izady, M. "Sufi Mystic Orders." (1995–2001) Online: http://www.hurdistanica.com/english/religion/sufism/sufism.html.

Jacobi, Jolande. *Masks of the Soul*. Ean Begg, trans. Grand Rapids, MI: Wm. B. Eerdmans, 1976.

Jacobs, Louis. "About Jewish Daily Life. *Halakhah: Sources and Development*." (1995) Online: http://www.myjewishlearning.com.

———. "Hasidic Ideas." (2002) Online: http://www.MyJewishLearning.com.

———. "Literature of and on Hasidim." (2002) Online: http://www.MyJewishLearning.com.

———. "The Baal Shem Tov, The Founder of Hasidism Is Shrouded in Legend and Mystery." (2002) *The Jewish Religion: A Companion*. New York: Oxford University Press, 1995. Online: http://www.MyJewishLearning.com.

———. "The Editing of the Talmud." (1995) Online: http://www.myjewishlearning.com/texts/talmud/Gemara/TalmudEditing_Prn.htm.

———. "The Influence of the Zohar." (2002) Online: http://www.MyJewishLearning.com.

Jaffé, Aniela. *The Myth of Meaning, Jung and the Expansion of Consciousness.*. R.F.C. Hull, trans. New York: Penguin Books, 1975.

———. *Apparitions, An Archetypal Approach to Death Dreams and Ghosts*. Irving, TX: Spring Publications, 1979.

James, Montague Rhodes. *The Apocryphal New Testament*. Oxford: The Clarendon Press, 1975.

James, William. *The Varieties of Religious Experience*. New York: Viking Penguin, 1982.

Jenks, Kathleen, Ph.D. " Rab'a al-'Adawiyya, an eighth Century Islamic Saint from Iraq." (2003) Online: http://www.mythinglinks.org/NearEast~3monotheisms~Islm~Rabia.html.

Jewish Virtual Library. "The Vilna Gaon – Rabbi Eliyahu of Vilna." (2002) Online: http://www.jewishvirtuallibrary.org/

Jin Technologies. "Nadva-tul-'Ulema of Lucknow" (2003) Online: http://www.storyofpaksitan.com/articletext.asp?arid=A028.

———. "Sir Syed Ahmad Khan." (2003) Online: http://www.storyof Pakistan.com/person.asp?perid=P001.

Johnson, Robert A. *Inner Work, Using Dreams & Active Imagination for Personal Growth*. San Francisco: Harper and Row, 1986.

Johnston, William. *The Inner Eye of Love, Mysticism and Religion*. New York: Harper & Row, 1978.

———, ed. *The Cloud of Unknowing and the Book of Privy Counseling*. New York: Image Books, 1973.

Jung, C. G. "A Psychological View of Conscience." (1958) R.F.C. Hull, trans. *The Collected Works of C.G. Jung*, Vol. 10. Princeton, N.J.: Princeton University Press, 1969.
——. "Conscious, Unconscious, and Individuation." (1939) R.F.C. Hull, trans., *The Collected Works of C. G. Jung*, Vol. 9i. Princeton, N.J.: Princeton University Press, 1969.
——. "Individual Dream Symbolism in Relation to Alchemy." (1943, revised 1952) R.F.C. Hull, trans. *The Collected Works of C.G. Jung*, Vol.12. Princeton, N.J.: Princeton University Press, 1969.
——. "Mysterium Coniunctionis." (1954) R.F.C. Hull, trans. *The Collected Works of C. G. Jung*, Vol. 14. Princeton, N.J.: Princeton University Press, 1969.
——. "On the Nature of the Psyche." (Revised 1954) R.F.C. Hull, trans. *The Collected Works of C. G. Jung*, Vol. 8. Princeton, N.J.: Princeton University Press, 1969.
——. "On Synchronicity." (1951, 1957) R.F.C. Hull, trans. *The Collected Works of C. G. Jung*, Vol. 8. Princeton, N.J.: Princeton University Press, 1969.
——. "Paracelsus the Physician." (1929) R.F.C. Hull, trans. *The Collected Works of C. G. Jung*, Vol.15. Princeton, N.J.: Princeton University Press, 1969.
——. "Psychology and Religion." (1938) R.F.C. Hull, trans. *The Collected Works of C. G. Jung*, Vol. 11. Princeton, N.J.: Princeton University Press, 1969.
——. "Psychological Types." (1949) R.F.C. Hull, trans. *The Collected Works of C. G. Jung*, Vol. 6. Princeton, N.J.: Princeton University Press, 1969.
——. "Symbols and the Interpretation of Dreams." (1961) R.F.C. Hull, trans. *The Collected Works of C. G. Jung*, Vol. 18. Princeton, N.J.: Princeton University Press, 1969.
——. "Symbols of Transformation." (1952) R.F.C. Hull, trans. *The Collected Works of C. G. Jung*, Vol.5. Princeton, N.J.: Princeton University Press, 1969.
——. "Synchronicity: An Acausal Connecting Principle." (1952, 1960) R.F.C. Hull, trans. *The Collected Works of C. G. Jung*, Vol. 8. Princeton, N.J.: Princeton University Press, 1969.
——. "The Meaning of Psychology for Modern Man." (1934) R.F.C. Hull, trans. *The Collected Works of C.G. Jung*, Vol. 10. Princeton, N.J.: Princeton University Press, 1969.
——. *The Undiscovered Self.* R.F.C. Hull, trans. New York: The New American Library, 1958.
Kabbani, Shaykh M. Hisham. "On Tasawwuf: al-Hasan as-Basri." *The Repudiation of "Salafi" Innovations.* (ASFA, 1996) Online: http://www.sunnah.org/tasawwuf/scholar1.htm.
Kahn, David and J. Allan Hobson. "Self-Organization Theory of Dreaming." *Dreaming*, Vol. 3, No. 3 (1993) Online: http://www.asdreams.org/journal/articles/3-3_kahn_hobson.htm.
Karp, Abraham J. "Shabbetai Zvi." (2002) *From the Ends of the Earth: Judaic Treasures of the Library of Congress.* Washington, D.C.: Library of Congress, 1991. Online: http://www.jewishvirtuallibrary.org.
Kavanaugh, Kieran and Otilio Rodriguez, trans. *The Collected Works of St. John of the Cross.* Washington, D.C.: ICS Publications, Revised Edition, 1991.
Kelsey, Morton T. *Dreams, A Way to Listen to God.* New York/Mahwah, New Jersey: Paulist Press, 1978.
——. *Encounter With God.* Minneapolis: Bethany Fellowship, 1972.
——. *God, Dreams, and Revelation, A Christian Interpretation of Dreams.* Minneapolis: Augsburg Publishing House, 1968.

———. *The Christian & The Supernatural*. Minneapolis: Augsburg Publishing House, 1976.
———. *The Other Side of Silence, A Guide to Christian Meditation*. New York/Mahwah, NJ: Paulist Press, 1976.
Kemerling, Garth. "Kant: Experience and Reality." (1997–2002) Online: http://www.philosophypages.com/ph/kier.htm.
———. "Søren Aabye Kierkegaard." (2002) Online: http://www.philosophypages.com/ph/moor.htm.
———. "George Edward Moore." (1997–2002) Online: http://www.philosophypages.com/ph/moor.htm.
———. "Moore: Analysis of Common Sense." (1998–2001) Online: http://www.philosophypages.com/hy/6k.htm.
———. "Bertrand Arthur William Russell." (2002) Online: http://www.philosophypages.com/ph/russ.htm.
———. "Alfred North Whitehead". (2002) Online: http://www.philosophypages.com.
———. "Ludwig Wittgenstein." (1998–2001) Online: http://www.philosophypages.com/ph/witt.htm.
Kennedy-Day, Kiki. "al-kindi, Abu Yusuf Ya'qub Ibn Ishaq." Online: http://www.muslimphilosophy.com/ip/kin.htm.
Kessels, A.H.M. *Studies on the Dream in Greek Literature*. Utrecht: HES Publishers, 1978.
Keyes, Margaret Frings. *The Inward Journey*. Millbrae, CA: Celestial Arts, 1974.
Khamush.com. "Al Hallaj Mystic and Martyr." (2004) Online: http://www.khamush.com/sufism/hallaj.html.
Khosla, K. *The Sufism of Rumi*. Longmead, Great Britain: Element Books, 1987.
Kimelman, Reuven. "Abraham Joshua Heschel: Our Generation's Teacher." *Melton Journal*, No. 15, Winter 1983. Online: http://www.crosscurrents.org/heschel.htm.
Kirjasto.sci.fi. "Bergson, Henri." (2000) Online: http://www.kirjasto.sci.fi/bergson.htm.
Knudson, Roger M. "The Significant Dream as Emblem of Uniqueness: The Fertilizer Does Not Explain the Flower." *Dreaming*, Vol. 13, No. 3 September (2003) Online: http://www.asdreams.org/journal/articles/13-3_knudson.htm.
Köçümkulkïzï, Elmira and Daniel C. Waugh. "Religion." (2001) Online: http://depts.washington.edu/uwch/silkroad/culture/religion/religion.html.
Koet, Bart J. *Dreams and Scripture in Luke-Acts. Collected Essays*. Leuven: Louvain University Press, 2006.
———. "Im Schatten Des Äeneas: Paulus in Troas (APG 16, 8–10)". *Luke and His Readers*, P.W. van der Horst, ed. (Leuven: Peeters, 2004).
———. "Trustworthy Dreams? About Dreams and References to Scripture in 2 Maccabees 14–15, Josephus' *Antiquitates Judaicae* 11, 302–347 and in the New Testament." *Persuasion and Dissuasion in Early Christianity, Ancient Judaism and Hellenism*, P.W. van der Horst, ed. (Leuven: Peeters, 2003).
———. "Why Does Jesus Not Dream? Divine Communication in Luke-Acts." In *The Unity of Luke Acts*, Joseph Verheyden, ed. Bibliotheca Ephemeridum Theologicarum Lovaniensium Series (Leuven: Leuven University Press, 1999).
Kohler, Kaufmann and Isaac Broydé, "Azriel (Ezra) Ben Menahem (Ben Solomon)." (2002) Online: http://www.jewishencyclopedia.com.
Koulack, David. *To Catch a Dream, Explorations of Dreaming*. Albany: State University of New York Press, 1991.

Kunkel, Fritz. *Creation Continues*. Elizabeth Kunkel and Ruth Spafford Morris, ed. Waco, TX: Word Books, 1973.
LaBerge, Stephen. *Lucid Dreaming*. Los Angeles: Jeremy P. Tarcher, 1985. Online: http://www.home.no/lucid/lucid/LaBergeStephen_LucidDreaming.htm.
———. "Reply to Foulkes." Online: http://www.sawka.com/spiritwatch/replyto.htm.
"Lahore Ahmadiyya Movement in Islam." Online: http://www.aaiil.org.
Lancaster, D.J. "Bell's Interconnectedness Theorem." (1999) Online: http://www.exmormon.org./boards/honestboard/messages/4049.html.
Lange, Rense; Michael Schredl; James Houran. "What Precognitive Dreams Are Made of: The Nonlinear Dynamics of Tolerance of Ambiguity, Dream Recall, and Paranormal Belief." (2000) Online: http://www.goertzel.org/dynapsyc/2000/Precog%20Dreams.htm.
Laszlo, Ervin. "Is There A Purpose in Nature? How to Navigate between the Scylla of Mechanism and Charybdis of Teleology." (1998) Ivan M. Havel, ed. A talk given to Charles University and the Academy of Sciences of the Czech Republic. Online: http:www.cts.cuni.cz/conf98/Procee-x.htm.
———. "New Concepts of Matter, Life and Mind" Online: http://www.physlink.com/Education/essay_laszlo.cfm.
———. "Subtle Connections: Psi, Grof, Jung, and the Quantum Vacuum." (1996) Online: http://twm.co.nz/subconn_laszlo.html.
———. "Toward a Physical Foundation for PSI Phenomena," (1996) 1994 J.B. Rhine Lecture, delivered at the 37th Annual Convention of the American Parapsychological Association, Amsterdam. Online: http://www.goertzel.org/dynapsyc/1996/ervin.html.
Lee, Dan. "A Brief Review of the Psychological Literature on Dreaming. (1998) Online: http:lightmind.com/Impermanence/Library/texts/files/DanLee-001.txt
Leiser, Pinchas. "On Dreams and Reality." (2002) Online: http://www.MyJewishLearning.com.
Lesch, Ann. M. "Zionism and Its Impact." Online: http://www.wrmea.com/html/focus.htm.
Lester, Toby. "What Is the Koran?" (1999) Online: http://www.theatlantic.com/issues/99jan/koran/htm.
Lortie-Lussier, Monique and Lucie Côté, Julie Vachon. "The Consistency and Continuity Hypotheses, Revisited through the Dreams of Women at Two Periods of their Lives." *Dreaming*, Vol.10, No. 2 (2000) Online: http://www.asdreams.org/journal/articles/10-2lortie-lussier.htm.
Ludwig, Arnold M "Altered States of Consciousness." *Altered States of Consciousness*, Charles T. Tart, ed. New York: HarperSanFrancisco, Third Edition, 1990.
MacAuliffe, M.A. *The Sikh Religion; Its Gurus, Sacred Writings and Anthems*. Oxford: Clarendon Press, Vol. 1, 1990.
MacRuaidh, Antoin. "The Compilation of the Text of the Qur'an and the Sunni-Shia Dispute." Online: http://debate.org.uk/topics/theo/dispute.htm.
Mafundikwa, Saki. "Afrikan Alphabets" (2000) Online: http://www.ziva.org.zw/afrikan.htm.
Mahoney, Maria F. *The Meaning in Dreams and Dreaming, The Jungian Viewpoint*. Secaucus, N.J.: The Citadel Press, 1980.
Malamat, A. "A Forerunner of Biblical Prophecy." Miller, Hanson, and McBride, ed., *Ancient Israelite Religion*. Philadelphia: Fortress Press, 1987.

Bibliography

Malone, Martin J. "Aranda." Online: http://lucy.ukc.ac.uk/EthnoAtlas/Hmar/Cult_dir/Culture.7827.

Maloney, George A, ed. *Pilgrimage of the Heart, A Treasury of Eastern Christian Spirituality*. San Francisco: Harper & Row, 1983.

MarDock, Mary Anne. "A Look into the Lives of My Ancestors." (1998) Online: http: www.utexas.edu/courses.wilson.ant304/projects.projects98/mardockp/mardocdp.htm.

Marks, Tracy. "Iroquois Dreamwork and Spirituality." (1998) Online: http://www.geocities.com/tmartiac/yupanqui/iroquoisdreams.htm.

Matz, Terry. "St. John Bosco." (1996–2000) Catholic Online, Saints & Angels. Online: http://www.catholic.org.

Mascarenhas, Fr. Fio. "St. Ignatius's Rules." (2004–05) Online: http://www.holyspiritinteractive.net/columns/fiomascarenhas/scripturallyspeaking/19.asp.

McDonald, Mark Alan. "Ancient Mari (Tell Hariri)." *The History of the Ancient Near East Electronic Compendium*. (2005) Online: http:ancientneareast.tripod.com/Mari_Hariri.html.

———. "Ancient Sumer History, Important City-States." *The History of the Ancient Near East Electronic Compendium*. (2005) Online: http://ancientneareast.tripod.com/Sumer.html.

McGrath, J.I. "Maturidiyyah Theology, Maturidi, Advanced Information." Online: http://mb-soft.com/believe/txw/maturidi.htm.

McNamara, Patrick and Jensine Andresen, Joshua Arrowood, Glen Messer. "Counterfactual Cognitive Operations in Dreams." *Dreaming*, Vol. 12, No. 3 September 2002. Online: http://www.asdreams.org/journal/articles/12-3_mcnamara.htm.

Meier, Carl Alfred, M.D. *Healing Dream and Ritual*. Einsiedeln, Switzerland: Daimon Verlag, 1989.

———. *Jung's Analytical Psychology and Religion*. Carbondale, IL: Arcturus Paperbacks, 1977.

Marvin, Chris. "Abu Al-Nasr Al-Farabi." (1995–2000) Online: http://www.trincoll.edu/depts/phil/philo/phils/muslim/farabi.html.

Meaningful Life Center. "The Besht: Rabbi Israel Baal Shem Tov." (2003) Online: http://www.meaningfullife.com/spiritual/mystics/The_Besht.php.

"Meeting Place of the Divine Council" Online: http://www.thedivinecouncil.com/MeetingPlaceDivineCouncil.pdf.

Merton, Thomas. *Conjectures of a Guilty Bystander, Personal Reflections and Meditations on Contemporary Issues*. Garden City: Image Books, 1968.

Metareligion. "Telepathy." Online: http://www.meta-religion.com/Paranormale/Telepathy.htm.

Metzger, Bruce, ed. "Introduction to the Apocrypha." *Oxford Annotated Apocrypha, Revised Standard Version*. New York: Oxford University Press, 1965.

"Michel Foucault — biography." Online: http://foucault.info/foucault/biography.html.

Michman, Dan. "A Historical Look at Religious Zionism." (1999) Online: www.biu.as.il/Spokesman?Tolerance/michman.htm.

Miles, Jack. *God, A Biography*. New York: Vintage Press, 1996.

Miller, Patricia Cox. *Dreams in Late Antiquity, Studies in the Imagination of a Culture*. Princeton, New Jersey: Princeton University Press, 1994.

Miller, P.D. *The Religion of Ancient Israel*. Louisville: Westminster John Knox Press, 2000.

Mindel, Nissan. "Rav Chisda."(2006) Online: http://www.chabad.org./library/article.asp?AID=112296.

Mishlove, Jeffrey, Ph.D. "Consciousness and Quantum Reality with Nick Herbert, Ph.D." (1998) An interview on *Thinking Allowed*. Online: http://twm.co.nz/Herbert.htm.

———. "ESP and Ceremonial Magic." (2006) Online: http://jeff.zaadz.com/blog/tags/lynn+thorndike.

———. "Medieval Explorations of Consciousness, Maimonides." Online: http://www.williamjames.com/History/MEDIEVAL.htm.

———. "Physics and Consciousness with Fred Alan Wolf, Ph.D." (1995-1999) An interview on *Thinking Allowed*. Online: http://twm.co.nz/wolf.html.

Monroe, Robert A. *Journeys out of the Body*. Garden City, NY: Anchor Books, 1971.

Montgomery, James A. "The Religion of Flavius Josephus." *Jewish Quarterly Review XI*, 1920-1921:277-305. Online: http://www.christianorgins.com/josephusreligion.html.

Moorcroft, William H. "Dream Sequences." (1998) Online: http://www.americanscientist.org/template/BookReviewTypeDetail/assetid/28658;jsessionid=baadhIyKmTs_u8

Moss, Robert. "Dreaming like an Egyptian" (2002) Online: http://www.mossdreams.com/egyptian.htm.

Murrell, Beatrix. "The Imaginal within the Cosmos: Natural Jesus (6): The Soul, Scientists & the Psi World." Online: http://www.bizcharts.com/stoa_del_sol/imaginal/imaginal_nj6.html.

Murzi, Mauro. "Rudolf Carnap." (2003) The Internet Encyclopedia of Philosophy. Online: http://www.iep.utm.edu/c/carnap.htm.

MyJewishLearning.com. "About Jewish Texts: Kitvei Kodesh." Online: http://www.myjewishlearning.com/texts/about_jewish_texts/TO_Sacred_texts120_Prn.htm.

———. "About Jewish Texts: Overview: Connections Through the Generations." Online: http://www.MyJewishLearning.com/texts/about_jewish_texts/TO_Connections200_Prn.htm.

———. "Halakhah: Jewish Legal Texts." (2002) Online: http://www.MyJewishLearning.com.

———. "Medieval Jewish History." (2002) Online: http://www.MyJewishLearning.com.

———. "Overview: About Talmud." Online: http://ww.myjewishlearning.com/texts/talmud/TO_AboutTalmud_3950Prn.htm.

———. "Overview: Early Jewish Conceptions of God." (2002) Online: http://www.MyJewishLearning.com.

———. "Overview: Gemara." Online: http://www.myjewishlearning.com/texts/Talmud/Gemara_Prn.htm.

———. "Overview: Jewish Conceptions of God in the Middle Ages." (2002) Online: http://www.MyJewishLearning.com.

———. "Overview: Kabbalah and Hasidism." (2002) Online: http://www.MyJewishLearning.com.

———. "Overview: Mysticism in Modern Times." (2002) Online: http://www.MyJewishLearning.com.

———. "Overview: the Origins of Jewish Mysticism." (2002) Online: http://www.MyJewishLearning.com.

———. "Talmud. Primer: Talmud." Online: http://www.myjewishlearning.com/texts/talmud/Primer_Talmud_3940_Prn.htm.

Mystica. "Precognition." Online: http://www.themystica.com/mystica/articles/p/precognition.html.

Bibliography

National Center for Policy Analysis. "Some Surprises in Religious Survey." (2002) Online: http://www.ncpa.org/iss/soc/2002/pd091902c.html.
National Muslim Student Association of the USA and Canada. "The Rightly-Guided Caliphs." Online: http://www.usc.edu/dept/MSA/politics/firstfourcaliphs.html.
Neihardt, John. *Black Elk Speaks*. Lincoln, NE: University of Nebraska Press, 1979.
Neimark, Jill. "Sledding at the Speed of Light." (2002) Online: http://www.science-spirit.org/articles/Articledetail.cfm?article_ID=286.
Neumann, Erich, Ph.D. *Art and the Creative Unconscious*. Ralph Manheim, trans. Princeton, NJ: Princeton University Press, 1974.
———. *Depth Psychology and a New Ethic*. Eugene Rolfe, trans. New York: Harper Torchbooks, 1973.
———. *The Origins and History of Consciousness*. R.F.C. Hull, trans. Princeton: Princeton University Press, 1973.
Neusner, Jacob. "Talmud. Talmudic Thinking. Monotheism and the sanctification of the trivial." (1998) Online: http://www.myjewishlearning.com/texts/talmud/Gemarra/TalmudicThinking_Prn.ht.
Nicoll, Maurice. *The New Man, An Interpretation of Some Parables and Miracles of Christ*. New York: Penguin Books, 1976.
Nietzsche, Friedrich. "Between Birds of Prey," found in C.G. Jung, "Symbols of Transformation" (1952), R.F.C. Hull, trans. The *Collected Works of C.G. Jung*, Volume 5, Princeton, N.J.: Princeton University Press, 1969. para. 459.
———. *The Birth of Tragedy and The Genealogy of Morals*. Francis Golffing, trans. Garden City, New York: Doubleday & Company, 1956.
———. *The Will to Power*. Walter Kaufmann and R.J. Hollingdale, trans., Walter Kaufmann, ed. New York: Random House (Vintage Books), 1967.
Nisbet, Matt. "The Best Case for ESP?" (2000) Online: http://www.esicop.org/genx/ganzfeld/
Noegel, Scott B. Review of Ruth Fidler, "Dreams Speak Falsely"? Dream Theophanies in the Bible: Their Place in Ancient Israelite Faith and Tradition." Journal of Hebrew Scriptures — Volume 6 (2006) Online: http://www.arts.ualberta.ca?JHS/reviews/review224.htm..
———. "Frances Flannery-Dailey, *Dreamers, Scribes, and Priests: Jewish Dreams in the Hellenistic and Roman Eras*." Journal of Hebrew Scriptures — Volume 5 (2004–2005) — Review. Online: http://www.arts.ualberta.ca/JHS/reviews/review202.htm.
Noffsinger, John. "Julian of Norwich and the Enigma of Divine Revelation." (1992) Spirituality *Today*, Spring, 1992, Vol. 44, No.1. Online: http://www.spiritualitytoday.org/spir2day/92441noffsinger.html.
O'Connor, J. J. and E.P . Robertson, "Gottfried Wilhelm von Leibniz." (1998) Online: http://www-history.mcs.st-andrews.ac.uk?Mathematicians/Leibniz.html.
———. "Sir Isaac Newton." (2000) Online: http://www-history.mcs.st-andrews.ac.uk?Mathematicians/Newton.html.
———. "Thomas Hobbes." (2002) Online: http://www-history.mcs.st-andrews.ac.uk/Mathematicians/Hobbes.html.
———. "Wolfgang Ernst Pauli." (2003) Online: http://www-gap.dcs.st-and.ac.uk/~history/Mathematicians/Pauli.html.
Odenheimer, Micha. "Challenging the Master: Moshe Idel's Critique of Gershom Scholem." *Jewish Action, the Magazine of the Orthodox Union*. Summer, 1990 (50:3). Online: http://www.MyJewishLearning.com.

O'Neal, Rev. Norman. "The Life of St. Ignatius Loyola." (2004) Online: http://www.luc.edu/jesuit/ignatius.bio.html.
Oppenheim, A. Leo. *The Interpretation of Dreams in the Ancient Near East*. Philadelphia: The American Philosophical Society, Vol. 46:3, (1956).
Oswald, Roy M. and Otto Kroeger. *Personality Type and Religious Leadership*. Washington, D.C.: The Alban Institute, 1988.
Otto, Rudolf. *The Idea of the Holy*. John W. Harvey, trans. New York: Oxford University Press, 1967.
Padgett, Doug. "Anthropology of Religion." Online: http://www.indiana.edu/~wanthro/religion.htm.
Pagels, Elaine. *The Gnostic Gospels*. New York: Vintage Books, 1981.
Parapsychological Association. "Who is Daryl J. Bem?" (1997–2005) Online: http://www.parapsych.org/members/d_bem.html.
———. "Who is Gertrude Schmeidler?" (1997–2005) Online: http://www.parapsych.org/members/g_schmeidler.html.
Park, Willard Z. *Shamanism in Western North America*. Evanston and Chicago: Northwestern University Studies in the Social Sciences 2, 1938.
Parry, Rabbi Aaron. "Ask the Rabbi: The Talmud & dreams." (2000) Online: http://www.virtualjerusalem.com/judaism/judaism_article.php?article_id=1451.
Pauli, Wolfgang. "The Influence of Archetypal Ideas on the Scientific Theories of Kepler" in *Atom and Archetype: The Pauli/Jung Letters, 1932–58*, ed. by C.A. Meier, Princeton, N.J.: Princeton University Press, 2001.
Peers, E. Allison, trans. and ed. *Dark Night of the Soul*. Garden City, New York: Image Books, 1959.
———. *St. Teresa's Complete Works*, Volume I and II. London: New Ark Library, 1963.
Pew Forum on Religion & Public Life. (2008) Online: http://religions.pewforum.org/reports.
Philips, Abu Ameenah Bilal, "Dream Interpretation." (1996) Online: http://www.bilalphilips.com/books/dream01f.htm.
Plato. *Plato's Theory of Knowledge*. Translated and commentary by Francis M. Cornford. New York: The Library of Liberal Arts (Bobbs-Merrill), 1957.
Pohlsander, Hans A. "Constantine I (306–337 A.D.)" (2004) Online: http://www.roman-emperors.org/conniei.htm.
Pollen, J. H. "St. Ignatius Loyola." (2002) Transcribed by Marie Jutras for *The Catholic Encyclopedia, Volume VII* (1910) Online: http://www.newadvent.org/cathen/07639c.htm.
Pratt, David. "David Bohm and the Implicate Order." (1993) Online: http://www.theosophy-nw.org/theosnw/science/prat-boh.htm.
Pusey, Edward B., D. D., ed. *The Confessions of Saint Augustine*. London: Collier Books, 1969.
Radin, Dean, Ph.D. "Can Science Seek the Soul?" A transcript from show 113 of *Closer to the Truth*. Online: http://www.closertotruth.com/topics/mindbrain,113/113transcript.html.
Radin, Paul. *The Trickster, A Study in American Indian Mythology*. New York: Schocken Books, 1976.
Rauschenbusch, Walter. *The Righteousness of the Kingdom*. Max L. Stackhouse, ed. Nashville, TN: Abingdon Press, 1968.

Reed, Henry, Ph.D. *Getting Help from Your Dreams.* Virginia Beach, VA.: Inner Vision, 1989.
———, ed. *Sundance Community Dream Journal.* Volume Two, Number 2. Virginia Beach, VA.: A.R.E. Press, 1978.
Reeves, David. "The Roots of Hypnosis." Online: http://www.mindtee.co.uk/hyp-art/roots.html.
Revonsuo, Antti. "The Reinterpretation of Dreams: An Evolutionary Hypothesis of the Function of Dreaming." In *Behavior and Brain Sciences*, Vol. 6 (2000) Online: ftp://ftp.princeton.edu/pub/harnad/BBS/WWW/bbs.revonsuo.html.
Richards, Mary Caroline. *Centering in Pottery, Poetry and the Person.* Middletown, Conn.: Wesleyan University Press, 1964.
Riginos, Alice Swift. *Platonica: The Anecdotes Concerning the Life and Writings of Plato.* Leiden: E. J. Brill, 1976.
Rilke, Rainer Maria. *Rilke's Book of Hours, Love Poems to God.* Anita Burrows and Joanna Macy, trans. New York: Riverhead Books, 1996.
Roberts, J.J. "Does God Lie? Divine Deceit as a Theological Problem in Israelite Prophetic Literature." (1986) Congress Volume, Jerusalem. J.A. Emerton, ed. (Leiden: E.J. Brill, 1988).
Robinson, B.A. "Comparing U.S. Religious Beliefs with Other 'Christian Countries.'" (2005) Online: http://www.religioustolerance.org/rel_comp.htm.
———. "Religious Identification in the U.S." (2005) Ontario Consultants on Religious Tolerance. Online: http://www.religioustolerance.org/chr_prac2.htm.
Robinson, George. "Early Kabbalah and the Hasidei Ashkenaz." (2002) Online: http://www.MyJewishLearning.com and taken from his book, *Essential Judaism.* New York: Atria Books, 2000.
———. "Gershom Scholem and the Study of Mysticism." (2002) Online: http://www.MyJewishLearning.com.
———. "Hasidic Mysticism." (2002) Online: http://www.MyJewishLearning.com.
———. "Kabbalah in Spain." (2002) Online: http://www.MyJewishLearning.com.
———. "Isaac Luria and Kabbalah in Safed." (2000) Online: http://www.MyJewishLearning.com.
———. "The Sefirot." (2002) Online: http://www.MyJewishLearning.com and taken from his book, *Essential Judaism.* New York: Atria Books, 2000.
———. "The Zohar." (2002) Online: http://www.MyJewishLearning.com and taken from his book, *Essential Judaism.* New York: Atria Books, 2000.
Robinson, John C, Ph.D. *But Where Is God? Psychotherapy and the Religious Search.* New York: Troitsa Books. 1999.
———. *Ordinary Enlightenment, Experiencing God's Presence in Everyday Life.* Unity Village, Missouri: Unity House, 2000.
Robinson. Paschal. "St. Francis of Assisi." (2002) Online: http://www.newadvent.org/cathen/06221a.htm.
Rollins, Wayne G. *Jung and the Bible.* Atlanta: John Knox Press, 1983.
Rolston, Holmes III. *Genes, Genesis and God.* Cambridge: Cambridge University Press, 1999.
———. *Science and Religion: A Critical Survey.* New York: Random House, 1987.
Roob, Alexander. *Alchemy & Mysticism.* New York: Taschen, 2001.

Rose, Daniel L., Psy.D. Review of "Children's Dreaming and the Development of Consciousness." by David Foulkes (2003) Online: http://mentalhelp.net/poc/view_doc.php?id=1623&type=book&cn=28.
Rosenthal, Franz. Trans. *The Muqaddimah*, Princeton: Princeton University Press, 1967.
Rosicrucian Archive. "Rosicrucianism." (1998) Online: http://www.cresite.org/printrosicruciansim.htm.
Rossi, Ernest Lawrence, Ph.D. *Dreams & the Growth of Personality, Expanding Awareness in Psychotherapy.* New York: Brunner/Mazel, 1985.
Rouselle, Robert. "Women's Dreams in Ancient Greece." *The Journal of Psychohistory*, V.26, N. 2, Fall 1998. Online: http://www.geocities.com/kidhistory/ja/womens.htm?200627.
Russell, Bertrand. *A History of Western Philosophy and Its Connection with Political and Social Circumstances from the Earliest Times to the Present Day.* New York: Simon and Schuster, 1965.
Russo, Richard, ed. *Dreams are Wiser Than Men.* Berkeley, CA.: North Atlantic Books, 1987.
Sahib, Maulana Aftab-ud-Din ahmad, "Phenomenon of Revelation." Online:http://www.aaiil.org. Sahib, Naseer Ahmad Faruqui. "Dreams." (1999) Online: http://www.aaiil.org.
Sahih Bukhari, Volume 9, Book 87, "Interpretation of Dreams." Online: http://www.usc.edu/dept?MSA/fundamentals/hadithsunnah/bukhari/087.sbt.html.
Saltet, Louis. "St. Jerome." (2005) Transcribed by Sean Hyland. Online: http://www.newadvent.org/cathen/08341a.htm.
Sanford, John A. *Dreams, God's Forgotten Language.* Philadelphia: J.B. Lippincott Company, 1968.
———. *Dreams and Healing, A Succinct and Lively Interpretation of Dreams.* New York/Mahwah, N.J.: Paulist Press, 1978.
———. *Healing and Wholeness.* New York/Mahwah, N.J.: Paulist Press, 1977.
———. *Mystical Christianity, A Psychological Commentary on the Gospel of John.* New York: Crossroad Publishing Company, 1996.
———. *The Man Who Wrestled With God, A Study of Individuation (Personal Growth Toward Wholeness)Based on Four Bible Stories.* King of Prussia, PA: Religious Publishing Co., 1974.
———. *The Kingdom Within, A Study of the Inner Meaning of Jesus' Sayings.* Philadelphia: J. B. Lippincott Company, 1970.
Schmidt, Andreas. "Martin Buber." (2000) Online: http://www.emanuelnyc.org/bulletin/archive/34.html.
Schmitt, Sarah. "Claude Levi-Strauss." (1999) Online: http://www.mnsu.edu/emuseum/information/biography/klmno/levi-strauss_claude.html.
Schniter, Eric. "The Jivaro and Shuar of the NorthWest Amazon: Who are they and what is their status?" Online: http://www.uweb.ucsb.edu/~eschniter/AMAZONIA/EJ.HTM.
Schoenberg, Shira. "Isaac Ben Solomon Luria." (2004) Online: http://www.us-israel.org/jsource/biography/Lauria.html.
Schwarz, Patricia. "The Official String Theory Web Site." Online: http://superstringtheory.com/basics/basic.html.
Senfelder, Leopold. "Theophrastus Paracelsus." (2001) Transcribed by Thomas J. Bress. Online: http://www.newadvent.org/cathen/11468a.htm.
Shamoun, Sam. "Muhammad's Alleged Night Journey to the Jerusalem Temple." (2002) Online: http://answering-islam.org.uk/Shamoun/nightjourney.htm.

Sharpe Meg. "Dream and Group, The Use of Dreams in Group Analysis, 'Touching Intangibles'. This paper is based on a lecture originally given to students on the London Introductory Course in Group Analysis. Online: http://www.funzionegamma.edu/magazine/2_engl_html/sharpe_ing.htm.

Shaw, Nanette. "Graduate Center Survey of Religion in America Complements U.S. Census." (2001) The Graduate Center of the City University of New York. Online: http://www.gc.cuny.edu?press_information/current_releases/october_2001_aris.htm.

Sheleg, Yair. "A Contemporary Spin on Judaism." (2004) Online: http://www.haaretzdaily.com

Shulman, David, translator. "10 Principles of the Besht." (2002) Online: http://www.kabbalaonline.org/\Chasidism\bescht/10_Principles_of_the_Besht.asp.

Shulman, David and Guy G. Stroumsa, ed. *Dream Cultures, Explorations in the Comparative History of Dreaming.* New York: Oxford University Press, 1999.

Siren, Christopher B. "Canaanite/Ugaritic Mythology FAQ, ver. 1.2." (1999) Online: http://home.comcast.net/~chris.s/canaanite-faq.html.

———. "Hittite/Hurrian Mythology REF 1.2" (1998) Online: http://home.comcast.net/~chris.s./hittite-ref.html.

Smith, H. Shelton, Robert T. Handy and Lefferts A. Loetscher. *American Christianity, An Historical Interpretation with Representative Documents, Volume II: 1820–1960.* New York: Charles Scribner's Sons, 1963.

Smith, Wilfred Cantwell. *The Meaning and End of Religion.* Minneapolis, MN: Fortress Press, 1991.

"Social Function of Dreams." Online: http://www.macalester.edu/~psych/whathap/UBNRP/dreaming/Functions6.html.

Sophocles. Online: http://www.island-of-freedom.com/SOPHOCLE.HTM.

Souvay, Charles. "Interpretation of Dreams," transcribed by Listya Sari Diyah. Online: www.newadvent.org/cathen/05154a.htm.

Spencer, Lloyd. "Horkheimer, Max." *The Icon Dictionary of Postmodern Thought.* Stuart Sim, ed. Cambridge: Icon, 1998. Online: http://www.tasc.as.uk/depart/media/staff/ls/Modules/Theory/Horkheimer.htm.

Spiegelman, J. Marvin. *The Divine WABA (Within, Among, Between, Around), A Jungian Exploration of Spiritual Paths.* Berwick, ME: Nicolas-Hays, Inc., 2003.

Starbuck, Scott R.A. *Court Oracles in the Psalms, The So-Called Royal Psalms in Their Ancient Near Eastern Context.* Atlanta, GA: Society of Biblical Literature Dissertation Studies, 1999.

———. "Like Dreamers Lying in Wait, We Lament: A New Reading of Psalm 126," *Koinonia* 1.2 (1989) 128–14.

States, Bert O. "Dream Bizarreness and Inner Thought." *Dreaming,* Vol. 10, No.4 (2000) Online: http://www.asdreams.org/journal/articles/10-4_states.htm.

Streck, M. *Assurbanipal und die letzten assyrischen Könige bis zum Untergang Niniveh's,* 3 vols (Leipzig: Hinrich, 1916) 2.1181ns.

Stretton, Kris. "Is e.s.p. real?" Online: http://www.viewzone.com/ESPl.html.

Sultzman, Lee. "Delaware History." (2000) Online: http://www.tolatsga.org/dela.html.

Tara's World of Islam. "Dreams." Online: http://www.angelfire.com/mo2/scarves/dreams.html.

Tart, Charles T. *Altered States of Consciousness.* 3rd edition New York: HarperSanFrancisco, 1990.

———. "Enlightenment and Spiritual Growth: Reflections from the Bottom Up." (2003) *Subtle Energies & Energy Medicine*, Vol.14 (1).
Taylor, Jeremy. *Dream Work, Techniques for Discovering the Creative Power in Dreams.* New York/Mahwah, N.J.: Paulist Press, 1983.
Telushkin, Joseph. "Hasidim and Mitnagdim." (2002) *The Most Important Things to Know About the Jewish Religion, Its People and Its History.* NY: William Morrow and Co., 1991 Online: http://www.jewishvirtuallibrary.org.
The Barna Group. "Surveys Show Pastors Claim Congregants Are Deeply Committed to God But Congregants Deny It!" (2006) Online: http://www.barna.org/FlexPage.aspx?Page=BarnaUpdateNarrow&BarnaUpdateID=206.
"The Liberian Post." (2001-2003) Online: http://liberian.tripod.com/Post8.html.
"The Life of Flavius Josephus." Online: http://ccel.org/j/josephus/works/autiobiog.htm.
"The Meeting Place of the Divine Council." Online: http://www.thedivinecouncil.com/MeetingPlaceDivineCouncil.pdf.
Thorndike, Lynn. *The History of Magic and Experimental Science, Vol. 5.* New York: Columbia University Press, 1938.
Thilly, Frank. *A History of Philosophy.* Third edition, revised by Ledger Wood. New York: Holt, Rinehart and Winston, 1964.
Tillich, Paul. *Systematic Theology.* Evanston, IL: The University of Chicago Press, Harper & Row, Publishers, 1963.
———. *The Courage To Be.* New Haven, Conn.: Yale University Press, 1966.
Tolaas, Jon and Montague Ullman. "Extrasensory Communication and Dreams." *Handbook of Dreams — Research, Theories and Applications.* Benjamin B. Wolman, ed. New York: Van Nostrand Reinhold Company, 1979. Online: http://siivola.org/monte/papers_grouped/copyrighted/Parapsychology_&_Psi/Extrasensory_Communication_and_Dreams.htm.
Torrey, E. Fuller, M.D. *Surviving Schizophrenia.* 3rd edition New York: HarperPerennial, 1995.
Turner, William. "Avicenna." (2002) Transcribed by Geoffry K. Mondello, Amy M. Mondello, and Stephen St. Damian Mondello. Online: http://www.newadvent.org/cathen/02157a.htm.
———. "John Scotus Eriugena." (2002) Transcribed by Diane E. Dubrule. Online: http://www.newadvent.org.
Ulanov, Ann and Barry Ulanov. *Religion and the Unconscious.* Philadelphia: The Westminster Press, 1975.
Ullman, Montague, M.D. "Dreams as Exceptional Human Experiences." Lecture presented at Exceptional Human Experiences Conference held in New York City, June 13, 1993. Online: http://www.aspr.com/ullm.htm.
———. "Psychical Research: A Personal Perspective."(1996) *The Psi Researcher*, August, 1996. Online: http://siivola.org/monte/papers_grouped/copyrighted/Parapsychology_&_Psi/Psychical Research.htm.
———. "The Experiential Dream Group: Its Application in the Training of Therapists." *Dreaming,* Vol. 4, No. 4 (1994) Online: http://www.asdreams.org/journal/articles/4-4_ullman.htm.
———, and Stanley S. Krippner, Ph.D.; Robert L. Van de Castle, Ph.D.; Mena E. Potts, Ph.D.; and Dominic J. Potts, Esq., J.D. "Maimonides ESP Dream Laboratory Experiments: Evaluating the Assault of the Calumniators." Abstract from lecture at the Association

Bibliography

for the Study of Dreams Conference, 2000 Online: http://www.fortunecity.com/westwood/vivienne/598/asd-17/abstracts/ullman_17.htm.

———, and Nan Zimmerman. *Working With Dreams*. New York: Laurel/Eleanor Friede Book, Dell Publishing Co, 1979.

Underhill, Evelyn. *Mysticism, A Study in the Nature and Development of Man's Spiritual Consciousness*. New York: E.P. Dutton & Co., 1961.

———. *The Life of the Spirit and the Life of Today*. Harrisburg, PA: Morehouse Publishing, 1994.

———. *The Spiritual Life*. Harrisburg, PA: Morehouse Publishing, 1994.

Understanding Islam. "Position of Dreams." (1999) Online: http://www.Understanding-Islam.com/related/text.asp?type=question&qid=58.

Van de Castle, Robert L., Ph.D. *Our Dreaming Mind*. New York: Ballantine Books, 1994.

Van Der Post, Laurens. *Jung and the Story of Our Time*. New York: Pantheon Books, 1975.

Van Henten, Jan Willem. "The Two Dreams at the end of Book 17 of Josephus' *Antiquities*." (2002) Online: http://josephus.yorku.ca/pdf/henten2002.pdf.

Varvoglis, Mario. "Ganzeld and RNG Research: A Memorial to Charles Honorton." Online: http:// www.psiexplorer.com/honorton2.htm.

Varon, Tz. "Misnato shel Harav Kook." (World Zionist Organization, Dept. of Torah Education and Culture in the Diaspora). Dan Michman, "A Historical Look at Religious Zionism." (1999) Online: http://www.biu.as.il/Spokesman?Tolerance/michman.htm.

Viereck, George Sylvester. "What Life Means to Einstein: An Interview by George Sylvester Viereck." *Saturday Evening Post*, October 26, 1929.

von Franz, Marie-Louise. *Alchemical Active Imagination*. Irving, TX: Spring Publications, 1979.

———. *Man and His Symbols*. C.G. Jung, ed. New York: Dell Publishing Company, 1970.

———. *On Divination and Synchronicity, The Psychology of Meaningful Chance*. Toronto: Inner City Books, 1980.

———. *On Dreams & Death, A Jungian Interpretation*. Emmanuel Xipolitas Kennedy and Vernon Brooks, trans. Boston: Shambhala, 1987.

Ward, Keith. *Religion and Revelation*. New York: Oxford University Press, 1994.

———. *God, Chance & Necessity*. Oxford: Oneworld Publications, 2001.

Ware, Corinne. *Discover Your Spiritual Type, A Guide to Individual and Congregational Growth*. Washington, D.C.: The Alban Institute, 1995.

Wei, Henry. *The Guiding Light of Lao Tzu*. Wheaton, Illinois: The Theosophical Publishing House, 1982.

West, Katherine Lee. *Crystallizing Children's Dreams*. Lake Oswego, Oregon: Amata Graphics, 1978.

Westar Institute. "David Friedrich Strauss." (1991) Online: http://www.westarinstitute.org/Periodicals/4R_Articles/Stauss/strauss.html.

Wheeler, J.A. and W.H. Zurek. "Law without Law," ed., *Quantum Theory and Measurement*, Princeton: Princeton University Press, 1983.

Whitaker, Andrew. "John Stewart Bell." (2002) Online: http://www-groups.dcs.st-and.ac.uk/~history.Mathematicians/Bell_John.html.

Whitmont, Edward C. *The Symbolic Quest, Basic Concepts of Analytical Psychology*. New York: G.P. Putnam's Sons for the C. G. Jung Foundation for Analytical Psychology, 1969.

Bibliography 141

White, Gregory L. and Laurel Taytroe. "Personal Problem-Solving Using Dream Incubation: Dreaming, Relaxation, or Waking Cognition?" *Dreaming*, Vol. 13 (4), 2003. Online: http://www.asdreams.org/journal/articles/13-4_white_taytroe.htm.
Whitmont, Edward C. and Sylvia Brinton Perera. *Dreams, A Portal to the Source*. New York: Routledge, 1989.
"Why do we dream?" Scientific America.com. (June 13, 2004) in the section entitled, "Ask the Experts: Biology."
Wicks, Robert. "Arthur Schopenhauer." (2003) The Stanford Encyclopedia of Philosophy, Edward N. Zalta, ed. Online: http://plato.stanford.edu/archives/sum2003/entries. schopenhauer/
Wikipedia. "Al-Ghazali" (2006) Online: http://en.wikipedia.org/wiki/Al-Ghazali.
———. "Artemidorus" (2005) Online: http://en.wikipedia.org/wiki/Artemidorus.
———. "Bell's Theorem." (2005) Online: http://en.wikipedia.org/wiki/Bell's_theorem.
———. "Eusebius of Caesarea." (2005) Online: http://en.wikipedia.org/wiki?Eusebius_of _Caesarea.
———. "Imam Abu Hanifa." Online: http://www.fact-index.com/i/im/imam_abu_hanifa .html.
———. "Jerusalem Talmud." (2006) Online: http://en.wikipedia.org/wiki/Jerusalem _Talmud.
———. "Mu'tazili." (2004) Online: http://en.wikipedia.org/wiki/Mutazilite.
———. "Labor Zionism." (2004) Online: http://en.wikipedia.org/wiki/LaborZionism.
———. "Revisionist Zionism." (2004) Online: http://en.wikipedia.org/wiki/RevisionistZionism.
———. "Samson Raphael Hirsch." Online: http://www.fact-index.com/s/sa/samson _raphael_hirsch.html.
———. "Timeline of Zionism in the Modern Era." (2004) Online: http://en.wikipedia.org.
———. "William II of England." (2006) Online: http://en.wikipedia.org/wiki/William_II _of_England.
———. "Zionism." (2004) Online: http://en.wikipedia.org/wiki/Zionism.
Wildman, Wesley. "Rudolf Karl Bultmann." (1994–2002) Online: http://people.bu.edu /wwildman/WeirdWildWeb/courses/mwt/dictionary/mwt_themes_760_bultmann. htm.
Wilkerson, Richard Catlett. "Dream Library: Dream Science." Online: http://www .dreamgate.com/dream/library/idx_science.htm.
———. "Dream Science and Dreamwork: Friends or Foe?" (1998) Dream Gate Publishing. Online: http://www.dreamgate.com/dream/articles_rcw/ed5-7drm_science.htm.
Williams, John Alden, ed. *Islam*. New York: George Braziller, Inc., 1961.
Wiseman, Anne Sayre. *Nightmare Help, A Guide for Parents and Teachers*. Berkeley, CA.: Ten Speed Press, 1989.
Wolf, Fred Alan, Ph.D. "A Conversation with Fred Alan Wolf." (2001) An interview by Guy Spiro. *The Monthly Aspectarian*. Online: http://www.lightworks. com?MonthlyAspectarian/2001/May/Conversation%20.htm.
———. "Global Awareness" An interview by Charlotte Clark on WOKR. Online: http: //www.ethoschannel.com/personalgrowth/wolf/science.html.
———. "Identity, Consciousness and the Soul." An interview by Charlotte Clark on WOKR. Online: http://www.ethoschannel.com/personalgrowth/wolf.dreaming.html.
———. "Physics and Consciousness," an abridged abstract from *Thinking Allowed*. Online: http://twm.co.nz/wolf.html.

"Wolfgang Ernst Pauli." Online: http://www-gap.dcs.st-and.ac.uk/~history/Mathematicians/Pauli.html.

Zeller, Max. *The Dream~The Vision of the Night*. Janet Dallett, ed. Los Angeles: The Analytical Psychology Club of Los Angeles and the C.G. Jung Institute of Los Angeles, 1975.

Zimmer, Heinrich. *The King and the Corpse, Tales of the Soul's Conquest of Evil*. Joseph Campbell, ed. Princeton, N.J.: Princeton University Press, 1973.

Subject/Name Index

A

Aaron, 54
'Abdel Muttalib, 52
Abelard, 103n
Abim'elech, 20
Aborigines, 69
Abram (Abraham), 15, 16, 17, 20–21, 52, 54
Achuar, 67n, 67, 169n
Acts (Book of), 34, 35, 36–37, 93n, 117
Adam, 52, 54
Adler, Alfred, 187n
Africa, 53, 63–64, 158n
Aguaruna, 169n
Akkadian, 2, 3, 4
Al-Akili, 59
Al-Bukhari, 137n
Al-Buraq, 54
Al-Ghazali, Abu Hamid, 52, 57, 120n
Al-Nasai, 137n
Al-Tirmidhi, 137n
Albertus Magnus, 42, 130n
Albright, Carol Rausch, 249n
Alchemy, 43
Alexander the Great, 9
Ali (Caliph), 133n
Almoli, Rabbi Solomon, 77n
Aisha, 116
Allah, 54–55, 57, 127n, 141n
Allegory, 52
Allport, Gordon, 187n
Ambrose, 38
American Religious Identification Survey, 2n
Aminah, 53
Amondson, Christian, x
Amorites, 18n, 15

'Anan, 70n, 40
Ananias, 37
Ancient Near East, 2–4, 22n, 16, 60n, 66n
Angel(s), 17, 18, 24, 61n, 35, 36, 37, 41, 42, 45, 53–54, 59, 125n, 115, 117
Another Perspective, 99–109
Anselm (Archbishop of Canterbury), 103n
Anthropology, 72, 83, 86, 90, 217n, 218n
Antipater, 51n
Antrobus, John S., 79, 192n
Anwandter, Rosa, 167n
Apache, 69
Appendix A, 111–13
Appendix B, 114–17
Apocalyptic Literature, 24, 73n, 74n
Apollo, 11
Apologists (Christian), 38
Aquinas, Thomas, 40–41, 42, 104n, 58
'Arabi, ibn, 57, 58, 146n
Aramaic, 10, 72n
Aranda People, 69
Araucanos People, 66
Arendt, Hannah, 185n
Arieti, Silvano, xxiii
Aristotle, 9, 10, 47n, 48n, 178n
Artemidorus, 9
Ark of Covenant, 18, 20, 75n
Aserinsky, Eugene, 78
Ashanti People, 64
Ashbrook, James B., 249n
Asher, Jacob ben, 83n
Asia, 37, 64–65
Asia Minor, 7, 10
Asibikaashi (Spider Woman), 65
Asklepian Temple, 10
Assurbanipal, King, 63n

Subject Index

Assyria, 4, 6, 63n
Atchity, Kenneth, 192n
Athanasius, 38
Augustine, 38, 39, 259n
Austin, J. J., 186n
Australia, 69
Austria, 185n
Ayer, Alfred, 186n
Azeez, Imam M. A., ix

B

Babel (Tower of), 62n
Babuya, Muhammad ibn, 138n
Babylon, 4, 6–7, 51n, 26, 28, 62n 67n, 82n, 88n
Bakr, Abu, 133n, 135n
Balaam, 18, 27, 114
Bambara, 64
Bandstra, Barry L., 39n, 61n, 62n, 69n, 72n, 73n, 74n, 92n
Bantu, 63
Barasch, Marc Ian, 165n
Barna, George, xvii, 4n
Barrett, Deidre, 199n
Barrows, Anita, 182n
Barth, Karl, 117n
Bassa Vah, 158n
Bassetti, Claudio, 80
Basil the Great, 38
Bear Dance, 69
Beauchamp, Betty Ann, ix
Beggiora, Stefano, 160n
Bell, John Stewart, 84–85, 228n, 229n, 230n
Bella Coola, 69
Bem, Daryl J., 212n
Berakhot, 26–28, 88n
Bergson, Henri, 74–75, 184n
Bergstrom, Peter and Vicki, ix
Berkeley, George, 180n
Bernard of Clairvaux, 103n, 106n
Bethel, 62n
Bhutan, 64, 157n
Bible/Scripture, Christian, 10, 24n, 39n, 57n, 62n, 70n, 75n, 34, 35, 39, 40, 44, 45, 46, 101n, 102n, 117n, 119n, 115, 117
Hebrew, 3, 4, 18n, 20n, 21n, 39n, 15, 16, 17, 20, 21, 22, 24, 25, 28, 57n, 70n, 78n, 89n, 35, 36, 101n, 102, 114, 117
Birgitta of Sweden, 106n
Bischof, Matthias, 80
Black Elk, 62n
Blackfoot, 69
Blagrove, Mark, 199n
Blake, William, 260n
Bluestone, Sarvananda, 107n, 65, 156n, 158n, 162n, 174n
Boghazkeui, 7
Bohm, David, 87, 228n, 235n
Borneo, 63
Bosco, St. John, 45, 116n
Bosnack, Robert, 199n
Bosnia/Herzegovina, 39
Boss, Medard, 187n
Brain, xxii, xxiii, 8, 158n, 80, 88, 89, 101, 105, 249n
Brazil, 66
Buber, Martin, 7n, 250n, 111, 112–13, 266n, 272n
Buddhism, xx, 159n, 74, 77,
Bukhari, 56, 128n, 141n, 116
Bukele, Momolu Duwalu, 158n
Bulawayo, 63
Bulkeley, Kelly, ix, xii, 147n, 152n, 154n, 219n
Bultmann, Rudolf, 117n

C

Caesar, 76n
Caillois, Roger, 219n
Caldironi, Luca, 160n
Caliph, 55, 133n, 135n
Campbell, Joseph, 8n, 99, 106, 241n, 250n, 112, 269n
Cameroon, 158n
Canaan (ite), 7, 39n, 15, 18
Canada, 65–66, 164n, 79, 199n
Carnap, Rudolf, 185n

Subject/Name Index   145

Carriere, Emile, ix
Cassidy, David, 225n
Catherine of Siena, 106n
Censorship, 4, 176n
Central America, 66–67
Chagigah, 28
Chamar, 64
Charting the Unchurched in America, xvii, 3n
Cherokee Indians, 69
Children / Infants, 45, 188n, 196n
Chile, 66, 167n
China, 8n, 64, 161n
Chippewa Indians, 164n
Chojnowski, Peter, 177n
Christian / Christianity, ix, xvi, xx, xxii, 2n, 9, 19n, 62n, 75n, 34–51, 114n, 116n, 117n, 130n, 131n, 63, 70, 76, 203n, 99, 100, 246n, 250n, 252n, 255n, 112, 114, 115, 117
Chittick, William C., 149n
Chronicles, Book of, 18, 40, 102n
Chrysippus, 51n
Chu'un Miano, 161n
Cicero, 9, 10, 43n, 48n, 49n, 50n, 51n, 34, 35, 39, 40
Clement, 38
Clustka, Chuck, ix
Colombia, 67n, 67
Condon, Gerard, 45–46, 102n, 118n, 119n
Confucius/Confucian, xx
Connections Local & Non-Local, 85, 89, 90, 105
Consciousness, xxii, xxiv, 13n, 3, 48n, 52n, 35, 43, 117n, 127n, 150n, 72, 77, 78, 79, 80, 86, 88, 89, 196n, 203n, 214n, 215n, 228n, 231n, 234n, 104, 105, 106, 114, 115, 116
  Altered State, 13n, 35, 74, 214n, 115, 116, 275n, 276n
  Un/Subconscious, xvii, xxv, 33n, 59n, 62n, 65, 75, 76, 81, 88, 196n, 199n, 228n
Constantine, 95n
Constantiople, 77n

Contemplation, xxi
Cornelius, 36, 46, 93n
Corinth, 37
Covenant, 15, 16, 17, 18, 20, 25, 75n
Covitz, Rabbi Joel, 77n, 88n
Cracow, 7n, 77n
Cratippus the Peripatetic, 51n
Crick, Francis, 192n
Crow Indians, 69
Cuna Indians, 66

D

Damascus, 37
Damasus (Pope), 40
Danel, 39n
Daniel, 4, 24, 73n
  Book of, 6, 7, 39n, 24, 72n, 73n
Darwin, Charles, 182n
David, King, 18, 64n
Dawood, Abu, 137n
Death, 7, 9, 21, 22, 83n, 38, 39, 45, 104n, 107n, 55, 56, 127n, 133n, 67, 208n
Dei Verbum, 45, 118n, 246n
Deism, 73
Delaney, Gayle, 199n
Delaware Indians, 69, 173n
Delusions, xxii–xxiii, 114
Dement, William C., 78–79
Democracy, 74
Democritus, 51n
Deral-Madineh, 5
Descartes, Renè, 72–73, 177n, 178n, 179n
Deuteronomy, Book of, 2, 22, 23, 60n, 61n, 69n, 70n, 78n, 35, 40, 69, 102n
Devereux, Charles, 219n
Dewey, John, 75, 184n, 185n
di Lonzano, Menachem, 77n
Di Widah, 158n
Dicaearchus the Peripatetic, 51n
Diderot, Denis, 74, 181n
Diogenes of Babylon, 51n

Discernment, xx–xxii, 9, 16, 17, 18, 41n, 19, 28, 70n, 55, 102, 245n
Divination/Diviners, xi, xxi, 8n, 9, 10, 43n, 47n, 48n, 49n, 50n, 51n, 16, 22, 35, 39, 40, 41, 102n, 48, 52, 112n, 119n, 83, 102, 109, 259n, 114
Divine Council, 7, 17, 24, 61n, 62n
Divino Afflante Spiritu, 102n
Dogon, 64
Dombeck, Mary-Therese B., 219n
Domhoff, William G., 80, 196n, 199n, 200n, 213n
Donatus, 39
Douay-Rheims, 102n
Dourley, John, 77–78
Dream,
    Historic Attitudes, 1–14
    Babylonian, 6–7
    Canaanite, 7
    Egyptian, 4, 5–6, 33n, 52n, 55n
    Greek and Roman, 8–10, 40n, 41n
    Hittite, 2, 5, 7, 10, 67n
    Near Eastern, 5, 17n, 21n, 22n., 27n, 16
    Anxiety, 1, 66n, 111
    Biological Function, xi, 28, 41, 43, 44, 56, 58, 65, 67, 68, 75, 76, 78, 79, 80, 99, 102
    Christian, 34–51
    Content / Messages, xi, xvi, xix, xxii, xxiv, 1, 2, 3, 5, 7, 11, 31n, 16, 17, 18–19, 20, 21, 22, 23, 24, 25, 27, 28, 63n, 67n, 70n, 34–35, 36, 38, 41, 43, 45, 52, 53–55, 56, 58, 59, 65, 66, 67, 68, 69, 70, 73, 76, 77, 78, 79, 80, 81, 82, 83, 86, 89, 102–3, 104
    Defined, xvi, 52n, 59n
    Examples, 1, 2, 6, 7, 8, 9, 10, 43n, 55n, 17, 18, 19, 20, 21, 24, 26–28, 63n, 76n, 83n, 34, 35–36, 37, 41, 42, 52, 53, 66, 73, 102–3
    Function, xv, 2–5, 7, 9, 11, 21n, 22n, 31n, 33n, 15, 16, 17, 22, 23, 24, 26–28, 66n, 38, 53, 57, 58, 59, 139n, 142n, 63, 64, 65, 66, 67, 68, 69, 70, 76, 77, 78, 79, 80, 81, 82, 86, 88, 89, 99, 100, 101, 102, 103, 104, 105, 106
God, xv–xxiv, xix, xxiii, 1, 2, 3, 5, 6, 7, 9, 10, 11, 20n, 33n, 15, 16, 17–25, 27, 28, 60m, 62n, 67n, 76n, 77n, 34–35, 36, 37, 38, 39, 40, 41, 43, 44, 45, 46, 91n, 102n, 118n, 52, 53–55, 56, 57–59, 125n, 129n, 139n, 140n, 63, 65, 66, 67, 68, 69, 70, 75, 77, 79, 81, 83, 84, 89, 90, 99, 100, 101, 102, 103–6
Handbooks, 4, 9, 11, 31n, 56, 152n, 104, 108
Healing, 5, 6, 10–11, 27, 67n, 37, 63, 66, 68, 69, 157n, 165n, 76–78, 82, 89, 211n, 212n, 213n
Images, xvi, xvii, xviii, xix, xx, xxiv, 4, 8, 10, 24, 38, 41, 102n, 53, 56, 58, 66, 75, 76, 81, 89, 101, 104
Incubation, 10–11, 55n, 18–19, 69
Initiation, xviii, xix, xxi, 33n, 24, 68, 83
Interpretation, xviii, 5n, 2, 4, 6, 8, 9, 10, 11, 22n, 27n, 17, 18, 22–23, 24, 25, 26, 27, 66n, 77n, 83n, 88n, 40, 42, 43, 45, 105n, 119n, 51, 53, 56, 57, 58, 59, 128n, 139n, 144n, 153n, 63, 64, 65, 66, 67, 68–69, 161n, 170n, 73, 75, 76, 77, 81, 87, 175n, 191n, 201n, 210n, 219n, 101, 102–3, 246n, 253n, 254n, 265n, 116
Islamic, 52–62, 98, 108
Judaism, 20n, 21n, 22n, 15–33
Language, xvii–xviii, xxiv, 27, 101, 102, 253n
Lucid, 48n, 39, 99n, 58, 148n, 79, 81, 86, 203n, 204n, 205n
Mantic, 2, 4–5
Message, 2–3, 4, 8
New Testament, 35–37
Nordic, 3
Nightmares, 1, 5, 19–21, 66n., 67n, 30, 38, 57, 65–66, 67, 79
Prediction / Prophecy, 1, 2, 4–5, 6, 8, 9, 10, 31n, 33n, 15, 16, 17, 18–19,

Subject/Name Index   147

20, 22, 23, 24, 27, 28, 60n, 67n,
71n, 73n, 76n, 88n, 35, 37, 39, 41,
42, 43, 45, 106n, 52, 53, 56, 57,
66, 67, 68, 79, 82, 105
Research xi, 9, 31n, 65, 72, 77, 78–79,
80, 81, 82, 89, 192n, 193n, 195n,
196n, 197n, 198n, 199n, 210n,
212n, 218n, 249n, 115
Royal, 2, 3, 5, 6, 7
Sacred and Mysterious, xv, xvi–xix,
5, 7n, 33n, 36, 39, 41, 43, 53,
129n, 65, 66, 68, 70, 88, 101, 106
Symbolic, xi, xvii, xix, xxiv, 3–4, 52,
67, 69, 75, 76, 78, 79, 101, 102
Temple, 5
Travel, 33n, 53–55, 129n, 130n, 64,
65
Warning, 4, 15, 20–21, 23, 24, 67n,
35, 36, 39, 128n, 66, 67
Dream Catcher, 65–66
Dreamtime, 69–70
Dunn, Jimmy, 34n
Durkheim, Emile, 217n
Dyak People, 63

E

Early Bronze Age, 1
Eckhart, Meister, 106n
Ecuador, 67n, 67, 169n
Edinger, Edward, 78
Ego, xx, xxii, xxiv, 191n, 102, 104, 112, 115
Egypt, 4, 5–6, 10, 33n, 34n, 37n, 52n,
55n, 15, 17, 18, 22, 59, 146n,
153n, 154n
Ehulhul, Temple, 7
Einstein, Albert, xxi, 10n, 11n, 85, 224n, 227n
Eisik, Rabbi, 7n
El, 7, 62n
Elam, 63n
Eli, 20–21
Eliade, Mircea, 7n, 83, 220n, 221n, 222n, 250n
Elihu, 23

Elisha, 27
Elizabeth, 117
Elohist, 16
Emerick, Yahiya, 122n, 123n, 124n
Empiricists, 70n, 23, 180n
England, xvii, 41, 107n, 73, 81, 87, 186n
Enlightenment, 72–73, 176n, 215n
Enoch, 54
Ephesians, Letter to, 111
Epidaurus, 10
Episcopal, ix, x, xv, 2n, 46
Erikson, Erik, 187n
Erinnu Temple, 3
Eriugena, John Scotus, 106n
Esdras, Book of, 24
Essences, 92n
Ester Book of, 24
Etemenanki, 62n
Eudemus, 9
Eusebius, 38, 39, 95n, 102n
Evans, Christopher, 192n
Evans, Don. ix
Exile, 23–24, 69n
Existentialism, 74
Exodus, 4, 18
    Book of, 25, 61n, 78n, 114
Ezekiel, 24–25
    Book of, 2

F

Fasting, xxii, 28, 42, 109n, 136n, 114
Fidler, Ruth, 22n, 65n
Field, Richard, 184n
Finland, 201n
Fiss, Harry, 192n, 199n, 249n
Flanagan, Sabina, 106n
Fletcher, Rev. John, ix
Foulkes, David, 79, 192n, 195n, 196n, 204n
Foy, Glenn, 2, ix, xv
France, 40, 102n, 103n, 109n, 68, 73, 74
Francis of Assisi, 42
Frazier, James, 217n
Free Will, 113
Frege, Friedrich, 185n

Freud, Sigmund, 77n, 76, 77, 78, 83,
   189n, 190n, 196n, 218n
Friedman, Maurice S., 250n

G

Gabriel, Archangel, 53–55, 125n, 126n
Galileo Galilei, 178n
Galilee, 76n
Gallup Poll, xvii
Garden of Eden, 62n
Garden of Gethsemane, 35
Gbili (Chief), 158n
Gendlin, Eugene, 187n
Genesis,Book of, 15, 17, 18, 20, 61n, 62n, 117
Gerar, 20
German, 42, 44, 103n, 117n, 73, 185n, 187n, 102
Ghana, 64
Giampà, Mario, 160
Gibeon, 18
Gideon, 18
Gilgamesh Epic, 7
Gill, Rev. John, ix
Gillespie, George, 81, 205n
Giovanni, Don, (See John Bosco)
Girgashites, 15
Globus, Gordon, 80
Gloucestershire, 11
Gnuse, Robert Karl, 76n
God
   Presence of, xv, xvi–xvii, xviii, xix, xx, xxi, xxii–xxiii, xxiv, 9n, 1, 2, 3, 4, 5, 6, 7, 9, 10–11, 20n, 24n, 55n, 15, 16–28, 57n, 61n, 62n, 63n, 67n, 69n, 70n, 74n, 75n, 76n, 77n, 79n, 89n, 34, 35, 36, 37, 38, 39, 40, 41, 42, 43, 44, 45, 46, 91n, 102n, 106n, 109n, 117n, 118n, 119n, 52, 53, 55, 56, 57, 58, 59, 129n, 133n, 140n, 150n, 63, 67, 68, 70, 72, 73, 74, 75, 76, 77, 78, 81, 83, 84, 86, 89, 90, 191n, 196n, 224n, 99, 100, 101, 102, 103, 104, 105, 106, 259n, 111, 112, 113, 266n, 270n, 114–17
   Will of xviii, xix, xx–xxii, 8n, 2, 3, 4, 5, 15, 16, 17, 19–19, 20, 22, 23, 24, 25, 26, 27, 61n, 62n, 67n, 69n, 70n, 73n, 74n, 76n, 89n, 35, 36, 37, 38, 39, 41, 42, 43, 44, 102n, 109n, 117n, 118n, 52, 53, 55, 59, 136n, 63, 73, 77, 78, 89, 99, 100, 101, 102, 103, 243n, 246n, 267n, 111–13, 114, 115, 253n
   Yearning for, xvi–xviii, xx, xxiv, 2n, 16, 18, 19, 20, 21, 22, 23, 24, 25, 27, 62n, 67n, 70n, 76n, 89n, 37, 38, 41, 42, 45, 58, 109n, 117n, 118n, 150n, 73, 74, 75, 76, 81, 182n, 245n, 100, 101, 102, 111, 112, 113, 114
Goethe, xiii
Goldberg, G.J., 76n
Goodenough, Donald R., 194n
Gras Ventres Indians, 69
Greece / Greek, 3, 6, 8–9, 10, 37n, 55n, 89n, 39, 40, 92n, 101n, 114
Greene, Brian, 233n
Gregory of Nyssa, 38
Gregory the Great, 38
Gross, Terry, 233n
Grossman, Cathy, 3n
Guajiro, 67n, 67, 170n
Gudea, King, 3

H

HaKohain, Yakov Leib, 78
Hadīth, 53, 55–57, 126n, 128n, 137n, 141n
Halakhah (see Jewish Law)
Haldane, Jane, 2n
Hall, Calvin, 78, 79, 80, 210n
Hallucination, xxii–xxiii, 114, 116
Hammurabi, 18
Hare Indian Nation, 69
Harney Peak, South Dakota, 62n
Harrison, David M., 228n
Hartmann, Ernest, 80, 202n

Subject/Name Index 149

Hathor Temple, 55n
Hattushili, King, 2, 7, 22n
Hayes, Roy, ix
Hearne, Keith, 81
Heavenly Host, 17
Hegel, Georg Wilhelm, 74
Heidegger, Martin, 185n
Heisenberg, Werner, 84, 225n
Hellenism, 24, 92n
Henein, Maryam, 157n
Herbert, Nick, 85, 231n
Hercules, Temple of, 8
Herod, 35
Herodotus, 6, 8, 37n
Hezekiah, 27
Hildegard von Bingen, 41, 106n
Himalayas, 64
Hindu, xx, 64, 155n, 76
Historic Perspective, 1-14
Hitler, Adolf, 102-3, 256n
Hittite, 2, 5, 7, 10, 15, 67n
Hivites, 15
Hobbes, Thomas, 73, 178n
Hobson, J. Allan, 192n
Hoffman, Valerie, 59, 154n
Holmes, Russell, 78
Homer, 8, 40n
Honorton, Charles, 212n
Hopi Indians, 69
Horney, Karen, 72, 188n
Horowitz, Rabbi, 83n
Howe, Elias, 105
Howells, William, 63
Huambisa People, 169n
Huaorani People, 169n
Hugo, 103n
Humanism, 42
Hume, David, 181n
Hunt, Harry T., 79, 194n, 249n
Huray, 7
Hurayrah, Aboo, 153n
Husserl, Edmund, 185n

I

Iban People, 69
Iliad, 8, 178n
India, xxiv, 56, 64, 65, 250n
Indonesia, 69
Ingram, Gordon, 168n, 170n
Innocent III (Pope), 42
Intertestamental Period, 105-6
Introduction, xv-xxvi
Irenaeus, 38
Iroquois Indians, 68-69, 171n, 172n
Isaiah, 21
  Book of, 17, 21, 27, 70n
Islam, xvi, xx, xxii, 62n, 52-62, 130n,
  131n, 132n, 133n, 136n, 139n,
  140n, 141n, 143n, 145n, 63, 70,
  99, 100, 114, 115, 116, 277n,
Islamic Perspectives, 52-62
Isḥāq, Muhammad ibn, 126n
Isra', 53
Israel / (ites), 2, 17, 18, 19, 21, 23, 60n,
  69n, 82n, 89n, 35, 114
Ištar, 63
Italy, 45

J

Jabal an-Nur, 125n
Jacob, 17, 18, 62n, 117
Jacobs, Louis, 78n, 83n
James, William, 13n, 75-76, 187n
Jebusites, 15
Jeremiah, 22-23
  Book of, 2, 21n, 17, 23, 70n, 35, 40
Jericho, Waters of, 27
Jerome, 10, 34-35, 38, 39-40, 46, 101n,
  102n
Jerusalem, 18, 19, 25, 26, 71n, 72n, 82n,
  88n, 36, 102n, 53-54, 55, 131n
Jesus, xviii, xxii, 1, 5, 22n, 62n, 35, 36,
  42, 46, 93n, 106n, 109n, 117n, 52,
  54, 125n, 180n, 246n, 252n, 113,
  114, 115
Jewish Perspective, 15-33
Jivaro People, 67, 169n

Job, Book of, 19–20, 21–22, 23, 114
Joel, 23, 24
    Book of, 24
Jocasta, 8
Joseph, 4, 17, 27
Joseph (Jesus' Parent), 35
Josephus, Flavius, 25, 76n
Joshua, 18
John the Baptist, 54, 117
John of the Cross, 43, 109n
John, Saint, 75n, 37
    Gospel of, 255n, 111
Johnson, Robert, ix, 78, 254n
Judah the Patriarch, 26
Judaism, xvi, xx, xxii, 4, 15–33, 70n, 77n, 36, 92n, 52, 63, 70, 99, 100, 114
Jude, Letter of, 37
Judges, Book of, 18
Juliana of Norwich, 41, 106n
Jung, C. G., xviii, 111n, 112n, 72, 75, 77, 175n, 190n, 191n, 196n, 228, 240n, 241n, 103–4, 106, 253n, 256n, 257n, 259n, 261n, 262n, 264n, 265n

K

Kabbalah, 27, 89n
Kadmonites, 15
Kagwahiv People, 66–67
Kalapalo People, 66–67
Kamiya, 192n
Kandemwa, Mandaza, 63
Kant, Immanuel, 44, 46, 73, 74, 176n
Karo, Yosef, 83n
Kaska Indians, 66
Kelsey, Morton T., 6n, 39, 40, 46, 94n, 96n, 97n, 98n, 100n, 102n, 113n
Kemerling, Garth, 185n, 186n
Kempe, Margery, 106n
Kenites, 15
Kenizzites, 15
Kepler, Johannes, 258n
Kerenyi, Carl, 187n
Kettner, Melvin, ix
Khaldun, ibn, 57, 59

Khamuas, Prince, 10, 53n
Khosla, K., 151n
Kierkegaard, Søren, 74
Kings (Book of), 18, 70n
Kiwai People, 69
Klamath Indians, 69
Kleitman, Nathaniel, 78
Knowledge, xi, xviii, xix, xx–xxi, 41, 57, 68, 72, 73, 74
    Discovered, xxi, 231n
    Revealed, xxi, 25, 41, 46, 118n, 57, 58, 135n, 69
Koet, Bart J., ix, 20n, 70n, 36, 91n
Kol People, 65
Konde People, 64
Kpelle People, 158n
Kramer, Donna, 192n
Kret, King, 7, 39n
Krippner, Stanley, 82
Kulaini, Mohammad, 138n

L

LaBerge, Stephen, 48n, 99n, 148n, 81, 203n, 204n
Labrador Peninsula, 65
Lactantius, 38
Lagash, 3
Lahore Ahmadiyya Movement, 56, 277n
Lakoff, George, 186n
Lakota Indians, 69
Lao Tzu, 248n
Law, Christian, 41, 43, 45, 119n, 105
    Islamic—see Shari'a
    Jewish / Halakhah, 25–26, 78n, 81n, 82n, 83n
    Secular, 84, 180n, 224n, 226n
Laszlo, Ervin, 88–89, 239n, 240n, 241n
Leibniz, Gottfried, 179n
Leivadia, Grove of, 55n
Lepcha People, 64
Levi-Strauss, Claude, 217n
Leviticus, Book of, 78n, 40, 102n
Lewis, 192n
Liberia, 158n
Liberius (Pope), 39

Subject/Name Index 151

Lightning, xv, xvi, 70n, 75n, 115
Little Big Horn (Battle), 62n
Locke, John, 73, 180n
Logic, 10, 40, 57, 64, 73, 75, 87, 89, 185n, 186n
Lombard, Peter, 103n
Lonzano, Rabbi Menachem di, 77n
Loreto, 33
Loyola, Ignatius, 43, 109n
Ludwig, Arnold M., 116, 275n
Lukács, Georg, 185n
Luke, 36, 37, 93n
    Gospel of, 36, 117

M

Macas, 67, 169n
Maccabees, 72n
    Books of, 24
Macrobius, 38–39
Macy, Joanna, 182n
Magallon, Linda L., 199n
Magi, 35
Maimonides, 83n, 82, 212n
Malamat, Abraham, 2, 20n, 21n, 23n
Malaysia, 69
Mali, 64
Malinowski, Bronislaw, 217n
Maja, Ibn, 137n
Mamu, 6
Mantia People, 69
Mapuches People, 66, 167n
Marah, Waters of, 27
Marett, R.R., 217n
Mari, 1, 2, 18n, 21n, 70n
Maricopa Indians, 69
Marks, Tracy, 68, 171n, 172n
Markus, Francis, ix
Martyr, Justin, 38
Marx, Karl, 217n
Mary, Jesus' Mother, 35, 109n, 125n, 113
    Gospel of, 130n
Maslow, Abraham, 187n
Matthew, Gospel of, 62n, 34, 35
Matz, Terry, 116n
Maurice, David, 194n

Maxentius, 38
Mayan People, 66
Mayawyaw People, 69
McCarley, Robert, 192n
McLuhan, Marshall, 249n
Meaning, xviii, xix, xxi, 2, 4, 44, 59, 65, 66, 67, 74, 76, 77, 78, 80, 87, 89, 196n, 202n, 212n, 213n, 102, 103, 106, 249n, 108, 257n, 264n, 111, 112, 268n, 116
Meaningful Orderedness, 103–4
Mecca, 53, 54, 55, 146n
Medinat al-Nabi
    (Medina), 55, 56
Meditation, xx, xxii, 25, 83n, 53, 212n, 114, 115
Mehwesekht, 10
Melchthon, 43
Meligai, 69
Merkavah, 24–25
Merton, Thomas, 117n
Mesopotamia, 1, 3, 4, 10, 27n, 62n, 67n
Mevlevi Order of Dervishes, 58
Mexico, 66
Miao People, 64, 161n
Michelangelo, 111
Midwinter Dream Festival, 68
Mikroat Gedolot, 77n
Mill, John Stuart, 180n
Miller, Patricia Cox, 17n, 40n, 41n, 42n, 45n, 46n, 47n, 90n, 102n
Miller, Patrick D., 16, 58n, 60n
Mindress, Harvey, ix
Mi'raj, 54
Miriam, 27
Mishlove, Jeff, 108n, 231n
Mishnah, 25–26, 28, 81n
Mitchison, Graeme, 192n
Miyuki, Mokusen, 78
Moffitt, Alan, 199n
Mohave Indians, 69
Mohammad—See Muhammad or The Prophet
Monroe, W. S., 192n
Montgomery, James, 76
Moore, George, Edward, 185n
Mormon, Book of, 45

Morocco, 64
Moroni, 45
Moses, 18, 25, 27, 69n, 78n, 36, 91n, 52, 54, 114, 115
Moss, Robert, 33n
Mozart, 117n
Muhammad, 62n, 52–55, 56, 59, 122n, 123n, 124n, 125n, 126n, 128n, 129n, 130n, 131n, 132n, 133n, 135n, 138n, 139n, 115, 116
Muqaddimah, 59, 152n
Murrell, Beatrix, 224n
Murshili, King, 5
Muslim, xvi, 1n, 52, 54, 55, 56, 57, 59, 129n, 131n, 133n, 134n, 136n, 142n
Mystic(al/ism), xi, xix, xxii, 15, 24, 28, 89n, 41, 42, 44, 106n, 118n, 53, 57, 59, 64, 155n, 73, 74, 75, 76, 89, 101
Mystery, xviii, xix, xx, xxiv, 107, 108, 111

N

Nabonidus, King, 7
Nanak, xx
Naskapi Indians, 65
Nathan, 18
Native American Perspectives, 68–69
Nazianzen, Gregory, 38
Ndebela, 63–64
Nebuchadnezzar, King, 4, 6, 62n
Necromancy, 16
Neihardt, John G., 62n
Neoplatonism, 76
Neurath, Otto, 185n
Neusner, Jacob, 25, 80n
New Guinea, 69
Newton, Isaac, 73, 84, 90, 183n, 224n
Nielsen, Tore, 199n
Nietzsche, Friedrich, 45, 74, 75, 89, 182n, 113, 273n
Nigeria, 64
Night Journey, 53–55, 129n, 130n
Njoya, Ibrahim (Sultan), 158n

Noegel, Scott, 22n
Non-Religious Perspectives, 72–98
Nootka Indians, 66
Numbers, Book of, 21n, 18, 91n, 114
Nyakyusa People, 64,

O

O'Connor, J. J., 178n
O'Nell, Carol W., 119n
Odyssey, 8, 40n, 178n
Odysseus, 8
Oedipus, King, 8
Ojibwe, 65, 164n
Oneirocritica, 9
Oppenheim, Leo, 2–5, 6, 10, 22n, 24n, 25n, 26n, 27n, 28n, 29n, 30n, 35n, 36n, 52n, 54n, 63n, 67n
Oracle, 6, 55n, 16, 63n, 64n, 63
Orenda, 68
Origen, 259n
Orlinsky, 192n
Orthodox / (y), xix, 15, 28, 89n, 41, 117n, 58, 146n, 83, 84, 100, 101, 102
Other Religious Perspectives, 63–71

P

Pacific Region, 69–70
Padgett, Doug, 119n
Pakistan, 140n
Palestine, 6, 26, 95n
Panama, 66
Papyrus Insigne, 5, 30n
Park, Willard Z., 220n, 221n
Parry, Rabbi Aaron, 26, 27, 28, 77n, 83n, 84n, 87n
Patiah, Yedudah, 27
Patmos, 37
Patriarch/(s), 17, 26
Paul (Saint), 6n, 37, 46, 111, 117
Paul the Hermit, 102n
Paul III (Pope), 109n
Paul VI (Pope), 45, 118n, 246n

Subject/Name Index   153

Pauli, Wolfgang, 84, 225n, 227n, 228n, 103, 258n
Paviotso Indians, 69
Penelope, 8
Peniel, 17
Pererius Benedictus, 43–44, 112n
Perizzites, 15
Perls, Fritz, 187n
Persia, 23
Peru, 67n, 67, 168n
Peter, 36–37, 93n
Peucer, Kasper, 43, 111n
Pew Forum on Religion & Public Life, 2n
Pharisees, 92n
Philips, Abu Ameenah, 153n
Philippines, 69
Philistines, 20, 21
Philosophical Perspectives, 72–75
Philosophy, 43, 72–75, 89, 180n, 185n, 186n
Philosophy of Science, 72, 84, 86–89, 90, 100
Physics, xvii, xxiii, 42, 72, 73, 84–86, 87, 88, 90, 224n, 226n, 228n, 234n, 101, 103, 104, 105, 106, 233n
Pilate's Wife, 35–36
Pius XII (Pope), 102n
Piute Indians, 69
Planck, Max, 224n
Plateau Indians, 69
Plato, 8, 9
Plautus, 39
Plutarch, 6
Polls, xvi–xvii, 2n
Posidonius, 51n
Prague, 7n
Pratt, David, 235n
Prayer, xxi, xxii, 9n, 10, 19, 26, 27, 86n, 42, 109n, 53, 54, 55, 126n, 127n, 136n, 68, 81, 87, 114
Pritchard, E. E. Evans, 217n
Promised Land, 17, 18, 89n
Prophet, The, 53, 55, 56, 59, 126n, 128n, 135n, 136n, 139n, 153n, 115, 116
Prophets, xi, 2, 23n, 16, 17, 18, 22, 23, 24, 28, 57n, 60n, 69n, 70n, 71n, 73n, 74n, 76n, 78n, 88n, 36, 39, 91n, 52, 54, 55, 57, 129n, 131n, 140n, 66, 73, 79, 89, 115
Psalms, 19, 22, 61n, 63n, 64n, 66n
Psyche, xviii, xx, xxii, 7n, 75, 76, 77, 84, 228n, 101, 104
Psychology, xvii, xviii, xxiii, 7n, 35, 42, 46, 72, 74, 75–82, 84, 86, 89, 189n, 228n, 101, 104, 106, 115
    Cognitive, 78, 79–80, 89, 194n, 196n, 199n, 200n, 213n, 104, 114
    Parapsychology, 72, 81–83, 87, 88, 206n, 209n, 212n
    Psychopathology/Psychosis, xxii, xxiii, xxiv, 82
    Research, 72, 78–79, 89, 196n, 198n
Psychophysical Parallelism, 103–4
Ptolemy, Soter, 55n
Pythagoras, 51n

Q

Quine, Willard, 186n
Qur'ān, 62n, 67n, 52, 55–57, 121n, 126n, 135, 136n, 141n, 115
Quraysh, 55

R

Rabbinic Traditions, 15, 26–28, 78n, 82n, 83n, 88n
Radin, Dean, 212n
Ragueneau, Paul, 68
Ramadan, 132n
Ramses II, 10
Ramsey, Glenn V., 78
Rapid Eye Movement (REM), 78, 79, 194n
Reason / Rationalism, xix–xx, 9, 10, 41, 44–45, 46, 117n, 72, 73, 74, 89, 176n, 179n,
Rechtschaffen, Alan, 192n
Reed, Henry, 82
Reeves, David, 32n, 56n
Rephaim, 15

Subject Index

Revelation, xv, xviii, xix–xx, xxi, xxii–xxiii, xxiv, 8n, 9n, 12n, 2, 5, 11, 23n, 16, 20, 25, 60n, 35, 40, 45, 46, 96n, 97n, 98n, 100n, 102n, 106n, 113n, 114, 117n, 118n, 52, 53, 56, 58, 59, 126n, 132n, 135n, 136n, 63, 65, 83, 87, 99–100, 101, 102, 103, 105, 106, 244n, 245n, 246n, 114–117
    Book of, 75n, 37
Revonsuo, Antti, 201n
Rhine, Joseph Banks, 81–82, 209n
Rhine, Louisa, 81–82, 210n
Richards, M. C., 112, 271n
Rif People, 64
Rilke, Rainer Maria, 182n
River Yuman Indians, 69
Robinson, John C., xxii, 15n
Robertson, E. P., 178n
Röcken, Saxony, 74
Roffwarg, H., 192n
Ròheim, Géza, 199n
Rolston III, Holmes, 87–88, 236n, 237n, 238n, 247n
Rome/Roman, 8–10, 11, 76n, 36, 37, 38, 42, 92n, 101n, 135n
    Catholic Church, 40, 42, 45, 102n, 104n, 109n, 176n, 102, 246n, 107
Romans, Letter to, 114
Rolle, Richard, 106n
Rousseau, Jean Jacques, 181n
Rumi, Julalu'd-Din, 14n, 57, 58, 59, 150n, 151n
Russell, Bertrand, 185n
Ryle, Gilbert, 186n

S

Sacramento Bee, 198n
Sacramento, California, lx, xxii
Sacred Texts, xxi, xxii, 79n
Sadducees, 92n
Sahib, Maulana Aftab-ud-Din Ahmad, xv, 1n, 274n
Sahih Bukhari, 56, 128n, 141n
Salaat, 142n

Samuel, 3, 20, 45
    Books of, 23n, 18, 20, 21, 60n, 114
San Blas Islands, 66
Sanford, John A., ix, 46
Sarah, 20–21
Sartre, Jean-Paul, 185n
Satan, xxii, 57, 59, 141n, 102
Saul, 21
Saxony, 74
Scherk, Joel, 85
Schlick, Moritz, 185n
Schniter, Eric, 169n
Schopenhauer, Arthur, 74
Schizophrenia, xxiii, 16n
Scholastics, 40–41, 42, 178n
Schwarz, John, 85
Science, xxi, 10n, 11n, 70n, 44, 108n, 56, 59, 141n, 72, 73, 74, 79–82, 84–88, 90, 181n, 193n, 194n, 201n, 214n, 219n, 224n, 228m, 236n, 237n, 238n, 100, 104, 247n, 249n
Scotland, 180n
Second Coming of Christ, 115
Sedar Zera'im, 26
Seereen/ Seerin, Muhammad ibn, 56, 59, 153
Septuagint, 101n
Serapis Temple, 55n
Setme Khamuas, 10
Shapiro, 192n
Sharī'a, 56, 136n
Shaykhut-Fa'ifa, 138n
Shaytān, See Satan
Shi'a, 55, 56, 138n
Shiloh, 20
Shiviar People, 169n
Shona People, 63–64
Shuar People, 196n
Shulman, David, 83, 223n
Sikh, xx
Simpson, David, 44
Sin, 17, 20, 61n, 117n
Sinai, 55n, 62n, 78n
Sinkyone Indians, 69
Sioux (Oglala) Indians, 62n
Siren, Christopher B., 39n
Smith, Joseph, 45, 114n, 115n

Subject/Name Index   155

Smoley, Richard, ix
Snyder, Fred, 79, 192n
Socrates, 8
Solomon, King, 18–19
Solomon, Wisdom of, 24
Solomon Islands, 69
Solms, Mark, 79, 80, 196n, 197n
Sonoyea, 158n
Sophocles, 8, 44n
Soothsaying, 16, 40
Soul, xv, 22, 27, 54, 57, 58, 59, 130n, 64,
   65, 67, 68, 99, 104, 107, 114
South Africa, 64
South America, 66–67
South Dakota, 62n
Souvay, Charles L., 105n, 119n
Space-Time, xxi, 86, 88, 89, 90, 206n, 105
Spain, 77n, 43, 167n, 169n
Sphinx, 6
Spiegelman, J. Marvin, 78
Spinoza, Benedict, 179n
Spirit/ual, xi, xvi, xviii, xix, xx, xxii, 24,
   41, 42, 43, 44, 46, 102n, 109n,
   53, 57, 58, 59, 129n, 142n, 150n,
   63, 64, 65, 66, 67, 68, 69, 158m,
   171n, 172n, 72, 74, 79, 82, 83, 86,
   87, 88, 89, 91, 183n, 191n, 214n,
   215n, 219n, 224n, 99, 100–1, 102,
   106, 247n, 115
Spirit of God, 3, 24, 34, 36, 93n, 246n,
   270, 114
   Discernment, xviii, xx–xxii, 9, 16, 17,
      18, 19, 28, 70n, 55, 102, 245n,
   Growth, xi, 89, 215n, 246n
St. Columba Episcopal Church, D.C., 2n
Starbuck, Scott, ix, 63n, 66n, 68n
Stapp, Henry, 84
Stein, Murray, 78
Stekel, Wilhelm, 187n
Stock, Rev. Joan, ix
Stoics, 51n
Strawson, Sir Peter, 186n
Stridonius, 39
String Theory, 85–86, 232n
Stroumsa, Guy G., 83, 223n
Stoyva, J., 192n
Sudan, 64

Sufi, 14n, 56, 58, 148n, 149n, 151n, 76
Sullivan, Harry Stack, 77, 189n
Sultzman, Lee, 173n
Sumeria / (n), 3, 6
Summary, 11, 28, 46, 59, 70, 89–90
Sun Dance, 69
Sunnī, 55, 56, 57, 58
Sūra, 62n, 67n, 54, 141n
Sweden, 106n, 212n
Swedenborg, Emanuel, 44
Switzerland, 65, 80
Symbols, xvii, xviii, xix, xxiv, 7n, 2, 3–4,
   24, 67, 69, 163n, 75, 76, 78, 79,
   89, 175n, 191n, 210n, 218n, 101,
   102, 250n, 253n, 265n
Synchronicity, 8n, 9n, 103–4, 263n, 114
Synesius of Cyrene, 38
Syria, 7

T

Talmud, 25–26, 27, 28, 77n, 80n, 82n,
   83n, 84n, 87n, 88n
Tanzania, 64
Taoists, xx
Tarot Cards, xxi
Tart, Charles T., 13n, 81, 82, 214n, 215n,
   116, 275n
Taylor, E. B., 217n
Taylor, Jeremy, 199n
Tedlock, Barbara, 219n
Tedrick, Jim, x
Temiar People, 69
Temple Mount, 54, 55
Temple, Jerusalem, 25, 72n, 117
Teresa of Avila, 43, 109n
Tertullian, Quintus, xvii, 38, 40, 46
Thaumaturgus, Gregory, 38
Thompson, Elisabeth, ix
Thutmose IV, 6
Tibet, 64
Tikopia People, 69
Tillich, Paul, 250n
Timaeus, 9, 46n
Time, Chinese, 8n
Tiv People, 64

Tobit, Book of, 24
Tolaas, Jon, 31n, 207n, 208n,
Tolkien, J. R. R., 56n
Torah, 18–19, 24, 25, 72n, 77n, 78n, 82n, 83n
Torrey, E. Fuller, 16n
Tosefta, 26
Tractates, 81n
Transcendent, xx, 42, 117n, 99, 101, 104, 106, 108
Trent, Council of, 102n
Trophonius, Cave of, 55n
Truth, xx, xxi, xxiii, 40n, 28, 118n, 58, 59, 141n, 143n, 63, 65, 73, 74, 77, 88, 211n, 100, 245n, 250n
Tsaphan, Mount, 62n
Turner, Paul, ix

U

Udm, 7
Ugaritic, 39n, 62n
Ullman, Montague, 31n, 82, 207n, 208n, 211n, 212n,
'Umar (Caliph), 133n
Uncertainty Principle, 84, 225n
Unconscious (see conscious)
United States, xvii, 117n, 164n, 75, 186n
Upanishads, 63, 155n, 74, 108
Urim and Thummim, xxi, 60n
Uruk, King, 4
USA TODAY, xvii
Utes Indians, 69
Uthman (Caliph), 133n
Utilitarians, 180n

V

Vai, 158n
Varvoglis, Mario, 212n
Vatican II, 45
Van de Castle, Robert L., 166n, 80, 82, 205n 213n
Van Der Post, Laurens, 256n
van, Gennep, Arnold, 217n
van Henten, Jan Willem, 76

Vedic, 64
Venezuela, 67n, 67
Verdone, Paul, 192n
Vesparian, 76n
Vienna Circle, 185n
Vietnam, xv
Virgil, 40n
Vision, xv, xxi, xxii, 1, 6, 9, 16–17, 18, 20, 21, 23, 24, 25, 59n, 60n, 62n, 66n, 71n, 73n, 75n, 77n, 35, 36, 37, 38, 39, 40, 41, 42, 43, 44, 45, 91n, 95n, 106n, 108n, 109n, 118n, 53, 58, 59, 130n, 154n, 63, 64, 67, 69, 72, 77, 106, 114, 115, 117
Voltaire, 181n
von Franz, Marie-Louise, 8n, 65, 163n, 257n
Von Gruenebaum, G.E., 219n
von Nettesheim, Heinrich Cornelius Agrippa, 42
Vulgate, 35, 102n

W

Wakan Tanka, 69
Ward, Keith, xxi, 9n, 12n, 245n, 246n
Wayúu Ethnic Group, 67
Weber, Max, 217n
Wei, Henry, 248n
Weserman, H.M., 81
Wesley, John, 44
Western Shoshone Indians, 69
Wheeler, John A., 226n
Whitaker, Andrew, 229n, 230n
White, Victor, 46
Whitehead, Alfred North, 185n
Whitman, R. 192n
Whitman, W., 76
Wilde, Oscar, 100–1, 248n
Wilkerson, Richard C., 194n, 201n, 219n
Willamette University, ix, xv
William II, King of England, xvii, 41–42, 46, 107m
Williams, John Alden, 126n
Wintu Indians, 69
Wisdom, John, 186n

Wittgenstein, Ludwig, 75, 186n
Wolf, Alan, 86, 234n
Woolverton, John, ix
Wounded Knee (Battle), 62n

X-Y

Yahweh, 16, 17
Yajnavalkye, 155n
Yaka People (Northern), 64
Yama People, 66
Yurok Indians, 69

Z

Zaire, 64
Zamzam (Well of), 52
Zealots, 92n
Zechariah (Elizabeth's Husband), 117
    Book of, 21n, 23, 71n
Zeller, Max, 78
Zepelin, 192n
Ziggurat, 62n
Zimbabwe, 63
Zimmer, Heinrich, 7n, 187n, 250n
Zion / Mt., 19, 21, 62n
Zionism, 15, 28, 89n
Zobo, Widoh, 158n
Zulu People, 64

www.ingramcontent.com/pod-product-compliance
Lightning Source LLC
Chambersburg PA
CBHW051931160426
43198CB00012B/2116